The Cambridge Introduction to
Early American Literature

The Cambridge Introduction to Early American Literature offers students a literary history of American writing in English between 1492 and 1820, as well as providing a concise social and cultural history of these three centuries. Emory Elliott traces the impact of race, gender, and ethnic conflict on early American culture, and explores the centrality of American Puritanism in the formation of a distinctively American literature. Elliott provides an overview of the oral and written literature of the Europeans who explored, settled on and colonized the North American continent. He goes on to focus on the New England Puritans and demonstrates the lasting impact of their thought and writing on early American literature. Elliott traces the evolution of forms and genres that have come to be seen as quintessentially American. This highly engaging and comprehensive study will be essential reading for students of the literature, history, and culture of early America.

Emory Elliott is University Professor of the University of California and Distinguished Professor of English at the University of California, Riverside where he is also the Director of the Center for Ideas and Society. His books include *Power and the Pulpit in Puritan New England* (1975), *Revolutionary Writers: Literature and Authority in the New Republic* (1982), and *The Literature of Puritan New England* (1994). He is the editor of *The Columbia Literary History of the United States* (1988), *The Columbia History of the American Novel* (1991) and the *Prentice Hall Anthology of American Literature*.

The Cambridge Introduction to
Early American Literature

EMORY ELLIOTT

CAMBRIDGE UNIVERSITY PRESS
Cambridge, New York, Melbourne, Madrid, Cape Town, Singapore, São Paulo, Delhi

Cambridge University Press
The Edinburgh Building, Cambridge CB2 8RU, UK

Published in the United States of America by Cambridge University Press, New York

www.cambridge.org
Information on this title: www.cambridge.org/9780521520416

First published 2002

A catalogue record for this publication is available from the British Library

ISBN 978-0-521-81717-2 hardback
ISBN 978-0-521-52041-6 paperback

Transferred to digital printing 2009

Contents

Preface

An earlier version of this book appeared as part of the first volume of *Cambridge History of American Literature* edited by Sacvan Bercovitch. That volume contains contributions by five different contributors and examines the development of culture and literature in the Americas from 1492 until 1820. My contribution to that work, on the literature of Puritan New England, was not the opening section of the volume, but rather, it followed one on the literature of the European exploration from 1492 through the 1700s. In opening this way, the *Cambridge History* makes very explicit the point that the English Puritans were not the first, nor the only, Europeans to live in and write about their experiences in the Americas.

This book is intended primarily to tell the story of the literature of the New England Puritans, but anthologies of American literature today no longer begin with the landing of the Pilgrims in Plymouth, Massachusetts in 1620. Quite properly, they follow the lead of the *Columbia Literary History of the United States* (1988) and the *Cambridge History of American Literature, Vol. I* (1994) that open long before Columbus first viewed the West Indies. The purpose of the first chapter of this book is to provide a concise overview of the long and complex history of Europe and the Americas of which the English Puritans were a small part when they set sail for America in 1620.

Acknowledgments

The following institutions provided financial support for the research and writing: the National Endowment for the Humanities, the University of California, and the Humanities Research Institute of the University of California. Early versions of the first chapter were presented at the University of Verona and at the Ecole Normale Superieure, and I thank my kind hosts, Professor Itala Vivan and Pierre-Yves Petillon respectively, and others who also commented on the work: Professors Viola Sachs, Dominique Marçais, Janine Dove-Rume, and Marc Chenetier. I am grateful to the former director, Mark Rose, and the staff of the Humanities Research Institute at Irvine for their support, and to the other members of the 1991–92 Minority Discourse Project for reading portions of the manuscript and offering most useful suggestions: Norma Alarcon, José Amaya, Vincent Cheng, King-Kok Cheung, Kimberle Crenshaw, Anne Dannenberg, Abdul JanMohamed, May Joseph, Clara Sue Kidwell, Smedar Lavis, Françoise Lionnet, Haiming Liu, Lisa Lowe, Lillian Manzor-Coats, Michael Sprinker, Sterling Stuckey, David Van Leer, and Clarence Walker. At the University of California, Riverside, I have benefited from the readings and guidance of Steve Axelrod, Carol Bensick, Georgia Elliott, Mark Elliott, Bruce Hagood, Deborah Hatheway, Carla Magill, Carlton Smith, Liam Corley, Christie Firtha, John Pinson and Jeffrey Rhyne. Michael Colacurcio of UCLA, Bernard Rosenthal of SUNY-Binghampton, and Heather Dubrow of the University of Wisconsin also contributed suggestions. I am also grateful for the support of friends, colleagues, and staff members of the English Department of the University of California, Riverside, and those of the Center for Ideas and Society: Trudy Cohen, Laura Lara, Antonette Toney, and Marilyn Davis who prepared the manuscript. I have appreciated the patience of Andrew Brown and Julie Greenblatt of Cambridge University Press, and of Ray Ryan who suggested the present volume. As always, my wife, Georgia, provided intellectual and emotional support, and my children, Scott, Mark, Matthew, Constance, and Laura, cheerfully indulged me over many years in my preoccupation with the people and events of another time and place.

Emory Elliott
Riverside, California

Chapter One

Brave New World

In 1611, Shakespeare wrote his last comedy, *The Tempest*, during one of the most perilous times in English political history. In 1603, Queen Elizabeth I had died, ending her reign of forty-five years. Throughout most of his career as a playwright, Shakespeare had benefited from and celebrated the period of economic growth and political stability credited to Her Majesty's strength and wisdom, and he and other writers were grateful for her support of the theater and of English literature in general. The ascendancy of James I to the throne sparked political and religious turmoil as both Catholic and Protestant reformers perceived the moment of transition to be an opportunity to reduce the power of the Anglican Church. With James' support, Church of England officials responded by increasing persecution of all religious dissenters.

Although England was emerging as a European power by virtue of its strong navy, global exploration, and colonization into the New World, Shakespeare and his audiences were conscious of the danger that civil war might be imminent. In fact, a bloody Civil War was on the horizon, but it would not begin for another thirty years. During those three decades, thousands of Puritans and Catholics suffered persecution, imprisonment, and torture, which finally led to the overthrow and execution of James' son King Charles I in 1649. Oliver Cromwell and the Puritans took control of the government and ruled the country for eleven years during which the theaters of England were closed. In 1660, the Puritans lost control of the Parliament, and King Charles II returned from exile in France to assume the throne and reestablish the English monarchy. In the form of veiled allegory, Shakespeare used his fanciful comedy of *The Tempest* to allude to some of the domestic and global issues that his country was facing as the play was being performed and to express national apprehensions about the future that many English people felt at the time.

Throughout the five decades of the Elizabethan monarchy (1552–1603), Spain, France, Portugal, and other European nations were vigorously competing in the Americas for control over the territory and wealth the New World offered. After John Cabot explored the coast of North America for England in 1598, Elizabeth displayed little interest in establishing a colony in America. Perhaps, Elizabeth believed that she could not afford the financial risks. Shortly after her death, however, James I commissioned the London Trading Company to establish a settlement in Jamestown, Virginia, in 1607.

With Elizabeth gone, the Spanish Armada defeated, and England emerging as the dominant Atlantic power, Shakespeare set his play in the Americas. He seems to have read the accounts that appeared in England in 1610 of the wreck of one of England's vessels in the Bermudas, islands that were said to be enchanted and inhabited by witches and devils. Envisioning the Americas as constituting either a "brave New World" that offered Europeans a new beginning or an exotic, dangerous place that threatened English stability and normality, Shakespeare imaginatively projected himself as artist into the role of his Columbus-like Prospero. Shipwrecked on an island off the coast of North America near the very spot on which Columbus had landed a century before, Prospero dreams that his beautiful daughter Miranda may have a secure future in a safe New World. But the presence already in America of Old World corruption, as well as local demonic spirits and monsters, undermines Miranda's safety. To triumph over such evils, Prospero must employ all of his knowledge of science, religion, and witchcraft in his encounter with a savage creature whose mother was a witch and whose father a devil. Although Prospero's real enemies are his evil brother Antonio and other malicious members of the courts of Milan and Naples, the play focuses upon the crude and offensive Caliban, a "savage and deformed slave." Because of the fantastic nature of the setting, Caliban functions less as a representation of Native peoples of America than as an inconceivable and grotesque challenge to the power of Prospero. Shakespeare makes Caliban's speeches and actions strange and disorienting – unsettling for Prospero and the audience. Some of Caliban's speeches even parody and mock those given earlier in earnest innocence by Miranda. The world seems upside down for Prospero for much of the play, so that the audience must have found rather absurd this story of a New World in which everything is distorted and where witches challenge scientists and aristocrats and slaves spurn their masters. For Shakespeare's audience, the play presents an ambiguous vision of the New World as a place full of promise but also threatening disaster and death. Underlying the attitudes of the people of Europe and the decisions of their leaders regarding the Americas would be the anxieties, fears, and dread of the exotic and the unknown that Shakespeare played upon so effectively in *The Tempest*.

When Christopher Columbus recorded in his journal on October 12, 1492, that "two hours after midnight appeared the land," he was gazing at the shoreline of the island he would name San Salvador in what would be called the Bahamas, meaning a place of splendor. Historians have long debated the question of exactly when the first people from across the Atlantic reached the Americas. Some scholars believe that around 1000 AD the Vikings landed in what is now Canada while others claim that Egyptian and Nubian people from Africa sailed on Atlantic currents to the Americas sometime around 1200 BC and left their traces in the cultural forms and facial features of the inhabitants whom Columbus met 2700 years later. For most historians, however, the arrival of Columbus marked an important moment as the beginning of continuous and accelerating connections between the people of the Americas and the rest of the world. The writings of Columbus initiated a vast literature of exploration and description that contributed to the European perceptions and understanding of the Americas. Many of these accounts provide quite accurate factual details while others are as fanciful as Shakespeare's *The Tempest* or present a blend of the actual and imagined.

Regarding the presence of people on the American continents in 1492, it is generally agreed among anthropologists that in pre-historic times a land bridge that existed between what are now Siberia and Alaska enabled people from Asia to migrate to the Americas. Between the time that the bridge was submerged about 20,000 years ago and Columbus' arrival, the population of the Americas grew to about 300 million people whose ancestors had developed over 300 different cultures in which were spoken as many as 800 different languages. Although sharing similar ethnic heritages, the peoples of the American continents were as diverse as those in Europe, Africa, and Asia in their religions, modes of social organization, economies, technical expertise, artistic expression, and military prowess and methods. Some communities, such as the Mayans and Aztecs in what is now New Mexico and Mexico and the Incas in South America, were extraordinarily advanced in science, mathematics, and engineering, and they built remarkable physical structures equal to those of the Egyptians in complexity. Other tribes and nations, such as those inhabiting the Northern plains, became expert hunter-gatherers while those living between the Atlantic seaboard and the Rocky Mountains lived in clans and villages and practiced highly developed forms of agriculture.

Although they appear not to have developed written languages, the oral languages of these native peoples were quite advanced, and they possessed language traditions that consisted of oral narratives, poetry, songs, and oratory. In the nineteenth and twentieth centuries, anthropologists, literary scholars, historians, and independent scholars of the indigenous peoples of the Americas have been determined to preserve what remained of these long cultural traditions. Researchers have recorded examples of the various forms of oral expression of Native Americans and have translated them into English. Nearly every anthology of American literature published in the last decade opens with a section devoted to Native American expression and contains selections of poetry, trickster stories, songs, and oratory.

Scholars of the field of Native American literature emphasize two important points that modern readers should remember about such written selections. First, English translations usually attempt to present these oral expressions in forms that resemble English literary genres of fiction and poetry, but most Native American artists adhered to generic traditions that are very different from those of the English and Europeans; these forms are also quite diverse among the Indians themselves, depending upon the particular tribal culture and the inclinations of the individual artist. Adherence to a strict form is not as much a feature of Native American genres as in English literature. Second, the very act of placing examples of the expression of the first inhabitants of the Americas at the beginning of a history or anthology suggests that their literary traditions existed only until 1492 and died away soon after Columbus arrived. But across America today, tribal cultures are alive and their artists continue to create new works of material culture and of oral and written literature both in English and in the tribal languages. These artistic productions are part of contemporary American art and literature, even as they also share an ancient heritage of Native America that extends back at least 25,000 years.

In a classic historical study which he titled *The Invasion of America: Indians, Colonialism, and the Cant of Conquest* (1975), the historian Francis Jennings dramatically shifted the modern perception of the arrival of the Europeans in America in the fifteenth and sixteenth centuries in order to make contemporary readers more aware of the genocide and cultural destruction that followed swiftly upon the arrival of Columbus. Millions of Native Americans died from diseases, such as smallpox, typhus, measles, and syphilis, that the invaders brought with them from Europe and for which the Native population had no immunities. By 1592 AD, only 100 years after the start of the European invasion of the Americas, twenty-three million Indians had died in central Mexico alone in the slaughter of battle, from the ravages of new diseases carried by Europeans, and under the brutal conditions of slavery to which millions were subjected.

Because Columbus came to be so idealized for his conviction that the earth was round, for his courage in sailing to the edge of what may have been a flat ocean emptying into a black hole of space, and for his "discovery" of a "New World" of fabulous wealth and natural resources, historians were long inclined to depict him as a scientist and an adventurer of great humanity, as very unlike the later conquistadors who led well-equipped armies against the poorly armed Native peoples. Yet, more recently, some historians have argued that Columbus was very much a participant in the system of eradication and plunder that generated a rapid return of European investment by transporting gold, spices, and other precious commodities from the Americas to the treasuries of Europe. Such a sense of urgency resulted in the killing of countless Indians and Africans who resisted being enslaved to work in the mines and the deaths of thousands of others from the brutal working conditions. Upon the news of what was at first thought to be Columbus's success in finding a passage to Asia, explorers from Italy, Portugal, and Spain followed in his wake.

In 1501, the Italian explorer Amerigo Vespucci made careful calculations to determine that the land that he and Columbus had reached earlier was part of a continent previously unknown to Europeans, and soon his own name became attached to the Americas. As word spread of the richness of the soil and the abundance of gold in the New World, European leaders recognized how resources from America would strengthen their own powers within Europe.

Throughout the sixteenth century, the Spanish, Portuguese and the French were especially active in trying to gain control over large portions of South America and Mexico and of the Southern portions of what is now the United States. The French built networks of colonies in Florida and along the Gulf of Mexico. The Portuguese controlled portions of South America that became Brazil, and the Spanish dominated much of Central America, Mexico, and the North American southwest. While the English did not settle Jamestown, Virginia, until 1607, the Spanish established a permanent settlement in St Augustine, Florida, in 1565. Moving across what is often called the Sun Belt, the Spanish established New Mexico (1598), Texas (1683), Arizona (1687), and California (1769). As they did so, they recorded their activities and some composed histories and even epic poems to preserve and celebrate their accomplishments. In 1542, Alvar Nunez Cabeza Vaca produced his *Relacion*, a personal narrative describing his adventures as one of the four survivors of an expedition of five hundred who then endured various hardships for eight years as they trekked from Florida along the Gulf coast to Mexico City. In 1610, Gaspar Perez de Villagra published his epic poem, *Historia de la Nueva Mexico*, which describes the regions settled and the feats of exploration and warfare in the New World.

In retrospect, it almost seems it was a cleverly designed plot of history that as the nations of Southern Europe were raiding the Americas, a religious revolution would be taking place in Northern Europe that would give rise to the Puritan Movement and thereafter the Puritan colonies in New England. However, the two events were not unconnected, for the economic changes produced by the wealth transported to Europe from the Americas in the sixteenth century helped to produce dramatic political and religious changes in Europe.

For centuries, the Catholic Church reigned as the single form of Christianity across Europe, and the Catholic faith was part of an elaborate theological system that explained every aspect of the universe in terms of the Great Chain of Being. At the top of the chain was God followed by the Pope, God's representative and spokesman on earth; next came the Kings of nations who lacked the supreme power of the Pope but who did possess the divine right of kings within their realms. The structure of the universe and ordering of the planets reflected the system of divine authority with the earth at the center and the sun and planets revolving around it.

The intellectual force of this theology and cosmology laid the foundation for the power of the church–states, which was buttressed when needed by methods of terror, such as in the Inquisition, and military power, such as in the Crusades. Historians have often noted that Columbus' ships were delayed in their departure for three days because in the harbor at Cadiz, Spain was blocked by the boatloads of Jewish refugees who were trying to flee Spain, which was expelling all Jews and Muslims to restore racial purity after the defeat of the Moors. In fact, the commissioning of Columbus' expedition was part of the celebration of the victory of Queen Isabella. While his explorations appeared to bolster the powers of the Church and the aristocracy, Columbus' discoveries confirmed the controversial theories of Copernicus and Galileo about the nature of the earth in relation to the rest of the solar system, thereby posing a major challenge to the idea of the Great Chain of Being and to the authority of the Pope. Such undermining of hierarchy would eventually make it possible for King Henry VIII to defy the authority of a Pope who would not grant him a divorce. When Henry made himself the head of the Church of England in 1533, he inadvertently encouraged religious dissenters all over Europe to consider that they might challenge the authority of Rome as well. Among those reformers the Puritans emerged as part of the Reformation movement, and they brought down the English monarchy by committing regicide against Charles I in 1649. But before that traumatic event, while the dissenters were still being persecuted by the Church of England, a small band of Puritans embarked for Holland and eventually sailed to America to seek religious freedom. In America, they imagined themselves to be fulfilling a sacred errand into the wilderness, and that act would come to be seen as the foundational event for the later establishment of the United States of America.

Before turning to the full story of the Puritans, however, there is one other European country that must be recognized for its strong presence in America decades before the Pilgrims landed. While the significance of "New France" has not held the attention of historians in the way that "New England" has, the relationships that the French established with the Indians in the sixteenth century had a major impact on the attitudes that the Native peoples had toward the English settlers when they did arrive in the early seventeenth century.

Neighbors to the Puritans in the northeastern part of North America, who are almost never mentioned in books about the English settlers, are the French. Nearly fifty years before the first Jamestown settlement was established in 1605, and seventy years before the Pilgrims landed in Plymouth, the French had two settlements in what would become Florida, Charlesfort in 1562 and Fort Caroline in 1564. Fort Caroline was destroyed by the Spanish in 1565 as part of a continuing rivalry between the two nations for control of the North American South and southwest. In 1605, the French established the first European colony in what would become Canada at Port Royal, and the destruction of that colony by the English in 1613 initiated a French-English contest for control of Canada. In 1627, the territory of New France was formally established in North America by a royal charter that designated the lands from the Atlantic to the Great Lakes and from Florida to the Arctic to be under French control. Of course, the Spanish and the English both took issue with that French proclamation. Because of a continuing war between France and England in Europe, intermittent fighting between the forces of these two countries occurred in North America, but in spite of these distractions, French traders and missionaries made considerable progress developing profitable business and farming in the areas around the Great Lakes near what would be, many decades later, the borderlands of Canada and the United States.

While there were many similarities between the colonizing done by the French Catholics and the English Puritans, there were also marked differences that reflect the two cultures as well as the physical circumstances of their differing geographic settings. Just as in Puritan New England where economic motives and religious fervor combined to inspire colonization, so too did the French combine trading and proselytizing in their efforts to serve God and country. Both colonies also were separated by an ocean and great distance from their home governments and thus were able to operate with a high degree of autonomy. In both cases, the result was that within a few decades of their beginnings, the attitudes, lifestyles, and cultural identities of those in America led them to seem to be nearly a distinct people from their European countrymen and women. It should be noted, however, that there were also a significant number of French Protestants, or Huguenots, who migrated to America in the seventeenth century to escape persecution in France, and the New England Puritans felt a strong alliance with them as a people who also had fled Europe to practice their own form of Christianity in a new land. But the Huguenots did not compose a substantially large enough community in New France to affect the relations between the French Catholics and the English Protestants of New England. For the most part then, there was no sense of alliance between the English in New England and the French colonists only three or four hundred miles to their west, since long-standing distrust between the two countries in Europe had persisted for centuries. In fact, by the end of the seventeenth century, the French presence in the upper mid-west had come to be viewed by the English as a barrier to their westward expansion, and the military engagements between the French and their Indian allies on the one side and the forces of the British Army and their New England militia grew into the devastating French and Indian Wars of the mid-eighteenth century.

All of which leads to this question: how did it happen that the French colonies were able to develop such positive relations with the Native peoples that they fought together as allies against the English in 1763, while associations between the Indians and the Puritans as well as the other English colonies along the eastern seaboard were more often hostile and verging on violence? There are several distinct reasons for these divergent relationships: religious, economic, and cultural.

The English were mainly farmers, fishermen, and manufacturers. They viewed land as something to be possessed, enclosed, cultivated, and protected, and they sought to establish towns and cities that required square miles of cleared land. Such a process of clearing and expansion meant that the English were constantly moving west, infringing upon tribal lands, and claiming new lands as their own. The French depended mainly on trapping, hunting, and trading and thus only set up small outposts and a few forts along the rivers of the New France territories. Indeed, they left the forests untouched since they needed the vast woods of the Northwest for the fur trade. Since the Native people themselves knew the forests so well, the French hired Indian guides to show them the richest trapping and hunting area. Thus, the French seemed to be taking very little and offering a profitable arrangement in return. The French also adapted themselves to the ways of the Indians; they became expert at living on the land and negotiating the complex web of waterways that enabled them to travel by canoe from the Saint Lawrence River to the Great Lakes to the Mississippi and on to the Gulf of Mexico.

Such differences in approach did not depend entirely upon economic interests, however. The French were far more inclined to adapt to the lifestyle and habits of the Native peoples than the English Protestants. For unlike the English, the French practiced "cultural relativism," and early on, they adopted the clothing, languages, food, and customs of the Indians, and encouraged intermarriage. While not giving up their religious beliefs or their identity as French people, the colonizers quickly blended with the Natives, and their priests converted far higher number of Indians to Catholicism. This was not achieved without great sacrifice and perseverance, for many of the Jesuits, or the "Black-Robes" as the Indians called them, were tortured and killed in America for their efforts. These devoted missionaries frequently found themselves at odds with the leaders of the French government who were more inclined to view the Native peoples as savages to be exploited rather than as human with souls to be saved. But unlike the Protestant clergy in New England who, as a rule, worked closely together with the civic leaders for the common goals of the community, the Catholic priests emphasized their independence from the state and persisted in their own mission of conversion long after most of the Protestant ministers in New England had abandoned that part of their errand into the wilderness. The English Puritans were far more insistent that Indian converts become more like white people culturally as well as spiritually. To be sure, there were examples of Puritans who were captured by the Natives and who became "Indianized" after living with a tribe for a long period, and there were some like Thomas Morton and Roger Williams who chose to live with the Indians and who came to appreciate their form of civilization. Not known for their tolerance for difference, however, Puritan clergy and magistrates viewed such "white Indians" as freaks or aberrations who had been bewitched and given up their identities as English.

The worldview of the Puritans, as this book will show, was not relativist at all. There were only two ways of doing things: God's way or the Devil's way. God's people were meant to live in enclosed communities surrounding a church, safe from the demons of the forests, and God's chosen were meant to marry among themselves. The rigorous requirements for proving oneself worthy to be a member of the congregation and of the chosen were, as we shall see later, quite demanding. Consequently, very few Indians could be identified as saved Christians, and thus there was little intermarriage between Natives and English in Puritan New England. For these reasons, the historian Edmund S. Morgan proclaimed that the Puritans were themselves the most "tribal" of all peoples.

When we look back today on the colonization of North America and examine the English Protestants in isolation, it appears inevitable that the English would soon abandon their plan to convert the Indians to Christianity and then initiate a process of expulsion and annihilation of the Native peoples from their lands that would not end until every indigenous nation had been destroyed. When we look at the ways in which the French and the Indians of the Ohio valley and upper Great Lake regions integrated, prospered, and fought together against the English, however, it is evident that there was an alternative model of behavior to the pursuit of the elimination of the Native peoples that became the goal of the English Protestants. It was, instead, the result of an inexorable coming together of cultural vision, religious values, particular government policies, and economic pursuits. As the Puritan scholar Sacvan Bercovitch has expressed it, the English Puritans looked at the land of North America and saw it in terms of Biblical types – the New Zion or Promised Land waiting for them to cultivate it for Christ. The French Catholics looked at it and saw it as an allegory, a stage on which several different narratives might be inscribed simultaneously. Clearly, a singleness of vision and purpose results in more direct and aggressive action with devastating consequences for those who stand in the way of its fulfillment.

Like the Spanish explorers, the French also published writings about their experiences in the New World. Authors whose names have rarely appeared in anthologies of American literature – such as Jean Ribault, Rene de Laudonniere, Marc Lescarbot, Jaques Cartier, Samuel de Champlain, Rene Robert Cavelier Sieur de La Salle, Gavbriel Sagard, and Jacques Marquette, and others – contributed important histories, personal narratives, and captivity narratives that describe experiences with the Native Americans and the New World from perspectives that are quite different from those of the English. The seventy-three volumes of the *Jesuit Relations*, which contain the reports from the Jesuit missions in North America over the course of the seventeenth century, describe the peculiarities of the human experiences of the Indians and the colonists in detail not found in many English texts. The works of these French writers are powerful in their own right and help to provide an important dimension of the cultural context into which the English settlers were entering as their ships arrived on the coast of New England.

It is important when examining the history and writings of the New England Puritans to remember that the Native peoples were always present in the daily lives and thoughts of the English colonists. Too many histories of early America have given the impression that the Europeans were settlers in a New World that was nearly devoid of other peoples or that the people who were there were unsophisticated and lacking in cultural traditions. A substantial body of scholarship now exists that demonstrates beyond any doubt that the Europeans and their descendents created the myth of the virgin land inhabited by primitive savages as one part of their strategy for justifying the invasion and occupation of the rich territories of the Americas.

When the English arrived in New England, they understood that the land upon which they settled had been occupied and disputed over by many tribes and clans for centuries. In the New England region, resided the nations of the Pequot, the Massachusetts, the Mohegan, the Narragansett, the Pocumtuck, the Wampanoag, the Algonquian, the Abenakis, the Niantic, and the Iroquois, among others. Each group spoke a different language or dialect and differed from others as distinctly as the peoples of different European nations did. The Native people knew very well of the technological superiority of the Europeans in war, for news had been circulating for decades throughout the Americas about the devastating effects of firearms.

Some of the Indians in New England had already managed to get possession of a few muskets. In their wisdom, however, they knew their military disadvantage and sought first to find a peaceful arrangement for accommodating the English.

In the first years of the settlement at Plymouth, the Wampanoag king, Chief Massasoit, and the English settlers established a treaty that led the Chief to bring ninety of his braves and a supply of venison to celebrate. This event was romanticized in the nineteenth century as part of a myth that characterized the Native people as willing participants in their own passive demise. In reality, the Indian toleration of English encroachment and the English restraint did not last long, and by the mid-1620s armed conflict was imminent. This pattern of a wary peace followed by armed conflict was established in the first decade of the English occupation, and it was repeated on an increasingly larger scale over the next century.

The English also learned about some bitter rivalries among the local Native tribes, and for a time they were able to exploit these differences among the Indians to their own advantage. From the time of the arrival of the first Europeans, firearms were highly valued as items of barter with the Indians who could gain a significant advantage over their tribal enemies with these new weapons. Fur traders and fishermen who were not Puritans were willing to trade guns to the Indians for furs and information that would help their fishing and hunting. Even before the Pilgrims arrived in Plymouth in 1620, some of the coastal tribes possessed a few guns. The first English settlers recognized the grave danger to their lives and communities of the growing number of guns, and by 1627, they were trying to put a stop to the spread of firearms among the tribes. One of the most famous rascals of Puritan New England was Thomas Morton who between 1625 and 1627 established a very anti-Puritan village near Plymouth that he called Merrymount where he held festivities with dancing and drinking for his fellow Englishmen and Indian women. In addition to his offensive morals, he also sold guns to the Native Americans in the region, and for that violation he was arrested and deported to England. This event was only the beginning, however, of increasing conflicts between the Indians and the Puritans that grew more frequent as the number of English colonists grew rapidly in the 1630s. The war between the colonists and the Pequot nation in 1637 was the first major conflict and an important turning point in the relations between the whites and the indigenous peoples. It culminated in horrific destruction in which the English surrounded Mystic Fort where about 500 Pequot men, women, and children were sleeping; they set fire to the fort with the result that all of the Pequot either burned to death or were killed trying to escape the flames.

From that day forward, the tribal peoples of the northeast avoided challenging the Puritans, but they also remained suspicious of them and anticipated that one day they would have to fight to defend their lands. There were many individual Indians who became friends with the English and a considerable number who were converted to Christianity and became "Praying Indians," as they were called, but the continual expansion of the English into the western lands increased tensions and led to periodic raids, skirmishes, and hostage taking. The number of New Englanders who were captured between 1675 and 1763 has been estimated to be over 1,600, giving rise to the literary genre of the captivity narratives of which there were many in New England Puritan writing.

After about fifty years of rising tensions between the English and the Native peoples, the surviving members of some of various tribes were brought together under Metacom, the sachem[1] of the Wampanoag tribe, to start what became a major war upon the English settlers. Metacom, or King Philip, as he was called by the English, managed to sustain armed conflict for about thirteen months. The English losses were severe with the death or injury of a higher percentage of the population than has occurred in any American war since. About ten percent of those who fought were killed, and the psychological and social impact of the war had lasting effects upon the New England colonies.

Although the Puritan community as a recognizable social entity ceased to exist by the later part of the eighteenth century, many of the Puritan concepts, rhetorical strategies, desires, beliefs, cultural attitudes, and imaginary projections upon the American landscape continued long after to have an impact on public policy. As the Europeans continued to expand into the Ohio Valley and to the Mississippi, the Native peoples became more resistant to what they then fully recognized to be a threat to their very survival. In response to the claims of the indigenous peoples to their right to live on the lands of their ancestors, the Anglo-Americans developed the ideological principle of Manifest Destiny that emerged from perspectives formed during the period of Puritan colonization in New England.

The Puritan notion that God had preserved the New World in isolation from the Old throughout human history because He wished to give His Chosen People a second chance for redemption was a powerful motivation and a justification for taking possession of America. The westward expansion of the United States in the nineteenth century under President Andrew Jackson and other leaders was rationalized to a large degree by the concept of Manifest Destiny. When, for example, Jackson authorized the military to remove the last remaining tribes from the eastern seaboard to the southwest, he based his arguments for doing so on Manifest Destiny. Violent aggression against the Native peoples of America became seen as God's will by most white Americans. During the first 350 years of European migration and conquest of the continents of the Americas, some of the European governments and some of the colonial leaders in America did make efforts to negotiate sales, treaties, and various mutually agreed upon exchanges which were legal in the minds of the Europeans. As their desires for more land and resources increased, so did their impatience with negotiation.

This is a story that continues today as throughout the United States tribal peoples still struggle to regain some degree of legal and moral status in a place where 500 years ago the idea of a white person was only a ghost story. Today, many Native people in America strive to rediscover, preserve, and celebrate their cultural heritages through local performances and literature and through research and teaching. Through their histories and art forms, they are recovering their tribal identities and enriching the culture of the United States as well.

Although both the Spanish and the French made significant inroads into parts of the southern section of the North American continent during the sixteenth century, it was primarily the English who settled the territories that would eventually stretch from what became Maryland to Florida and would spread westward from the coastline to the Smokey Mountains. The beginnings were quite inauspicious, however, for after John Cabot explored the North American coast for England in 1598, England conducted little activity in the Americas until the Jamestown settlement in 1607. When that village was quickly devastated by disease, starvation, and Indian attacks, England appeared to become more determined, and the London Company sent more men and supplies under Captain John Smith who was able to establish stability. In 1612, John Rolfe joined the colony and successfully cultivated the first tobacco crop there. The Indians still remained unsure of the English until 1614 when Rolfe married Pocahontas, the daughter of the chief Powhatan, thereby bringing peace and prosperity and generating one of the most romantic tales of English-Indian relations in America.

Quickly, the tobacco crop became a staple of the English colonial economy in the South and the need for cheap labor rapidly increased with the result that indentured servants and slaves became an economic solution. Slavery had been introduced into the New World by the Portuguese and the Spanish who first enslaved the Indians they conquered in the West Indies and Latin America. Because the Native Americans usually knew quite well the lands in which they were held and they possessed deep hatred for their recent conquerors, they refused to work and were often able to escape. Since 1440, the Portuguese explorers to Africa had been engaged in the exploitation of Africans as slaves. As agricultural crops such as sugar, coffee, rice, and tobacco became crucial trading commodities in the Americas, planters who sought to increase the size of their plantations sought out African slaves to work the fields. Thus, as the Virginia Company came to prosper, the first shipload of African slaves arrived in the English southern settlements in 1619, one year before the arrival of the Pilgrims at Plymouth.

The plantation economy prospered during the seventeenth century in the South and with growth came more slaves. Religious tolerance prevailed in the South resulting in a greater diversity of religious groups and perspectives and a gradual separation between the clergy and secular leaders. The South also had a hierarchical social system of landed gentry who possessed the leisure to develop their taste for the finer pleasures of music, dance, and *belle lettres*. Although there was also considerable religious literature in the South as in the North, Southern readers and authors favored classical literature and the more secular English literature. Thus, the South of the seventeenth and eighteenth centuries produced a considerable body of lyric and epic poetry, satire, and comedy. Written primarily by aristocrats of classical training, the literature of the South is witty, sophisticated, and artistically self-conscious. *The History of the Dividing Line* (w. 1729–38) by William Byrd II, which is often anthologized today, is an elegantly written description of life on Southern plantations. Robert Beverley's *The History of the Present State of Virginia* (1705) contains humor and satiric commentary on the foibles of the planters and their families.

The regions between New England and the Chesapeake usually referred to as the "Middle Colonies" were less well defined by ethnicity or religion than those societies to their north and south. The Dutch settlements of New Amsterdam (later Manhattan), and New Netherlands (now New York and New Jersey) prospered in the early decades of the seventeenth century until they were captured by the English government forces in 1664. To their southwest, William Penn was able to procure a charter from the English government in 1681 to establish a settlement, which became Pennsylvania, where religious freedom was an established right. This settlement became a safe haven for persecuted people, such as the Quakers and the Mennonites. With the strong emphasis on brotherhood and toleration, immigrants who were drawn to Pennsylvania in huge numbers in the 1680s avoided conflict with the Indians and opposed slavery. Penn himself insisted that all land allocated to Europeans first be legally purchased from the Native peoples. During the eighteenth century, Philadelphia, the adopted home of Benjamin Franklin, developed into the leading cultural center in the colonies, and the region produced many fine writers such as John Woolman, who produced powerful abolitionist texts. Among the best authors of poetry, plays, and fiction, writers such as Thomas Godfrey, William Smith, Hugh Henry Brackenridge, and Charles Brockton Brown, lived in Philadelphia and contributed to its reputation for intellectual life. The region that became the State of Maryland began to take shape as a colony when Charles I granted a charter to Lord George Calvert in 1632. The territory was named Maryland in honor of Henrietta Maria, the Queen Consort of Charles I. Calvert's son was a Catholic and undertook the colony as a refuge for persecuted Catholics. The land was occupied by the Algonquin-speaking peoples who withdrew peacefully, sparing Maryland from a potentially devastating war. From the time that the Puritans took control of the government in England, the legal rights and religious freedom of Marylanders were in jeopardy. As the Puritans grew more numerous in America and more powerful in Parliament, a local civil war paralleling the one in England ensued in the colony in which the Puritans emerged as the victors in 1655 and took control of Maryland territory. In 1657 the weakened Protectorate of Oliver Cromwell imposed a compromise, but the Maryland Colony remained in peril until the Glorious Revolution in England in 1688 when the control of the Colony passed to the Crown who established the Church of England as the official church. The most notable work of literature to emerge from Maryland in the seventeenth century is the comic poem, *The Sot-Weed Factor*, by Ebenezer Cook. It is a mock epic that satirizes social life and the political chaos of the colonial marketplace, and its tone and spirit were captured in the modern novel by John Barth also entitled *The Sot-Weed Factor* (1960).

Note

1 The wise man or philosopher of the tribe.

Chapter Two

The language of Salem witchcraft

Few events have captured the imaginations of Americans as powerfully as the Salem Village witchcraft trials of 1692. Assessments of the entire Puritan period have achieved their sharpest focus through an analysis of the Salem trials, which have served as a litmus test for theories about the nature of life in early America. Some social historians find the reasons for the trauma in economic causes, with the jealous resentment of the disadvantaged leading them to strike out against their circumstances as well as against particular social enemies. One localized version of this argument focuses upon the feuding factions of Salem Village, whose long-term battle seems to have predetermined the would-be accused and accusers. Cultural anthropologists and psycho historians have read the Salem records as discursive expressions of anxieties brought on by the rapid succession of political and economic events in the 1680s, which were exacerbated by a series of crises, including fires, floods, disease, and Indian attacks. Other accounts emphasize the role of the common people, who discovered demonism to be a weapon with which to threaten the established powers. Because a high percentage of those tried and punished were women, a number of whom owned property under challenge, some interpretations present evidence of the efforts of jeopardized male authorities to repress rising female independence and economic autonomy. In different ways, most interpreters share the assumption that the Salem incident marks a critical turning point in New England history when old religious values were in question and new secular ones were being formed. Accordingly, the witchcraft delusion is most often perceived as the site of a profound cultural transformation.

Although all of these arguments enliven our conversations about New England history, each is but another attempt to re-create in our imaginations the realities of that former time through words. Indeed, then as now, we must turn to words and expression if we are to grasp the connections between shadowy motivations and their often shocking and brutal public results. In Salem Village, language and imagination were the central components in the catastrophic events that marked the last days of an aspiring Christian utopia. Words projected a network of evil conspiracy in which anyone might be a scheming villain. The accused were suddenly transfigured in the minds of their neighbors into demons, monsters, enemies, aliens – exotic others from a dark world. Having survived, and even prospered, during decades of natural disaster, political persecution, and bloody war, the residents of Salem discovered their most terrifying menace within their borders. In a tragic summer that left twenty dead and scores imprisoned, the citizens acted out a bloody judicial process that would become paradigmatic of all subsequent forms of "witch-hunting."

No case better illustrates the crucial role of language in the formative events of Salem than that of Rebecca Nurse. During Nurse's trial, the jury at first found her innocent of witchcraft but then reversed its decision when the magistrates refused to accept the verdict. The judges declared that the jury had failed to consider a "self-incriminating" statement Nurse had made on the witness stand. In itself, the statement was actually very ambiguous: Nurse had merely questioned why two confessed witches, Abigail Hobbs and her daughter Deliverance, were allowed to testify against her when they were, in her words, people who "used to come to her." For no apparent reason, the magistrates chose to interpret her words as an admission that she saw these women regularly at witch gatherings. The jury heard differently, at least initially. The court clerk, Thomas Fitch, recorded that "after the honored court had manifest their dissatisfaction of the Verdict, several of the jury declared themselves desirous to go out again, and thereupon the honored court gave leave." When the jury appeared to not comprehend the "proper" meaning of Nurse's words, the magistrates provided them with an official interpretation. As Fitch reports, "these words were to me a principal Evidence against her."

Upon learning later about the confusion over her phrasing, Nurse petitioned the court to take into consideration what she really meant in her statement – that because Goodwife Hobbs and her daughter were imprisoned with her in the Salem jail, they were allowed to come into her company there and question her, thereby gathering incriminating material for testimony against her in court. She was incredulous that the statements of these unreliable prisoners were used as the critical evidence in her conviction. When she was questioned about this matter in court, she had been totally unaware that her words were being misinterpreted, for, as she explained, "being hard for hearing, and full of grief, none informing me how the court took up my words, and therefore, [I] had not the opportunity to declare what I intended when I said they were of our company." In spite of this plea and a petition signed by over forty citizens on her behalf, she was hanged on July 19, 1692. Words, and interpretations of them, could be fatal.

The only facts that can ever be known about the disturbing events at Salem are the words left to describe them – the verbal codes, now three centuries old, that were charged with associations and meanings that modern vocabularies have attempted to recast and make discernible for contemporary readers. The various analyses of the texts produced by those events have raised questions about a range of issues that the language of the Salem trials verbalized: questions about social and political authority, gender roles, religious order, theology, economics, and literary matters themselves – narrative structure, imagery, typology, and class-coded dialogues. Yet many questions remain: for example, before that fateful year, charges of witchcraft were nearly always treated by the clergy and the magistrates with great skepticism and dealt with in protracted proceedings that served to quell emotions and remove matters to distant courts, where they usually ended months later without resolution. In contrast, the Salem documents indicate that although many of the clergy were initially wary, especially on point of evidence, the magistrates appear to have joined forces with the accusers and confessed witches and inexplicably to have become themselves caught up in the frenzy of the hunt.

During those tumultuous months, some of the condemned citizens presented reasonable pleas to the officials imploring them to reexamine the process and the rules of evidence. In July, as he awaited execution, John Proctor desperately wrote to five Boston clergymen that "the magistrates, ministers, juries, and all the people in general, are so much enraged and incensed against us by the Delusion of the Devil, which we can term no other, by reason we know in our Consciences, we are all innocent persons." After describing in precise and deliberate terms how the accusations of confessed witches and suspicious persons had been accepted as fact and how young people, including his son, were tortured until they confessed to witchcraft, Proctor begged the Boston clergy to have "these magistrates changed and others put in their place who must conduct fair trials."

In September, knowing she was to die, Mary Easty tried to save others when she wrote:

> I petition your honors not for my own life, for I know I must die and my appointed time is set, but the Lord he knows it is that if it be possible no more innocent blood may be shed which undoubtedly cannot be avoided in the way and course you go in. . . . I know that you are in the wrong way . . . and if your honors would be pleased to examine these afflicted persons strictly and keep them apart some time . . . I am confident that several of them [would have] belied themselves and others [who are lying] will appear.

Why were these reasonable requests ignored?

There are other mysteries. The texts of the accusations and the responses of the accused are quite varied and full of amplification between February and May, but the complaints during the summer months became increasingly more formulaic and the trials more theatrical, as though played out by set scripts. In these enactments, the roles of the magistrates and the bewitched accusers seem to become intertwined in a sustained effort to torment and harass the accused into confessions. Quite often the judges seem to employ verbal manipulation to obtain guilty verdicts. Indeed, what emerges from a chronological reading of the *Salem Witchcraft Papers* is an increasing similarity over several months in the tone and diction of the magistrates, the accusers, and the confessing witches, and a sharpening contrast between the tense, emotional, and strident language of those who confessed and the more objective, reasonable, and surprised tone of those who refused. The more sensible an accused person sounded, the greater the possibility that he or she would be executed, as concessions quickly became the only route to survival.

With these matters in mind, it is possible to approach the question of the vigorous engagement of the magistrates from a new historical perspective. Throughout the seventeenth century, the ministers claimed special rights and power in interpreting the language of the supernatural. In the scriptures, in nature, and even in daily events and in ordinary words, the learned clergy discerned hidden and arcane meanings of divine purpose. Through typological interpretations of the Bible, events, and various narratives, the clergy had formulated a Puritan linguistic system that gave meaning and purpose to the unknown. Law and government bestowed secular powers upon the magistrates, but the secular leaders deferred to the clergy in supernatural matters and in all things in which God's will could be discovered.

By the 1690s, however, the realities of New England life could no longer be made to conform to the symbolic projections of the ministers. Perhaps for this reason and for all of the political and economic reasons so often cited, the people and magistrates of Salem and surrounding villages were short on patience with clerical deliberations. Suddenly, the residents of the village embraced the language of witchcraft – a verbal legacy long available through the cultural heritage of Europe, where witchcraft episodes had been rampant for three centuries. In this parallel world of witchcraft, the people of Salem discovered an alternative linguistic system, and although the substance of what was being said may not have made any rational sense, the very fact that it confounded those in authority made it a source of political power. Through this form of discourse, those who embraced the language of witchcraft possessed a means of challenging the authorities in a society where such defiance had not been permitted in the churches or in the courts since the 1630s when the positions of Anne Hutchinson and Roger Williams were suppressed.

When confronted with the verbal outburst of 1692, the clergy found that their stock responses and practiced evasions would not serve, and without the support of the clergy in this supernatural matter, the magistrates were bewildered. Seeking higher secular authority for support, the magistrates turned to the newly appointed governor, William Phips, who in May authorized the Court of Oyer and Terminer (meaning literally "to hear and determine") to begin trials and later embarked on an extended trip, not to act on the matter again until October. Once testimony was being taken, the magistrates were exposed to the tremendous energy and psychic power of the accusers without the buffering devices of the clergy, who seemed temporarily stunned. As the judges were repeatedly forced to engage the accusations and denials, they themselves became locked into a discursive battle in which there was no neutral ground. Presented with no apparent alternatives, the magistrates followed the course of least resistance and appropriated to themselves the powerful vocabulary of witchcraft, thereby permanently eclipsing the clergy's privileged linguistic role in New England. So potent was the discourse of witchcraft that even a minister like the Reverend George Burroughs of Maine, who had been the minister of Salem Village from 1680 to 1682, was not safe from its destructive force; he was hanged in August 1692. Thus, the accusers and the confessed witches engaged their leaders in a new form of public drama – a primal dialogue through which the actors and audiences could speak to one another – a form of discursive exchange through which the powerless might engage, threaten, and even destroy their rulers. And before it was all over, so they did.

As events progressed under these conditions, the only way for the magistrates to maintain their authority and control the proceedings was to become unrelenting witch-hunters. Although it can never be known whether some interrogations were consciously designed to save or destroy lives, it is interesting that the pattern the magistrates followed in taking extreme measures to force the accused to confess might well have been the only method for saving the life of an accused. The defendants who tried to counter their prosecutors' charges with logic and reason and who treated the bewitched as sick or deranged were nearly all found guilty; ironically, those who defended themselves within the terms of the discourse of witchcraft survived. The psychological process that the magistrates employed for exacting confessions closely approximated the well-established linguistic formula for proving the presence of grace in religious conversions. Just as a minister might prepare the hearts of those yet to be saved and lead them in stages toward the moment of inner light, so in this inverse world of witchcraft, the magistrates might save an innocent life by coaxing a person to confess to imagined crimes.

Some of the petitions for the freedom of those still in prison in December and January, long after the panic had ended, indicate the increasing realization that confession was the only possible means for an accused to escape execution. The plea for the release of Mary Osgood and others who had confessed is quite direct on the point:

> By the unwearied solicitations of those that privately discoursed with them both at home and at Salem, they were at length persuaded publicly to own what they were charged with, and so submit to that guilt which we still hope and believe they are clear of. And, it is a probability, the fear of what the event might be, that confessing was the only way to obtain favor, might be too powerful a temptation for a timorous woman to withstand, in the hurry and distraction that we have heard.

The tactful and considered term "unwearied solicitations" used here rather than some more derogatory expression may suggest awareness that such solicitations saved Osgood's life.

Along with these observations regarding the verbal tactics of the magistrates, an examination of the dynamics of the dialogues in two famous cases reveals important dimensions of the pattern. When Susannah Martin entered the courtroom on May 2, it was still early enough in the trials that she felt free to laugh when the afflicted girls cried out and fell down at her appearance. To her mind, good sense and shared adult understanding of the silliness of children would prevail over such nonsense. She quickly learns, however, that the magistrate, who is not identified but is most likely John Hathorne, is not a neutral participant; he is her prosecutor:

> "Why do you laugh?"
> "Well, I may at such folly."
> "Is this folly? The hurt of these persons?"

Assuming that her reputation as a civil member of the community will be a valid defense, Martin answers:

> "I never hurt a man, woman, or child."

At this point the drama heightens as Mercy Lewis cries out against her, and the clerk reports:

> "And she laughed again."

Perhaps impatient and eager to end the proceedings quickly, Martin addresses the court with what is for her a statement of fact:

> "I have no hand in witchcraft."

But to accumulate evidence against her, the magistrate ignores this declaration and pursues the issue of the children's suffering:

> "What ails them?"
> "I do not know."

Now that he has Martin engaged in a dialogue about what are assumed to be the results of witchcraft – assumptions that are already entertained by the audience – the magistrate springs a verbal trap. Martin is now enough on guard to try to evade it:

> "What *do you think* [ails them]?" (italics in original)

Knowing that whatever answer she gives to this query will be turned against her, Martin begins to show an awareness of the danger of her situation:

> "I do not desire to spend my judgement upon it."

But he persists:

> "Do you think they are *bewitched*?" (italics in original)

Martin had reached a pivotal moment here because were she to say that they were bewitched and then accuse others of bewitching them and herself or were she to confess her own guilt and participation, she might still save herself, leave the anxious bench, and join the chorus in the gallery. But she disdains to engage in the language of witchcraft and bravely, but fatally, persists in declaring her innocence:

> "No, I do not think they are."

Now the magistrate knows that he has enough of a verbal commitment from her to turn her words upon her:

> "What *do* you think about them?" (italics in original)

At this point, Martin appears to realize her mistake, but it is too late, for she has engaged in the fatal discourse of witchcraft even by denying its effects. In one of the most interesting acknowledgments of the power of words in the records, she says:

> "My thoughts are my own, when they are in, but when they are out, they are another's. I desire to lead myself according to the word of God."

In other words, the only safety is in silence. Without her own words to use against her, the magistrates would have had to concede that her case was based only on spectral evidence. Although she was naive in her initial presumption that her innocence could save her, Martin is not ignorant of the principles of Puritan theology as they apply to witchcraft cases, for she attacks the use of spectral evidence by reminding the court of past arguments against it: that when dealing with the world of the supernatural, no living person can be certain of the meaning of particular signs or appearances. She tells the magistrate:

> "He that appeared in someone's shape or in a glorified shape can appear in anyone's shape."

Her argument here contends that even if the court grants the honesty of the children's report and even if it is believed they saw a vision of her that seemed to injure them, there is still no valid proof that she was involved personally and is a witch, for Satan may use the image of a goodly person as well as an evil one to do harm, and, in fact, that wily deceiver may be more likely to do so.

At this point in the proceedings, the magistrate is not about to dispute theology with a witch. Perhaps hoping to catch her off guard, he directly accuses her of dishonesty. Calmly and firmly, she responds:

> "I dare not tell a lie if it would save my life."

Perhaps she understood that this is exactly what a lie would do. The magistrate's parting statement is significant both for what he says and for what he does not. His words are "Pray God discover you, if you be guilty"; however, the meaning of this coded language may be restated thus: "I hope that if you are guilty, as I think you are, God will cause you to confess your guilt, for that is the only chance you have to save your life." This seems to be the meaning that Martin takes, for she answers:

> "Amen, Amen. A false tongue will never make a guilty person."

By this, she seems to mean what other condemned prisoners might have articulated to friends and loved ones from the Salem prison: "Even if I confess to being guilty, I will know that I am innocent, and the lie that will save my earthly life will condemn me to eternal damnation. Better to die and be saved than to live now and perish eternally in hell." Susannah Martin was executed two months later on July 19.

In the early weeks of the trials, many of the accused were completely startled that the judges could take the absurd accusations of disturbed people seriously. The curt, straightforward replies of the accused contrast sharply with the ranting of their accusers and the verbal machinations of the magistrates. Examined on March 21, Martha Corey was one of the first to undergo interrogation. Questioned by both John Hathorne and Nicholas Noyes, Corey tried to persuade her jurors of her innocence with calm and sensible answers to the charges. Again Hathorne begins with an assumption of her guilt:

> "You are now in the hands of Authority. Tell me why you hurt these persons."
> "I do not."
> "Who doth?"

> "Pray give me leave to go to prayer. [This request was made several times.] I am an innocent person: I never had to do with witchcraft since the day I was born. I am a gospel woman."

Corey then makes a temporary verbal escape from the apparent lie against her by saying that she did not know how the children were injured but only *thought* or *speculated* about the matter, but a child exclaims that "there is a man whispering in her ear." Hathorne takes this assertion as truth and asks Corey:

> "What did he say to you?"

Corey attempts to establish some kind of bond with Hathorne by assuming that the two of them recognize that children can be mischievous. She says:

> "We must not believe all that these distracted children say."

Maybe Hathorne does have sympathy for her at this moment, for he gives her perhaps the best advice he can under the circumstances.

> "If you expect mercy of God, you must look for it in God's way by Confession."

But like Susannah Martin, she spurns the language of witchcraft by replying logically:

> "Can an innocent person be guilty?"

As the rigorous questioning continues and as other members of the court join in the proceedings, the clerk records: "It was noted that she bit her lip several times and at the same time several of the afflicted bit their lips." It was also observed that when her hands were unbound, all of the afflicted girls were pinched by unseen hands, but when Corey was tied again, they were at rest. Noyes asks her: "Do you not see these women and children are rational and sober as their neighbors when your hands are fastened?" With this Corey grows weary and begins to give up the fight:

> "When all are against me, what can I help it? If you will all go and hang me, how can I help it? You are all against me, and I cannot help it."

At this point, Magistrate Noyes takes up the questioning and asks her if she was in covenant with the Devil for ten years. When she laughs at this suggestion, the children cry out that they see a yellow bird with her. When Hathorne asks her about the bird, she again laughs. To provide conclusive evidence of her guilt, Noyes asks her a series of catechism questions, which she readily answers until he gets to the mystery of the Trinity:

"How many gods are there?"
"One."
"How many persons are there?"
"Three."
"Cannot you say so there is one God in three blessed persons?"

The clerk notes at this point: "She then was troubled." The sacred language of Christian theology has become a weapon in this battle of deadly words. From late spring until fall, efforts continued to persuade Martha and her husband, Giles, to confess to several crimes, but they refused to avail themselves of the language of the authorities and their accusers. Giles was pressed to death during questioning on September 19 and Martha was hung on September 22 along with six other women and one man.

During the summer of 1692, it became evident that confession – the acknowledgment of the power of the court and of the bewitched – was a defendant's only means of survival. Indeed, once it became evident that mimicry of confessed witches was the key to earthly salvation, the task for the accused was to create engaging and convincing confessional narratives. Since there seems to have been relatively little actual occult activity in New England before 1692, there were few sources for provocative details to embellish the testimony and confessions. For this reason, the testimony of Tituba, a slave woman from the Caribbean, early in March proved a fount of occult images from the African and Caribbean traditions. Her reward for her titillating testimony was not only her life but the contribution of her narrative details to many of the trials. During the summer, the confessions became more elaborate and were sprinkled with the same repeated occult phantasms: the yellow bird, the black man with the black book, pins and puppets, witch meetings in the forest, and spectral appearances of all of the previously accused witches, with a few new names usually added. The language of witchcraft also took on distinctly racial dimensions as the Devil was often identified as black and many activities of the witches occurred in the forest, where the witches interacted with Indians. Cotton Mather believed that the rise in witchcraft had "some of its Original among the *Indians*, whose chief *Sagamores* are well known unto some of our Captives, to have been horrid *Sorcerers*, and hellish *Conjurers*, and such as Conversed with *Daemons*" (italics in original).

After the horrifying event of the several executions of July 19, there commenced an orgy of confessions. On July 21, Mary Lacy, Sr. confessed to riding on a pole through the sky before falling into the water, where the Devil baptized her; on August 10, Elizabeth Johnson, Jr. confessed to using puppets to torment others; on August 30, Elizabeth Johnson, Sr. answered yes to every accusation made against her and then described a white bird and a black man who came to her; on September 1, Stephen Johnson confessed to being baptized by the Devil when he was swimming and to tormenting others himself. The most remarkable outpouring of witchcraft language came from fifteen-year-old Mary Lacy, Jr. who on July 21 – which surely must have been a day of terror for those in custody because of the outpouring of new accusations against them as well as new victims – accused her mother of making her a witch. The prolific Mary provided several pages of testimony in which she described several events: conversations with the Devil; drinking hard cider with Richard Carrier, whom she also accused; seeing black cats, which she believed sucked the body of Goody Carrier; riding on a pole above the trees; knowing of the killing of children with puppets; and attending a black mass in the forest celebrated by the Reverend George Burroughs, who served communion of brown bread and red wine from earthen cups. When asked why she and her fellow witches sought to hurt the people of the village, Mary gave an answer – cast in the jeremiad rhetoric of the Puritan pulpit – that became the standard response to this otherwise bewildering question: "The Devil would set up his Kingdom here and we should have happy days and it then be better times for me if I would obey him."

In a process that we would call today troping or parodying the established Puritan religious language and typology, William Barker borrowed the terms of an election day sermon in his confession: "And the design was to destroy Salem Village, and to begin at the minister's house, and to destroy the church of God and to set up Satan's Kingdoms, . . . and to destroy that place by reason of the people's being divided and their differing with their ministers." Such interweaving of the profane language of witchcraft with the sacred idiom of the Puritan sermon articulated the doom of a once vital and energizing verbal system that had been sustained for seven decades through the course of religious belief and clerical power over language. Moreover, it signaled that the trials had become the site of a dangerous discursive field in which power circulated through language.

A critical question confronts social and literary historians engaged in interrogating the experience and the discourse produced by the Salem witchcraft episode: how did it happen that such a violent verbal explosion occurred in a community that had been dedicated to fleeing persecution for the joy of Christian fellowship and peace? By 1695, the New Englanders wanted to look back upon the events at Salem as constituting a rupture, a delusion, an aberration, in an otherwise glorious history that Cotton Mather and others were steadfastly in the process of transforming into myth. Examination of the record and of the historic development of the language and literature of Puritan New England reveals that the seeds of the Salem tragedy were planted at the start and that the fruit it bore resulted from decades of cultivation of symbolic meanings, verbal inventions, and discursive descriptions. In many ways, the story of the literature of Puritan New England reads as a cautionary tale of how – through grand design, through conscious decisions and unconscious delusions, through sincere or self-serving verbal stratagems – the utopian dream of joyful fellowship metamorphosed into the realities of confusion, accusation, terror, and lamentation of 1692. Though frequently with the best of intentions, the lawmakers and word-makers of Puritan New England inadvertently guided their experiment from the promise of John Winthrop's utopian dream of 1630 to the failures of the 1680s and 1690s. Along the way, Puritan authors captured in their writings the experience of a people who sought perfection in this world and salvation in the next but who, from the beginning, deeply feared that their realities were falling short of their dreams.

Chapter Three

The dream of a Christian utopia

In fascinating ways, the literature of the New England Puritans reveals – and at times conceals – the remarkable number of contradictions in their religious, social, and political ideas, and it demonstrates how they managed to balance opposing aspirations and ideals to sustain a society that was from the start fragmenting from internal conflicts. Despite their tenacious struggles to achieve clarity in their expressions of purpose and design, the Puritans were frequently ambiguous and paradoxical. This chapter attempts to account for the compulsions, dissensions, and convergences within their culture and to demonstrate the intellectual complexity of their thought and writing. Language and literary forms both generated and formulated narrative expressions of the experiences of individuals and their communities as the generations journeyed from the bleak landing at Cape Cod to the flourishing of the New England Federation in 1642 to the tragic events at Salem in 1692.

Over the past forty years, scholarship on the American Puritans has been so rich and various that there is hardly a statement one can make about the Puritans today without arousing controversy. Scholars in every area of the humanities and social sciences have employed new theories and methodologies in their studies of Puritan New England. Because many see the Puritans as having established certain ideas and structures that are fundamental to later American society – although even this point is much debated – scholars are attracted to the study of seventeenth-century New England, and interpretations of that culture frequently have larger political and ideological implications for the United States as a whole. Competing interpretations of complex historical or theological matters are related to arguments over whether the Puritans were militant ideologues and the originators of all that is problematic in America or whether they were gentle religious idealists who earnestly sought to create a utopian community that could not be further from the realities of modern America.

In Puritan studies, disputes begin over the very meaning of the word "Puritan," to whom it could be applied, and for how long a period, if ever, a recognizable "Puritanism" existed. Originally, "Puritan" was a term of derision that moderate English Christians and Catholics cast upon radical

Protestants, who later embraced it as a badge of honor. Because there were so many competing reformist sects in England, however, it is difficult to determine exactly which groups "Puritan" described. In New England, the situation is somewhat clearer because the two larger gatherings of congregationalists established fairly homogeneous colonies. Still, scholars disagree over how long these New England Protestants adhered to the doctrines of "Puritanism"; some say for only six years, others say for sixty years, others say well into the eighteenth century, and still others claim that (lower case) "puritanism" persists in America today.

The one set of statements regarding the New England Puritans that scholars do generally agree upon is that the descriptions of the "Puritan Founding Fathers" presented by historians of fifty years ago and earlier need revision. The Puritans were neither "founders," since the land was already inhabited, nor all "fathers," since mothers, sisters, and daughters played critical roles too. Nor were the Puritans the only invaders of what the Europeans called the New World in the sixteenth and seventeenth centuries; explorers and opportunists from Spain, Holland, France, Portugal, Italy, and Africa were also here, as were members of numerous other English religious groups. The mythic picture of the Pilgrims setting foot upon a pristine new land in 1620 has been categorically rejected. On Cape Cod in 1605, the French had already killed several Native Americans in hostilities over a stolen kettle.

The implications of these recently established historical perspectives are clear. A fresh approach to the literary history of the Puritans necessarily must engage with the fact of the presence of the Native-American cultures on the land that was renamed New England and the impact of the indigenous peoples upon the Europeans and the Europeans upon them. Similarly, a current survey of Puritan writing must look more closely at the complex issue of gender in the patriarchal Puritan society and the importance of women writers who persisted in writing in spite of the pervasive strictures against them. Discussions of Puritan literature must acknowledge that no single monolithic interpretation of Puritan history exists and that every statement one makes about the subject involves a choice among several competing, but not necessarily contradictory, interpretations.

Why were certain Protestant reformers labeled "Puritans" in the late sixteenth century? The answer to that question requires a brief review of their origins in the Protestant Reformation. From the time of early Christianity, church councils resolved theological disputes, defined heresies, and submitted their opinions to the pope for final judgment. Between 1378 and 1417, however, the Catholic Church underwent a major split known as the Great Schism, which resulted in the election of two popes, one based in Rome and the other in Avignon, France. In 1414, the Council of Constance resolved the schism by deposing both acting popes and electing Martin V to be the one pope in Rome. The deeper effect of this period of schism, however, was the diminished power of the Roman church and the start of the Reformation, led by a number of important theologians, among them Martin Luther, John Huss, Jerome of Prague, Ulrich Zwingli, John Knox, and John Calvin. The religious programmes of each of these reformers engendered independent Christian churches that separated from Rome.

Within the context of this period of rebellion, King Henry VIII rejected papal authority when he was denied the pope's permission to divorce his wife, Catherine, in order to marry Anne Boleyn. In 1534, Henry declared the autonomy of the Church of England and made himself its head. Many English Catholics objected and continued to practice their Catholic faith, and when Henry's Catholic daughter, Mary, assumed the throne in 1553, she launched a reign of terror against the Protestants that earned her the designation Bloody Mary. John Foxe recounted these persecutions in his *Book of Martyrs* (partially published in 1554, with the complete edition in 1559), which helped galvanize the Protestant movement and thus became a classic for the Puritans.

When the Protestant Elizabeth I was crowned in 1558, she reestablished the Church of England as the official state church. Throughout her long reign until her death in 1603, Elizabeth held at bay the rebellious Catholics on her political right and a growing number of radical reformers on her left who wanted the English church to discard the accoutrements of the Roman church, such as the vestments, Latin chants, rituals, statues, and other icons. Elizabeth's compromise was to encourage the reformers in theory but to retain the externals of Catholicism in practice. Those English reformers who most adamantly opposed the compromise were labeled "Puritans" for their insistence on returning to the pure forms of the early Christians.

Scholarly debate over the reasons that large numbers of people were attracted to reformist congregationalism focuses and divides primarily upon the issues of spirituality and pragmatism. The declared motives of the ministers and their followers were completely idealistic: they profoundly believed that the Church of England was wrong to retain "popish abominations"; they feared for their own and their children's souls because they were forced to practice a corrupted form of Christianity; they embraced the congregational organization of the early Christians and held that the Bible contained the actual words of God, which preachers of the English church treated cavalierly.

However, many social and economic histories support an alternative view: that the people drawn to Puritanism were those financially burdened by the sixteenth-century population growth, such as second sons disenfranchised by the laws of primogeniture and landholders of rent-controlled properties whose taxes were being increased. When Puritan ministers preached family discipline, social order, and God's spiritual and temporal calling of his saints, the disgruntled heard an empowering religious–moral–economic message. Certainly, Elizabeth I and later James I recognized that the reformers represented a political threat that exceeded the bounds of theological disputes. By 1600, those attracted to congregationalism had become a persecuted people who felt themselves to be martyrs in their own country. Fired by religious fervor and political anger, they sustained an underground struggle that would erupt in civil war in 1642 and regicide in 1649. Matters of landholdings, representation, taxes, and property values were very much involved in the parliamentary debates that led up to the war. Although the Puritans constantly warned themselves against materialism and punished merchants for overpricing, their mixed religious and economic motives would lead both to their financial success and to personal and communal distress.

With few doctrinal differences dividing them, the Anglicans and the Puritans actually shared many beliefs. Both postulated an ordered universe, with God heading a great chain of being of all creatures, and both believed that the Gospels contained God's word, to be interpreted by the ministry. Although the Anglicans retained some externals of Catholicism, they joined the reformers in rejecting the Latin mass, which they saw as empty performance, and in abhorring the Catholic clergy's general lack of Gospel preaching. Yet their differences, although minor in theory, were emotionally charged. The Anglicans believed in a church hierarchy, with the monarch as head, and the Puritans believed in congregations, with elected ministers and magistrates leading each church. In the early years, they insisted that each congregation be fairly independent, relying on occasional synods to check serious errors, but later, especially in England after 1649, the reformers moved toward the presbyterial structure of churches under one supreme court of elected magistrates. Ultimately, the English Puritans' inability to settle this issue of polity contributed to their demise and the Restoration of Charles II in 1660. Regarding the Bible, Anglicans believed that the scriptures were composed at different times and places and were to be construed on broad principles. They held that God gave people the power of reason for applying Biblical precepts to matters of ethics and morals, which change over time. The Puritans believed that the words of the Bible literally contained all truth and that the corrupt reason of fallen humanity was unreliable. The Anglicans viewed the Puritans as narrow literalists, and the Puritans perceived the Anglicans to be blind to human corruption and ignorant of Christ's law.

Among the several major theologians whose writings influenced the English Puritans, John Calvin was preeminent. English theologians such as John Preston, Richard Sibbes, and William Ames modified Calvin and formulated many specific doctrines of congregationalism, but the five tenets of Calvin's *Institutes of the Christian Religion* of 1536 remained basic: (1) total depravity – the complete corruption of humanity resulting from Original Sin; (2) unconditional election – the predestined salvation or damnation of every individual; (3) limited Atonement – Christ's gift of life through His death but only for those already predestined for heaven; (4) irresistible grace – necessary for conversion but which can be neither earned nor refused; (5) perseverance of the saints – the enduring justification and righteousness of the converted. Despite the assurances that the conversion experience and church membership seemed to provide, every Puritan understood that the possibility for self-delusion was strong and that even the most confident saint should constantly search his or her heart for signs of self-deception, sin, and hypocrisy.

If interpreted to their extremes, these fatalistic principles, with their emphasis upon helplessness and dependence, would appear to engender either despair or hedonism, and for that reason, the challenge for Puritan ministers was to guide believers along a spiritual and psychological middle way. When the people cried out, "What must I do to be saved?" Puritan theologians offered them Calvinism modified by the doctrine of preparationism, which held that although a person could not earn grace, the individual could prepare for grace. Certain signs in the life of the sincere penitent, such as a yearning for grace, moral and virtuous actions, and rapt attention to sermons, could provide hope of impending conversion. Although preparationism appears to contradict the doctrine of unconditional election, it eventually became a central tenet in the evolving system of spiritual nourishment and social control in the pioneer communities of Puritan New England.

To some, preparationism appeared to approach the heresy of Arminianism (that works could merit grace), and the clergy often accused one another of this error. At the other extreme, an overemphasis upon free grace moved toward antinomianism – the heresy that grace, conversion, and study of the scriptures were sufficient for salvation so that a church, a clergy, and proper conduct were superfluous. Anne Hutchinson's antinomianism was the most notorious case, but many were accused of this heresy in England and New England. Efforts to sustain the balancing act between the excesses of preparationism and conversionism correspondingly generated tortuous struggles for the clergy and engendered some of the most dramatic and engaging texts of Puritan literature.

To understand certain nuances of Puritan writings, it is necessary to examine a number of other ideas held in common by the majority of Puritans in America by 1645. With their insistence upon the need for a highly trained clergy, the Puritans considered a gift for metaphor and imagery and even a knowledge of classical literature and the arts to be valuable assets for an effective preacher. Although it is true that the Puritans valued a "plain style" of speaking and writing over the sometimes florid Anglican preaching style, they also appreciated language that could warm the affections, prepare the heart, and allude to the implicit meaning inherent in ordinary events. Language and art always had to be utilitarian, however, serving a spiritual purpose and never presuming to eclipse the Bible.

An important dimension of the Puritans' mastery of language was their use of Biblical typology. In strictest terms, typological hermeneutics involved explicating signs in the Old Testament as foreshadowing events and people in the New. This produced interesting consequences; for example, Jonah's three days in the whale typologically parallels Christ's three days in the tomb, and Job's patience prefigures, or is a *figura*, of Christ's forbearance on the cross. Applied more liberally and figured more broadly, typology expanded into a more elaborate verbal system that enabled an interpreter to discover Biblical forecasts of current events. Thus, the Atlantic journey of the Puritans could be an antitype of the Exodus of the Israelites; and the New England colony, a New Zion, to which Christ may return to usher in the Millennium. The first settlers were conservative, cautious typologists, but as Edward Johnson's *Wonder-Working Providence of Sion's Saviour in New England* (1654; composed c. 1650) demonstrates, by the 1640s New England's sacred errand into the wilderness and the approaching Apocalypse were accepted antitypes of sacred history. Claiming to strive for plainness, Puritan writers created instead a subtle and complex language system. The great Puritan poet Edward Taylor was the consummate typologist (see Chapter 4).

Nature was another area wherein Puritan thought made evident its affinity for the paradoxical. Along with the Bible and occasional instances of direct divine revelation, nature was for the Puritans a third channel of communication from God to humanity. An angry God might send violent storms or earthquakes to warn backsliders. Should God wish to alert a single saint to a personal failing, He might have a sparrow fall into the saint's path or even take the life of a loved one. The Puritans were living in the age of Francis Bacon, the "New Science," and the founding of the Royal Society in 1662, and their views of divine intervention into natural events might appear to be in conflict with any objective or scientific view. Science would inevitably challenge the authority of religious systems, but the Puritans discerned little conflict between the objective recording of observed natural phenomena and the discovery there of divine providences. Cotton Mather sent frequent reports to the Royal Society while searching the heavens and forests for God's messages.

For students of Puritan writing, the definition of "literature" has traditionally been broad. In addition to a relatively small corpus of self-conscious imaginative writing such as history, poetry, and captivity narratives, "Puritan literature" also includes sermons, diaries, letters, trial transcripts, religious tracts, and broadsides. Of course, most of the Puritans were reared and educated in the England of Shakespeare, Donne, Spenser, and Sidney. Thus, the Puritans did recognize and appreciate literary artistry, but their religious scruples made them suspicious of all products of the flawed human imagination. When they came to power in England, they closed the theaters, which they condemned as offering sinful entertainment that distracted people's attention from the preaching of God's word. Puritan schools emphasized the study of rhetoric to prepare for practical uses of language as in the pulpit or at the bar. Unless a poem or narrative has a pedagogical, religious purpose, its composition was seen as a waste of the author's time. Anne Bradstreet had her manuscript taken from her without her knowledge and published in England because she would never have dared publish in America; Edward Taylor did not circulate his poetry, which was not discovered until the 1930s; and Cotton Mather was forever apologizing for writing another of his over 400 titles. Even most of the works of the great Puritan poet John Milton qualified as religious writing.

Yet, as is apparent in the imaginative works they did produce and in the richness and eloquence of much religious and political discourse, there were many Puritans who possessed literary talent. During the first three decades of colonization, the major contributors to the literary record were those in public positions who grappled with the thorny issues of church and state: William Bradford, John Winthrop, John Cotton, Roger Williams, Thomas Hooker, Thomas Shepard, and, through her powerfully spoken words, Anne Hutchinson.

In England in the 1580s, Robert Browne despaired of the English government ever reforming the church along congregational lines, and he published his *Reformation without Tarrying for Any* (1582) urging nonconformity and complete separation from the Church of England. In 1609, a large number of separatists (also called Brownists) moved to Holland, but by the mid-1610s, they became convinced that all of Europe was corrupt and that the Continent provided an unfit environment for raising their children. With a charter under the title of the Plymouth Company, about 100 separatists departed in the *Mayflower* for Virginia. In 1620, they accidentally landed to the west of Cape Cod, where they established a settlement they named Plymouth. Realizing that they had put ashore far from the territory designated in the charter, they drew up their own charter, the Mayflower Compact, which declared their loyalty to the king but established their own government by majority rule. The first governor, John Carver, died in 1621, and William Bradford assumed the post, in which he served, except for a five-year sabbatical, until his death in 1657. The colonists negotiated a treaty with Massasoit, chief of the Wampanoag tribe, and sustained tranquil relations with them for fifty years. Contacts with other tribes were not so peaceful, as when the Pilgrims used military force to appropriate lands from the Narragansets. Prospering mainly on the fur trade, which required the cooperation of the Wampanoags, the community grew and expanded. Plymouth Colony joined the New England Federation in 1643.

Following the foray of the Brownists into the New World, there came a much larger band of congregationalists of more moderate political and religious positions under the leadership of John Winthrop. Born into a land-holding family in Suffolk, England, Winthrop studied at Trinity College, Cambridge, where he considered entering the ministry before deciding to become a lawyer. Establishing a prosperous practice, he retained strong religious convictions throughout his life. In 1629, he negotiated an agreement with the English government to establish the Massachusetts Bay Company and was elected its governor by its Puritan stockholders. In 1630, the group sailed the *Arbella* to New England and founded a colony that became Boston. Such a departure was dangerous, physically and emotionally arduous, and politically controversial, for they left behind their persecuted compatriots, who viewed the emigrants as escapists. But they found consolation and justifications for their flight in the scriptures, where they read that the things of this world, including parents, children, and friends, were insignificant compared to salvation.

In Boston, Winthrop and his colleagues established a theocracy in which the clergy had great political influence and the status of freeman was limited to male church members. In the original Pauline spirit, the leaders encouraged like-minded religionists from England to join them, and between 15,000 and 20,000 persons arrived during the "Great Migration" of the 1630s. Because of the considerable expense involved in making the ocean crossing, the vast majority of these early arrivals were people of wealth and status who also brought with them indentured servants and African slaves. The colonizers flourished through agriculture, fishing, and the fur trade, and soon a growing merchant class thrived as well. With their esteem for literacy and a learned clergy, they established the Boston Latin School in 1635 and Harvard College a year later.

The Massachusetts Bay Puritans differed from those at Plymouth by being nonseparating congregationalists. Clinging to some hope that the English church might yet reform, they wished to remain a loyal opposition in exile. In the interim, they sought refuge from persecution and the opportunity to establish an example for their English colleagues of how model congregational communities could be formed. Indeed, many of these colonists expected their stay in America to be temporary, and hundreds did return in the early 1640s to join the English Civil War and the Puritan Commonwealth. In spite of these departures, however, the large families of the first generation and a steady flow of new immigrants rapidly increased the English population in Massachusetts by the 1650s.

Among the Native-American tribes inhabiting the territories that the Puritans eventually acquired were the Wampanoags, Massachusetts, Pokanokets, Capawicks, Mohegans, Nipmucks, Pequots, Patuxets, and Narragansets. Before the first English arrived, numerous Europeans had visited the coast of America and some had begun ill-fated settlements. During these early contacts, Europeans captured and enslaved many Native Americans and stole their food and property. Then an epidemic of smallpox in 1616 killed 75 to 90 percent of the native population along the coast between Penobscot Bay and Cape Cod. By the 1620s the plague had reduced the Pokanoket tribe of Cape Cod from 20,000 to 2,000, and they were being tyrannized by the Narragansets, who had been spared the pox by virtue of their geographical location. When the Pilgrims' first winter claimed nearly half of the colony, the Pokanokets, who saw the Pilgrims as technologically advanced potential allies, sent the Patuxet Squanto, a prisoner of the Pokanokets who had been captured by whites years before and taken as a slave to England, to form a treaty with Bradford's group. Between 1620 and 1622, Squanto was a guide, interpreter, and diplomat for the colony, helping the English arrange treaties with other Native-American tribes and trade for food and furs. Because Squanto's entire tribe had been destroyed by smallpox when he was in England, he remained within the Plymouth Colony until his death in 1622. On his own, he would certainly have been enslaved by other tribes. The highly romanticized tale of Squanto's spontaneous aid to the Pilgrims has for many decades stood as an example of the myth of immediately friendly relations between the English and the Indians. An examination of the details of his association with the whites, however, reveals a more pragmatic and ambiguous relationship.

Before leaving for America and for some decades after, the Puritans proclaimed one of their major intentions to be the religious conversion of the native inhabitants. With the exception of the persistent missionary efforts of John Eliot and Thomas Mayhew, however, the Puritans abandoned their proselytizing attempts rather early. Since the relations between the Europeans and the native peoples were so thoroughly centered around trade, land acquisition, and political maneuvering, perhaps it appeared to the English clergy in the initial years of the settlement that there was little time for proselytizing. In addition, the Native Americans' suspicion and wariness made them rather unreceptive to the white God. Nonetheless, some were converted to Christianity, and by the 1670s, there were several villages of "praying Indians." Despite these successful conversions, however, most Puritan clergy viewed the Indians as hopeless pagans. Indeed, the very attitudes and preconceptions that the Puritans brought with them prevented

many from seeing the original inhabitants of the New World as human beings. For most Puritans, the "howling wilderness" outside their "enclosed
gardens" was a territory under Satan's power, and amid this dangerous landscape the Indians were obviously children of the Devil. Although the English
did occasionally purchase land from the native tribes, they soon began to
perceive the Indians as "savages" and "animals," and this verbal and imaginative projection enabled them to conceive of the land as essentially vacant
of human occupation and thus available for the taking. John Winthrop interpreted the smallpox plague as God's generous land clearing to prepare it
for His saints.

In the first few years of colonization, the settlers found the Native inhabitants very useful in the fur-trading business because of their knowledge of
the land, their experience as hunters, and the willingness of some to sell furs
cheaply to the New Englanders, who made large profits exporting them
to England. As exploitation rapidly devastated the animal population near
the colony, however, the fur trade became a less vital part of the English
economy. Agriculture became more important, and the English began to
take more land by force, leading in 1636 to the first major "Indian War,"
with the Pequots.

The events leading to the confrontation and the resulting massacre of
between 400 and 700 Pequots is vividly described by Captain John Underhill
in his *News from America* (1638), an extraordinary text depicting an early
American holocaust. Beginning in 1632, the Dutch and the English were
claiming ownership of the Connecticut Valley by right of discovery. The
Pequots claimed prior discovery and right of conquest because they had
defeated weaker tribes to gain control of the valley. While disputes and negotiations continued over the next few years, English colonists continued
to move into the area. After a series of complex events about which there
is much dispute among historians, the Puritans authorized an attack upon
the Pequots. An army of English and their Mohegan allies surrounded the
Pequot village and shot and burned the people, mostly women and children.
As Underhill recounts, at the first volley of English shots, the Pequots "brake
forth into a most doleful cry so as if God had not fitted the hearts of men
for the service, it would have bred in them a commiseration towards them."
God seems to have fitted those Puritan hearts quite well, and the English fe-
rocity so terrified the other tribes that a general peace was sustained between
the English and the Native peoples until the 1670s when the Narragansets,
led by Chief Sachem Metacomet, nicknamed King Philip, mounted a final
stand (see Chapter 3). Because of the limited strife between the English and
the Indians during the long middle period, Puritan writing may give the impression that the Indians disappeared until the war of the 1670s. Considerable
interactions between the colonizers and the colonized continued, however,

accompanied by sustained discussions on both sides about the nature of the troubling "other." Numerous contemporary accounts delineate the benefits and detriments of interaction with alien peoples, as the New Englanders ceaselessly interrogated the subject of the savage. Accounts of such troubling realities as these conflicts with the Indians were nearly always interwoven with myths and dreams of the possible.

So intense were the Puritan expectations that they began to generate a prophetic literature even before the English arrived at the New England site of their project. At sea on board the *Arbella* in the spring of 1630, for example, John Winthrop composed one of the most significant texts of Puritan writing, his sermon "A Model of Christian Charity," and he began another, his *Journal*, which was published in 1825–26 as *The History of New England from 1630 to 1649* (an earlier version was published in 1790). In the early years, it was not unusual for lay people like Winthrop to deliver sermons, but the practice was forbidden after the 1636 trial of Anne Hutchinson. In 1629 in his *Reasons to be Considered . . . for the Intended Plantation in New England*, Winthrop described the "excess of riot" and the "multitude of evil examples of the licentious government" in England, and he began to formulate the framework for his own Christian government based upon the "law of the gospel." For Winthrop, these hours of composition must have been euphoric, for his text looks optimistically and hopefully toward a golden future in which the harsh New England conditions and the divisions and contentions of his governorship were as yet unimaginable.

As both an idealistic blueprint of the structure of the Puritan community and an expression of Winthrop's cherished convictions, "A Model of Christian Charity" opens by proclaiming that "God Almighty in his most holy and wise providence" has designed the human condition in such a way that social inequality is natural: "as in all times some must be rich, some poor, some high and eminent in power and dignity, others mean and in subjection." Leaving questions of social justice to the Divinity, Winthrop explains that God's plan for His community is fair and orderly and will work perfectly when His people heed the rules of the Gospel. For "every man might have need of other, and from hence they might be all knit more nearly together in the bonds of brotherly affection." Following the "two rules . . . justice and mercy," the rich will help the poor, the strong aid the weak, the people follow their leaders, and the leaders labor for their people. Imitating Christ, heeding the "law of grace or the gospel," and practicing the "duty of mercy," the community of saints will be joined into a holy unity by the love of Christ, for "Love is the bond of perfection."

Noting parallels between the Puritans and the Old Testament Hebrews, Winthrop's sermon culminates in a vision of the sacred covenant between God and His saints for this divine enterprise. With a warning that would be repeated in many sermons, Winthrop says that God "hath taken us to be his after a most strict and peculiar marriage, which will make him the more jealous of our love and obedience." Just as God told the "people of Israel" that they were the only ones he would recognize, so "God now gives a special commission" to the Puritans. If God allows the *Arbella* to reach New England, that will be the sign that "he ratified this covenant and sealed our commission," "and should the people later become greedy, ambitious, and carnal" – "seeking great things for ourselves and our posterity" – "the Lord will surely break out in wrath against us . . . and make us know the price of the breach of such a covenant." In his conclusion, Winthrop emblematically employs the famous image of the Puritans as the exemplary society: "The God of Israel . . . has set up this people that we shall be as a city on a hill. The eyes of all people are upon us."

Scholars disagree over whether or not at the time of their departure Winthrop and his congregation had already conceived of themselves to be embarking on a sacred errand. Some argue that the Puritans arrived with such a fully developed teleology and that Puritan ministers used typology to elaborate the Biblical parallels to their present, and others insist that Winthrop was simply using stock sermon rhetoric and had no such conception of an ordained American destiny. At stake in this interpretive issue is the very foundation of what has been called "American identity." One image of these English "founders" is that Winthrop and his colleagues were, in spite of their denials of the things of this world, actually early American precapitalists who were about to initiate a process of divinely supported material progress that would lead to violent conquest, unquenchable imperialism, and self-righteous and self-obsessive nationalism. At the other extreme is a picture of a pietistic people struggling to escape a corrupt modern world to a holy utopian haven for which Winthrop's image of the "city on a hill" was really an inappropriate trope because he and his people sought a primitive medieval retreat. Debates over which of these scripts better describes the evolution of Anglo-European North America have polarized historians and literary scholars. Perhaps the only resolution is one that accepts both descriptions as somewhat accurate, that depicts Winthrop's mission as utopian in conception but necessarily flawed because of its dependence upon the language of expansionism and a teleology of perfectionism.

Winthrop's text expressed a paradox that would be a constant source of confusion and strife for the Puritans: the saints must reject the allure of this world and yet labor in their temporal callings with such diligence that they would produce material success, which, in turn, would endanger the moral integrity and spiritual perfection of the community. As another important Puritan text, *The Last Will and Testament* (1653) of the merchant Robert Keayne, makes evident, the Puritans' linking of spiritual and temporal callings was troubling. A devout member of John Cotton's church, Keayne was brought to court in 1639 for overcharging for a bag of nails. Keayne's text reveals that he was shocked and humiliated by this "deed and sharp censure," and he piously accepted God's justice since he knew that he had committed other sins that deserved penance. However, Keayne also argues that his pricing was a trivial act, compared to sins of others, and that it was only natural that merchants would follow the laws of supply and demand in setting prices. He cites the jealousy of those who envied his success as the reason for his censure. In Keayne's mind, being part of a city on the hill meant not only attending to sermons but also succeeding in the marketplace. As a result of such apparent contradictions, Winthrop's design of a loving, sharing community of saints was short-lived. Keeping their covenant would prove every bit as difficult as Winthrop had warned, perhaps even more difficult than he feared. As his *Journal* testifies, discontent and disputes would quickly and repeatedly threaten to destroy his fragile utopia.

The most frequently examined sections of Winthrop's *Journal* are those pages that record one of the Massachusetts Bay Colony's most destructive religious tumults. The trial of Anne Hutchinson is a landmark narrative in women's history. Hutchinson's New England experience began when she and her family emigrated to Boston in 1634 to follow their minister, John Cotton. Her husband, William, was elected deputy to the Massachusetts General Court, and Hutchinson continued her community service as a nurse-midwife and spiritual adviser to women. Sometime during her first years in Boston, she began to hold weekly meetings in her home to discuss the sermon of the previous Sunday. These gatherings soon grew to have sixty or more people, including the then governor, Henry Vane, and other prominent figures. After a time, Hutchinson began to criticize some of the leading clergy for preaching a covenant of works instead of grace. She accused them of being "legalists" who suggested that people could earn salvation and that the conversion process could be charted and anticipated, and she insisted upon the Calvinist doctrines of divine sovereignty and free grace. She declared: "Here is a great stir about graces [earned for works] and looking into hearts, but give me Christ; I seek not for graces, but for Christ; I seek not for promises, but for Christ; I seek not for sanctification, but for Christ; tell me not of meditation and duties, but tell me of Christ." In their efforts to offer people encouragement and promote moral order through preparationism, some of the clergy had allowed their rhetoric to slip toward Arminianism. Hutchinson keenly detected this shift, and her followers agreed. The group then began efforts to replace John Wilson, pastor of the Boston church where Cotton was the teacher, with Hutchinson's brother-in-law John Wheelwright. This move sparked support for Wilson from other parishioners and countercharges that the Hutchinson group were antinomians who were rejecting authority and the importance of law and order in every aspect of life. Some called Hutchinson and her party licentious fanatics. Convinced that the very foundation of the theocracy was at stake, the authorities convened the first synod in the colonies.

In private meetings with Hutchinson and finally during her trial, the magistrates and ministers urged her to admit her errors, but she firmly held her ground. In her view, the piety that was central to the Pauline spirit of the Puritans was being replaced by a mechanical system of social morality and rewards. So essential were these issues for her that she was prepared to be excommunicated and banished rather than to live in error in Massachusetts. The record of her trial constitutes one of the most stirring prose works in Puritan literature. Hutchinson's wit and keen intelligence are evident as are the frustrations and desperate maneuvering of her opponents. In these disputations, the intersections of discursive formations and power relations are revealed.

Although John Cotton was not on trial, many authorities were deeply suspicious of his teachings. However, since it would only further embarrass the already beleaguered government to accuse Cotton of heresy, the leaders pressured him to denounce Hutchinson. Cotton refused, but he also refused to defend her. Aware of Cotton's predicament and of the court's desire to avoid political embarrassment by separating Cotton's position from her own, Hutchinson listened as they sought grounds for condemning her teachings without implicating Cotton. She knew she could protect Cotton by claiming that her ideas came not from him but directly by divine revelation, a presumption for which she could be punished. Although it is evident throughout the trial that Hutchinson was eminently capable of eluding her questioners with complex replies and Biblical citations, she finally conceded to having experienced a direct and divine revelation. In this manner, she empowered herself in a way that was necessarily intolerable to the patriarchal authority. Yet, even as she confessed to the revelation, she chose her words judiciously so that they could be interpreted either as a confirmation or as a denial: she said she received the message "by the voice of his [Christ's] own spirit to my soul." By saying "soul" rather than "ear," she left the question of whether the voice was literal or constructed unanswered. However, with their own power founded upon the literal nature of language, the judges took her statement to mean that she claimed to have heard Christ speaking to her through the senses, and they condemned her. The court then urged Cotton to acknowledge her guilt, but his reply was so evasive that some members of the court remained unsatisfied. Forced to settle the matter, Governor Winthrop asserted that "Mr. Cotton is not called to answer to any thing."

The fact that Hutchinson was a woman is very important in any interpretation of the texts of the case and in later writings about her. The

Puritan authorities resented all defiance, but they were doubly disturbed by her assertions of spiritual independence because of her gender, for in English society at the time women were expected to be submissive to their husbands and all other male authorities. In many contemporary and later Puritan writings, Hutchinson is referred to as a Jezebel, and much is made of her giving birth to a deformed child months after the trial as proof of her female "misconceptions." There were rumors that she was promiscuous and in love with John Cotton. After she and her family were banished in 1638, they spent five years in Rhode Island and then moved to New York, where she and all of her family but one were killed in an Indian raid. This outcome satisfied her old enemies, who saw the work of Providence both in manifesting God's judgment upon her and in confirming that events of human history are signs of the divine plan.

In the first years of the colony, Anne Hutchinson was not the only rebellious Puritan to disturb the peace of Winthrop's holy garden. Born in Smithfield, London (c. 1603), Roger Williams prepared for the ministry at Cambridge and migrated to New England in 1630. A staunch separatist, he turned down a position in a nonseparatist Boston church to accept a post in Plymouth. Strongly committed to the idea of converting the Indians, he developed close ties with the Narragansets, and unlike most other English, he recognized the natives to be people who possessed complex cultures, religions, and traditions of their own. His sympathy with them and his strict religious principles led him to challenge the legality of the charters that were being used by the whites to confiscate Indian lands. Moving to Salem in 1633, he also began to insist that the New England Way (or what has been called federal theology), which linked church and state, was fallacious. Asserting that religion was a private matter between each individual and God, he charged that laws and courts should not attempt to fuse spiritual and public issues.

When John Cotton heard Williams preach in 1633, the two ministers initiated a long debate over questions of church and state. Williams insisted that the idea of nonseparating congregationalism was absurd, for to be a congregationalist was to believe in individual church autonomy and thus to be a separatist necessarily. He perceived the nonseparationism of the Massachusetts Bay Colony to be a blatant political compromise of faith and reason in order to retain the favor of the English reformers. So unsettling were his charges that, in 1635, the Massachusetts General Court ordered Williams returned to England, but he and a dozen supporters fled to Rhode Island, where they founded Providence. There he lived among the Native Americans, learned their languages and customs, and published *A Key into the Language of America* (1643), which provides both a history of the Native Americans and information about their lives, ideas, and religion. Suggesting that the whites had much to learn from the more highly civilized natives, this work denied the myth of the native peoples as savages and heathens and shamed the Massachusetts Bay Puritans into expanding their missionary efforts.

When Williams was in England in 1644 to obtain a charter for Providence, Cotton published a letter he had written to Williams eight years before, upbraiding him for his errors. Williams responded with his essay *The Bloody Tenent of Persecution, for Cause of Conscience, Discussed* (1644), to which Cotton replied in *The Bloody Tenent, Washed, and Made White in the Blood of the Lamb* (1647), which Williams answered several years later in *The Bloody Tenent Yet More Bloody* (1652). In these works, Williams developed more fully his attack upon nonseparating congregationalism and federal theology. A stricter Calvinist than Cotton, who saw nonseparation as a liberal and generous gesture to the English church members, Williams insisted that the truest form of Christianity is that of separatist congregations where individuals and parishes can follow their own inclinations. Although not as radically individualist as Anne Hutchinson, Williams charged that the New England clergy were intolerant and persecuted those whose views varied even slightly from state-approved doctrines. Like Hutchinson, Williams also recognized in the New England Way a leaning toward Arminianism. Williams accused Cotton of "swimming with a stream of outward credit and profit, and smiting with the fist and sword of persecution such as dare not join in worship with him." Williams reasoned that government officials were elected by the people and that for them to intrude into religious affairs was a violation of the sacred world by the profane. Because he called for political authorities to stay out of religious issues, he is recognized as the first advocate in America for the principle of the separation of church and state.

From a literary viewpoint, a most interesting feature of the "Bloody Tenent" exchanges is the key role of typology in the arguments, for the debate related to the ways that Old Testament types may or may not be applied to current political matters. Puritan ministers and magistrates frequently drew upon Old Testament texts in their arguments to justify their authority, as Cotton in his *Tenent Washed* where he draws parallels between the government of ancient Jerusalem and that of New England. Williams insists that with the establishment of Christ's new covenant and the writing of the New Testament, the Old Testament types have been fulfilled and are not applicable to secular history. Maintaining a conservative position on the use of types, Williams argues that the only valid reading of Old Testament types is as foreshadowings of New Testament antitypes. By insisting on a stricter use of typology, Williams mocks the notion of the Puritans as a chosen people; he believes that Christ's spiritual army is worldwide and not confined to a "New Israel" in New England. In a sense, Williams emerges as a true fundamentalist; for him the language of the Old Testament was not metaphorical and thus was not open to broader interpretation. The irony of his case is that he was a theological conservative who viewed all issues with narrow Calvinistic logical consistency and yet he is often remembered as the most liberal-minded Puritan New England leader.

As is already apparent from the discussions of Hutchinson and Williams, John Cotton was the most important minister of the first generation and often at the center of controversy. Born in 1584 into the family of a wealthy attorney in Derby, England, Cotton attended Cambridge and then the Puritans' Emmanuel College and became vicar of St Botolph's in Boston, England, in 1610. At first, he gained his popularity from his elegant and ornamented preaching style, but then he fell under the influence of the reformer Richard Sibbes and henceforth emulated Sibbes' plain style. Although his nonconformity was evident early, he was protected from persecution for twenty years by family friends. He preached the farewell sermon to Winthrop's departing company in 1630, and in 1633, when he was forced to resign his post at St Botolph's, he too migrated to America.

Cotton's sermon of 1630 *God's Promise to His Plantation* was an important political statement because of his own eminence in England and because of the suspicions among English Puritans that colonizing New England involved an abandonment of their English cause at home. Although at the time Cotton did not plan to join in the migration, his rationalization of nonseparation established him as a prominent champion for the Massachusetts Bay venture. Fending off another criticism some had made about English encroachment on Native-American territories, he also articulated the arguments for the usurpation of the American lands:

> God makes room for a people in three ways: First, when he casts out the enemies of a people before them by lawful war with the inhabitants... Secondly, when he gives a foreign people favor in the eyes of any native people to come and sit down with them either by way of purchase... or else when they give it in courtesy... Thirdly, when he makes a country though not altogether void of inhabitants, yet void in the place where they reside.

Realizing that missionary work was necessary for justifying the English occupation of the natives' territories, he advises the colonists to "offend not the poor natives, but as you partake in their land, so make them partakers of your precious faith; as you reap their temporals, so feed them with your spirituals." In Cotton's rhetoric, the language of Puritan theology found resonance with the colonial project: native "others" were destined by God to be transformed and displaced.

Cotton also employs several Old Testament types to suggest parallels between the Hebrews and the colonists, but although he allows for the possibility of envisioning their journey as an errand to "the land of Canaan," he shrewdly reminds them and those remaining behind that England was also part of the New Zion: "Be not unmindful of our Jerusalem at home, whether you leave us or stay at home with us." This sort of conscious diplomacy would characterize Cotton's position in the Hutchinson trial and his preaching over the years, but it would also anger critics like Roger Williams who perceived in Cotton's language a similarity to the smooth words of the double-tongued Deceiver.

Cotton's most important works in New England include his *The Way to Life* (1641), which employs preparationist doctrine to describe how a believer moves toward salvation by way of hearing the Gospel preached, and *The Way of the Churches of Christ in New England* (1645), which is a thorough description and justification of the New England Way. By 1642, the English Civil War had begun, and Cotton was convinced that a dramatic change was occurring in the history of Christianity and that the Second Coming and the Millennium of Christ's rule on earth were at hand. In *The Pouring Out of the Seven Vials* and *The Church's Resurrection* (1642), Cotton elaborates this vision and urges New Englanders not to return to England but to keep their covenant with God in America. Although Cotton was one of three New England ministers invited to participate in the Westminster Assembly in 1642 to reform the Church of England, he declined. Instead, he reacted against the developments in English Puritanism, and at the Synod of 1646 in Boston, he helped to draft the Cambridge Platform, a definition of New England congregationalism based largely upon his writings. After his death in 1652, several more of his works were published, and his influence on New England church polity remained strong for several decades.

Second only to Cotton in stature and perhaps the most effective preacher of his time in New England, Thomas Hooker was born in England in 1586 into the family of a yeoman about whom little else is known. Like Cotton, Hooker began his training at Cambridge and moved to Emmanuel College, where he remained a tutor until 1618. After serving in two churches over the next fourteen years, he fled to Holland and then New England in 1633 on the same ship with John Cotton and Samuel Stone, another leading clergyman. Hooker and Stone became the first ministers in the church in New Town, soon to be Cambridge.

In 1636, Hooker and Stone made a startling and unorthodox decision to relocate their church to Hartford, Connecticut. When Hooker's petition to the Massachusetts magistrates for permission to move was denied, he left anyway. Although Hooker explained his departure by citing the people's need for more land, some critics – then and now – have speculated that Massachusetts was not big enough for the egos of both Hooker and Cotton; the two had frequent disputes over church membership. Hooker favored a more liberal membership policy, and he devised an elaborate preparation process that involved precise psychological stages on the way to conversion. The six essential stages of this morphology of conversion were contrition, humiliation, vocation, implantation, exaltation, and possession; and these he subdivided further. He required that a prospective member demonstrate to him and then to the congregation a successful passage through these stages. This rigorous public ritual was intimidating to many later arrivals to New England because such practices never existed in England. Hooker believed, however, that his method assisted the individual to discover what to expect in the experience of grace and that this process reassured the elect and discouraged hypocrites. Most ministers agreed that the worst psychological condition was that of persons who deceived themselves about having a conversion experience only to despair later upon discovering their error. Between 1635 and 1645, many of the New England churches developed stricter tests for church membership, some requiring a lengthy public description of every detail of the conversion experience. Some historians suggest that the large influx of new colonists during the 1640s put pressure upon the towns and churches to accept new members, who, in turn, were rewarded with land and political privileges; some have suggested that economic factors, as well as religious zeal, led to more demanding membership requirements.

Hooker's sermons provide some of the best illustrations in the literature of the ways in which the Puritan inclination toward the system of logic of the French reformer Petrus Ramus affected expression and actions. It remains unclear how fully Puritan thinkers consciously embraced Ramistic logic, but the structure of many sermons suggests that many clergy found it useful. In opposition to the complex syllogistic reasoning of the Catholic Scholastics, Ramus established a Manichean strategy in which one reasoned through established sets of opposites or contraries. An example of this rhetorical strategy can be found in the much-debated question as to whether or not all who claim to be saved should be admitted into the church. Since the most liberal admission policy would result in admitting hypocrites who sought membership entirely for the political and economic advantages of franchise, then logically, it followed that it was safer to exclude some. Yet the either/or nature of Ramistic logic tended to foster polarization and extremism: a person is either saved or damned, saint or sinner, virtuous or sinful; there is no purgatory between heaven and hell. The world can be divided into the holy community of the theocracy and the "others," who are inherently and fatally flawed by the corruption of this world. The dualism of Ramus worked well enough for resolving complex theological problems quickly, but when extended into other areas of life such as race relations or politics, this Manichean logic proved to be highly problematic for the Puritans, and has remained so for Americans. Indeed, much of the history of American expansionism may be said to have been cast in similar oppositional terms.

In his work *The Application of Redemption* (1656), Hooker employs this logic to set up a series of true versus false ways of looking at sin, and he suggests that in the mind of God and in His kingdom polarization is the rule: "Imagine thou sawest the Judge of all the World sitting upon a Throne . . . the Sheep standing on his right hand, and the Goats at the left: Suppose thou heardest that dreadful Sentence, and final Doom pass from the Lord of Life (whose Word made Heaven and Earth, and will shake both) *Depart from me ye cursed*; How would thy heart shake and sink, and die within thee?" Hooker's most important works were *A Survey of the Sum of Church-Discipline* (1648), a major defense of the New England Way, and *The Soul's Preparation for Christ* (1632), a full elaboration of his conversion morphology.

Although Cotton and Hooker were much admired for their reasoning and preaching, not everyone in New England appreciated their absolutism and plain style. There were those with a sense of humor who visited New England and openly criticized the Puritans. Thomas Morton, an Anglican, established a settlement at Mount Wollaston (now Quincy), Massachusetts, but which the Puritans called Merrymount. Morton annoyed the Puritans for three years by allowing dancing and maypole festivities in his community, but he disturbed them more when he began to sell whiskey and firearms to the Indians, thereby threatening the fur trade and the incorporation of the natives into the Puritan cultural economy. In 1628, Captain Miles Standish of Plymouth led an attack upon Morton's group and arrested him, but Morton was tried and found innocent. In 1630, John Endecott arrested Morton again, burned his house, and confiscated his property. Morton was deported to England, where he attempted to have the Massachusetts charter revoked and where he published his *New English Canaan* (1637), a satiric attack upon Puritan religious practices and their tendency to compare themselves to the Israelites. He also provided descriptions of Native Americans, whom he found to be noble and superior in character to the Puritans.

A more piously motivated critic of Puritan New England was the devout English Puritan Thomas Lechford, who came to Massachusetts in 1638. He attended a congregational church in Boston and practiced law until 1641, when he returned to England. Many were repatriating at this time to support their coreligionists in the impending Civil War, but Lechford made it clear that he did so because he could not abide what he considered to be the bizarre developments in theology and church polity in New England. In 1642, he published *Plain Dealing, or News from New England*, a relatively moderate and dispassionate, but nonetheless critical, description of his experience, which he subtitled *A Short View of New England's Present Government, both Ecclesiastical and Civil, compared with the anciently-received and established*

Government of England, in some material points fit for the gravest consideration in these times. In particular, he was disturbed by the "public confessions and trials," which seemed to him extreme: "By what rule, I ask them, are faults of men to be so publicly handled before all the world?" He also notes that although the New Englanders claim to be congregationalists, they have already constructed a formidable state-church hierarchy. With the Civil War just beginning, Lechford's reservations about the New England Way were shared by many English Puritans. As the English revolutionaries debated the polity of the reformed church and state they hoped to establish, Boston's "city on a hill" was for them a deeply flawed model.

Not all of the satire produced from New England was aimed at the Massachusetts Puritans, however. Nathaniel Ward arrived in New England in 1634, at the age of fifty-five, after he was expelled from his ministry at Essex, England. He settled at Ipswich and was drafted in 1641 to compose what became the Massachusetts Body of Liberties. Returning to England in 1645, he published *The Simple Cobbler of Aggawam in America* (Aggawam had been the Native-American name for Ipswich). A conservative Puritan, Ward satirized the emerging religious toleration of the English reformed churches, which he regarded as examples of political opportunism and compromise. Deriding the knotty theological debates being conducted in Parliament to justify such deals, he said the Devil "cannot sting the vitals of the Elect mortally" but he can "fly-blow their Intellectuals miserably." Going through four editions in its first year, this lively work is the first satire of England from the vantage point of New England, although it is clear that Ward still thought of himself as English. It also reveals a Puritan male's patriarchal views about gender identifications and his concern that established gender roles not be breached. For example, Ward repeatedly uses metaphors of female dress to talk about modern corruptions in society, and he is especially adamant that the gender divisions not be blurred. Men who lose their civil rights, he says, "are but women." For him, the fate of Anne Hutchinson is a warning to all women who overstep the boundaries of their female roles, and he advises: "Let men look to't, least women wear the Spurs." For Ward, religious tolerance – with its blurring of strict theoretical distinctions – was implicated in the tolerance of powerful women. Women who sought to expand their limited, gender-defined roles were sinners, seeking to find salvation on their own terms. To Ward, the social, religious, and political upheavals of mid-century England seemed to threaten even these most fundamental aspects of human nature and God's design.

Beginning with the confidence of Cotton's *God's Promise* and Winthrop's "Model of Christian Charity" in 1630, the Puritans rapidly found that their theological doctrines and church and civil policies were so complicated and unclear that the very sincerity and piety of believers generated such divisions and contentions that the dream of a loving fellowship soon proved unrealizable. By 1645, they had produced a substantial body of literature, but much of it is inspired by disagreement, strife, and defensiveness. Ministers debated, social idealists pleaded, juries hounded, and satirists carped. Only later would Puritan historians, such as Edward Johnson in 1654 and Cotton Mather at the turn of the century, reconstruct these first years in ways that would "spiritualize" (later readers would say romanticize) the past and transform defeat into a myth, imagining enduring and even harmonious victory. The power of language would triumph, yet again, over the "facts" of experience.

Chapter Four

Personal narrative and history

As many historians admit, a record of past events is the hybrid product of facts and interpretation. The Puritans, convinced of the flawed and fallen nature of humanity, distrusted all accounts of the past except those of the Bible. At the same time, they produced a host of personal narratives of individual lives and histories of the corporate New England enterprise because they believed that, even in its corrupted state, human reason is one of God's primary vehicles for communicating His lessons to humanity. A record of God's dealings with His people could be spiritually beneficial. Funeral sermons rehearsed the lives of deceased saints, and election sermons recounted the spiritual record of the community. Biographies, autobiographies, diaries, and conversion narratives recorded the saint's fulfillment of a single destiny, but histories charted the progress of God's larger design.

Although the specific focus of a particular text might be on the one or the many, Puritan authors and audiences believed that the lives of the individual and of the group were inseparable. The church represented the body of Christ, with every member such an integral part that if one person were in distress the entire body writhed. Conversely, if the spiritual community were troubled, each individual was afflicted. The spiritual journey of a single soul became a community drama that served as a paradigm for the plight of the congregation just as the well-being of the congregation was reflected in each member. With the prescribed interdependence of communal and personal history, good times would generate not only personal assurance but also the self-righteous aggression of the group against enemies and outsiders. During sunnier days in Winthrop's enclosed garden, the harmony of the saints emboldened every heart, and the fellowship of the Lord celebrated the glory of every saint. But troubled times produced paralyzing, even suicidal, doubts for the individual and communal self-castigation; during the darkest days, the people would search the depths of their souls for the causes of God's anger and scrutinize the behavior of each other for signs of spiritual offenses. Once even a single sinner or hypocrite entered the body of saints, that individual was as dangerous as a witch or an Anne Hutchinson and capable of spreading a fatal infection among them. Depending upon events and perspectives, the bond between the self and society could be empowering or it could be debilitating and destructive. The community could band together to purge the one or the few, as at Salem in 1692, or an individual like Roger Williams could excoriate the body. Given the basic corporal algorithm, imagery of sickness and death proliferated in Puritan writing.

With the conversion experience established as the essence of Puritan religious life, the spiritual relation became a basic rite of passage and verbal model that provided the psychological pattern for other genres. The psychomachy of the soul's struggle against the body, sin, and Satan and of its journey toward grace and salvation was a fundamental scenario repeated in diaries and autobiographies as well as in histories, where the subject is the whole community's trauma. Because it was one of the earliest and most powerful personal narratives, the autobiography of Thomas Shepard I (1604–49) served as an important model for the many that followed.

Shepard was born in Northampton, England, and attended Emmanuel College, where he was ordained in 1627. Silenced by Bishop Laud in 1630, he emigrated to Massachusetts Bay in 1635, where he was chosen pastor at New Town (later Cambridge). In the early 1640s, he began to publish treatises on the conversion process, notably *The Sincere Convert* (1640), and he started keeping a personal journal of his own spiritual experience, which was published much later, in 1747, under the title of *Three Valuable Pieces...A Private Diary* and again in Edinburgh as *Meditations and Spiritual Experiences of Mr. Thomas Shepard* (1749). In the late 1640s, he composed a retrospective account of his life in the autobiographical form, and this was published in 1832 in Boston as *The Autobiography of Thomas Shepard*.

Shepard seems to have begun his journal at the point in New England Puritan history when pressures upon the communities were moving ministers to require public tests for church membership. These tests consisted of a recounting of the details of a person's struggles toward salvation through the power of divine grace. Although Shepard had been a severe critic of Anne Hutchinson, she believed he was one of the few ministers who preached a covenant of grace. But Shepard's anger at Hutchinson, like Cotton's withdrawal of support for her, indicates the clergy's realization, perhaps unconscious, that a subtle compromise with the doctrine of grace had to be achieved to preserve ecclesiastical order and that the doctrine of preparationism was essential. In his journal, Shepard charted his own preparation in order to instruct others in discovering the signs of grace. The agonizing paradox that logically one can do nothing to be saved and yet emotionally one feels the need to act is at the core of Shepard's journal. Charting the alternations between moments of ecstasy and periods of doubt, the journal demonstrates a pattern of psychological self-manipulation and emotional swings that came to characterize the conversion narrative as a genre.

Shepard's early life had been especially unsettled. When he was three, his mother died of the plague; then he lived for a time with his grandparents, who neglected him, and later with an uncle. When his father remarried, Shepard moved back home, but he said of his stepmother that she seemed "not to love me but incensed my father often against me." When he was ten, his father died in spite of Shepard's desperate prayers: "I did pray very strongly and heartily for the life of my father and made some covenant, if God would do it, to serve him [God] the better as knowing I would be left alone if he was gone. Yet the Lord took him away by death, and so I was left father less and mother less." Adding to his trials was a harsh schoolmaster whom Shepard described as being so cruel he often wished himself in "any condition to keep hogs or beasts rather than to go to school and learn." At his darkest childhood hour, however, he was saved by his older brother, John, who took him in, ensured his education, and became "both father and mother unto me." Under a new schoolmaster, he gained confidence: "it so fell out by God's good providence that this man stirred up in my heart a love and desire of the honor of learning, and therefore I told my friends I would be a scholar."

In the context of this background of emotional alternations between chaos and calm, Shepard was prepared psychologically to understand the nature of the conversion process. At college, he began to view his nature as sinful and longed to repent, but he continued his "lust and pride and gaming and bowling and drinking." The day came, however, when "[I] drank so much one day that I was dead drunk . . . and awakened late on that Sabbath and sick with my beastly carriage." Fleeing into the fields to meditate upon his condition, he experienced the presence of Christ, who did not "justly . . . cut me off in the midst of my sin [by death]" but who "did meet me with much sadness of heart and troubled my soul for this and my other sins." After this revelation, Shepard began "daily meditation about the evil of sin and my own ways" and was thereby prepared to attend to the words of John Preston's sermons in a new way: "the Lord so bored my ears that I understood what he spake and the secrets of my soul were laid upon before me . . . all the turnings and deceipts of my heart . . . my hypocrisy and self and secret sins." After the conversion experience, he resolved to become a minister, but as his narrative confirms, he never stopped doubting and searching his heart. At one point "for three quarters of a year," he was so tormented that he "had some strong temptations to run my head against walls and brain and kill myself," until finally "the Lord dropped this meditation into me: Be not discouraged therefore because thou are so vile, but make this double use of it: loathe thyself the more; (2) feel a greater need and put a greater price upon Jesus Christ."

Once he was in New England and undertook his pastorship, Shepard's external life became more settled as duties consumed much of his personal apprehension and anguish. But sainthood remained for him a process rather than a static experience, and throughout his life he continued to have what he called "renewed conversions" upon rediscovering his vile nature. The nature of God's narrative plan for the single soul and for His people was to "show his Power by the much ado of our weakness" so that "the more weak I, the more fit to be used." As Shepard observed, "When I was most empty, then by faith I was most full."

In Shepard's public works, such as *The Sound Believer. Or, a Treatise of Evangelical Conversion* (1645), he established for the colony the process by which the elect should expect to come to saving grace. Shepard preached that it is far better for a soul to face its misery now than to "perish everlastingly," and he insisted that human will plays a role in the process: "every man that perishes is his own Butcher." By the time that the Cambridge Platform was adopted in 1648, a relation of the conversion experience before the entire congregation was required of all who would join a congregational church, and ministers and church members knew exactly what they should hear from the converted. A precisely coded language and narrative text became requisite for salvation, as well as for the social and political benefits of church membership.

One remarkable document in this respect is *The Diary* (published in 1965) of the eminent minister and poet Michael Wigglesworth (1631–1705) (for Wigglesworth's poetry see Chapter 5). Born in Yorkshire, England, in 1631, Wigglesworth moved with his parents to New England in 1638 and settled in New Haven. A brilliant student, he studied with the famous schoolmaster Ezekiel Cheever and was writing compositions in Latin by the age of nine. After an interruption in his education resulting from his father's five-year illness, he went on to Harvard, where he studied medicine as well as theology, finished first in his class, obtained an AB and an AM, and remained as a tutor until 1654. In 1655, he married his cousin Mary Reyner, and in 1656 he was ordained as the minister of the church at Malden. Then he entered a long period of painful and mysterious disease that so weakened him that he could not perform his clerical duties. In 1659, when Mary died, Wigglesworth's debilitation deepened. He declined the presidency of Harvard because he did not think his "bodily health and strength competent to undertake ... such a weighty work." According to Cotton Mather, Wigglesworth turned to writing poetry because it was the only way that he could continue to serve the church and community: "that he might yet more *Faithfully* set himself to Do Good, when he could not *Preach* he *Wrote* several Composures, as are for Truth's dressed up in a *Plain Meter.*"

In 1686, however, Wigglesworth experienced a remarkable rejuvenation. "It pleased God," wrote Cotton Mather, "wondrously to restore His *Faithful Servant.* He that had been for nearly Twenty years almost *Buried Alive,* comes abroad again." Wigglesworth resumed his duties in Malden, but when he shocked the community by marrying his housekeeper, Martha Mudge, who was twenty-five years younger than he and not a member of the church, his congregation reduced his salary. But, as the marriage endured and produced six children, Wigglesworth ultimately regained the respect of his congregation and of the broader Puritan community. Wigglesworth was married a third time, following Martha's death, to Sybil Avery in 1691, when he was sixty.

Wigglesworth's *Diary* for the years 1653 and 1657 documents his youthful fears of damnation brought on by sexual desire, masturbation, and nocturnal emissions and his guilt feelings over his anger toward his father, especially about his inability to feel sorrow over his father's death. Wigglesworth's *Diary* is filled with the kind of statements that have given the Puritans a reputation for obsessive gloom: "Innumerable evils compass me about, and prevail against me, wherefor I am afraid and ashamed and unable to see God still loving me with an everlasting love. I find so much of my spirit go out unto the creature, unto mirth, that there is little savour of God left in my soul." His accounts of his interactions with his students suggest that "mirth" was probably fairly rare in Wigglesworth's life: "I set myself this day to wrestle with the Lord for myself and then for my pupils . . . but still I see the Lord shutting out my prayers . . . for he whom in special I prayed for, I heard in the forenoon with ill company playing musick, though I had solemnly warned him but yesterday of letting his spirit go after pleasures." The lamentations of Puritan diaries sometimes appear forced and formulaic, but the specificity of Wigglesworth's descriptions gives convincing evidence of mental anguish.

The *Autobiography of Increase Mather* (1962) is more dispassionate than the Wigglesworth *Diary*, but it too makes clear that even those who had the strongest reasons to expect sanctification endured years of severe doubt before conversion and then experienced periodic uncertainty throughout life. Often called the "foremost American Puritan," Increase was the son of the first generation minister Richard Mather. He graduated from Harvard in 1656, completed a master's degree at Trinity College, Dublin, married the daughter of John Cotton, and was pastor of Old North Church, Boston, for almost sixty years. A prolific author, he published over 100 works, including histories, sermons, tracts, treatises, and a biography of his father. The most eminent minister in New England from about 1670 to the early 1700s, Mather socialized with the highest government officials and the wealthiest merchants. From 1685 to 1701, he served as president of Harvard, which he guided through severe legal and financial crises. In 1688, he was chosen for a mission to England to entreat James II to restore the charter, and when William and Mary became the new sovereigns in 1689, Mather negotiated a new charter with them. Although he probably obtained as much for Massachusetts as was possible at the time, some criticized him for yielding too much and for using his political position to help his friends, especially his nominee for governor, Sir William Phips. After Phips's mediocre administration, Mather became embroiled in nasty political battles and suffered a decline of influence from about 1700 until his death in 1723.

Over the course of his life, Mather kept a diary, but in 1685 he decided to compose a formal autobiography from his many diary volumes. Writing for his children with no intention of publishing, he declared his purpose was to show them how his faith had been sustained through trials and doubts. One of the most interesting features of this work is the way in which the idea of God's covenant with an individual developed, at least in Mather's mind, into a two-sided agreement in which God had certain obligations. At a low point in his youth, when he was awaiting both his spiritual calling to grace and his temporal calling to the ministry, he wrote that "the Lord broke in upon my conscience with very terrible convictions and awakenings. . . . I was in extremity of anguish and horror in my soul." After reading the scriptures in search of help, Mather actually dared to threaten God:

> I that day begged of God, that He would give me leave to plead with Him, (and with Tears and meltings of heart I did plead with Him) that if He should not answer me graciously, others after my decease, that should see the papers which I had written which I had kept as remembrances of my walking before God would be discouraged. For they would say "Here was one that prayed for bodily and spiritual Healing, yea and believed for it also, and yet he perished in his affliction without that Healing."

Given Mather's subsequent career, it is evident that God recognized the power of this argument and bestowed the needed grace. What is perhaps most surprising about this passage is that the forty-six-year-old pastor chose to present his children with this example of his youthful brashness.

To a great degree, Puritan diaries and autobiographies tend to be formulaic, for the individual was almost always attempting to relate each personal experience to an accepted teleology: as in John Bunyan's *Grace Abounding to the Chief of Sinners* (1666), the life of the saint follows an expected course to salvation. Many extant spiritual narrations, diaries, and autobiographies follow the paradigm rather closely. The experiences of conversion, doubt, and spiritual growth were forced to conform to narrative archetypes, gaining their authority from earlier linguistic models. Individual personality was less important than God's general ways of dealing with humanity. Given the autobiographers' inclination to record common human experiences, the unique and surprising acts of divine Providence in particular lives have special significance and give Puritan autobiographies, such as Increase Mather's, their drama. Over the course of the seventeenth century, the diaries became less formulaic so that the diaries of Cotton Mather and Samuel Sewall, for example, are more secular and express more private and individual concerns.

The *Diary of Cotton Mather for the Years 1681–1708* (published in 1911–12) and *The Diary of Cotton Mather, D.D., F.R.S. for the Year 1712* (published in 1971) show a sophisticated blending of the ritualistic and the mundane. Cotton Mather (1663–1728) was the grandson of patriarchs Richard Mather and John Cotton and the son of Increase Mather. He was educated at Harvard and assumed a post as his father's assistant in the Second Church of Boston, where he served under his father except for the five years after Increase's death in 1723 (for Cotton Mather's life, see Chapter 5). Mather's diaries are filled with what had become by the 1680s the standard laments over physical temptations and spiritual weaknesses, although they appear to have been quite genuine for him. He explains how he fights sexual temptations by fasting until he is so weak that the desire fades, and he expresses his distress over his stammering speech, which disturbed Increase and jeopardized his expected career in the pulpit. Mather also records daily observations of fashion, politics, finances, and such vanities as his longings to become a member of the Royal Society, which he did, and the president of Harvard, which he did not. The most memorable and poignant sections of Mather's diaries are those in which he reports bitter personal tragedies, such as the deaths of his closest brother, Nathaniel, and of two wives and several children. Particularly affecting are the passages on the madness of his third wife, which shocked and bewildered him, and the profligacy and finally the disappearance at sea of his favorite but rebellious son, "Creasy" (Increase II), whom he had hoped would follow him into the ministry.

Although not as famous as the frequently anthologized *Diary of Samuel Seawall* (see Chapter 5), Mather's diaries exemplify more lucidly the ways in which the convictions and passions of late Puritanism shaped a life and a writing style. With each tragedy, Mather was more determined not to abandon his faith in the divinely ordained role that he and his people had in the world. The more he suffered, the more energy he threw into his writing and his pastoral work. Every event was a sign; every adversity could be turned to good; every seeming indication of New England's demise could contain a sign that Christ was preparing His Second Coming to be in this American New Jerusalem, where He would rule for a thousand years in glory. If Mather's grandfathers had not fully conceived of their venture in such providential terms, there is no question that Mather interpreted the Puritan experiment as a sacred mission and that he found Old Testament types being fulfilled in much of New England's history.

The move from diary and autobiography to biography is a significant step toward Puritan artistic consciousness and the creation of distinctive literary styles. As a genre, the biography occupies a middle territory between the study of the inner life of the individual recorded in personal narratives and the examination of communal progress that is the subject of Puritan history. On the surface, the purpose of biography was not very different from that of the funeral sermon – to present a holy model of one who had practiced *imitatio Christi*. As in John Bunyan's *A Pilgrim's Progress*, the life of the saint should follow the course of piety of a *figural* Christian. In Puritan biography, the narrative of the model saint also became a story of the community of saints so that inner and outer worlds were linked in the exemplary life.

Within that framework, Puritan biographers did manage to craft particular narratives that are varied in detail and remain engaging. One feature that was unique to the Puritan biographies of the first-generation saints was the unusual inclusion of a substantial discussion of why they left England. The earliest known American Puritan biography to be printed is John Norton's *Abel Being Dead Yet Speaketh* (1658) on the life of John Cotton. In his explanation of Cotton's coming to America, Norton set a pattern for later biographies by establishing several parallels between Cotton's experiences and those in the Bible: "No sooner had Christ received his mission into his public ministry, but he is led into the wilderness to be tempted by the Devil." Old Testament types foreshadow that God "transplants many of his Faithful servants into this vast Wilderness [and] giveth *Moses* the pattern of the Tabernacle in the Wilderness. *Ezekiel* seeth the forms of the House in exile. *John* receivth his Revelation in *Patmos*." Through such typologizing, England becomes Egypt, the Atlantic, the Red Sea, and New England a New Zion. Despite the heavy typology and hagiography, Norton does manage to convey some glimpse of Cotton's personality by drawing upon his letters and diaries and upon anecdotes conveyed to Norton by Cotton's wife.

Twelve years after Norton's life of Cotton was published, Increase Mather advanced the form of Puritan biography with his book on his own father, *The Life and Death of That Reverend Man of God, Mr. Richard Mather* (1670). Increase not only compares Richard to the Old Testament patriarchs but praises him as one who embodied Puritan ideals that Increase feared would never be so fully represented again. Although he remains anonymous as biographer, he does sign the dedication letter that precedes the text. There he elaborates upon his father's virtues and rakes the opportunity to suggest how far short Richard's congregation falls in their attempts to imitate their pastor's holiness: "Remember his Farewell Exhortation, which is now in many of your Houses, and Oh that it were in also your Hearts."

Following the formula established by Norton in the Cotton biography, Increase includes a long document by Richard in which he elaborates his reasons for leaving England. At the center of Richard's arguments are the need for a father to be able to govern his own family as he wishes and for a minister to guide his own congregation, neither of which were permitted in England. England's corruption threatened family order as well as proper religious worship. It is significant, even ironic, that Richard places such emphasis upon family order given Increase's famous defiance of his father's authority in the 1660s over church membership rules.

This family dispute was part of a generational one that gave rise to the Half-Way Covenant, as it was derisively called by its opponents. The modification in membership rules was instituted by the Boston Synod of 1662 to counter declining conversions among the children and grandchildren of the original saints. The new membership provision allowed that "if a person born and baptized in the church did not receive faith he could still continue his membership and have his own children baptized, by leading a life free from scandal, by learning and professing the doctrines of Christianity, and by making a voluntary submission to God and His church." The communion table was still reserved for full members, but the children of unregenerate parents (mostly grandchildren of the first settlers) could be baptized, and both these children and their parents could attend services. Those who favored this provision, like Richard Mather, assumed that it was very likely that the children and grandchildren of the founders would eventually receive grace and that the best environment for preparing their hearts was inside the fellowship of the church. Opponents, like Increase, perceived this accommodation to involve a serious break with the original rules and insisted that the unregenerate, regardless of family credentials, should not be worshipping among the elect. So opposed were the members of Richard's own parish at Dorchester to the change that they rejected it during Richard's lifetime in spite of his advocacy. After his death, they recanted.

Both Increase and his brother Eleazar opposed the Half-Way covenant and opted for keeping the churches pure by granting baptism only to the children of full church members. Mather was still against it when he wrote the biography. In the text, he uses Richard's deathbed prayer as a rhetorical device for urging the new generation to avoid the need for new membership rules by finding the grace in their souls and experiencing conversion. Increase recalls his father's words: "A special thing which I would recommend to you, is Care concerning the Rising Generation in this Country, that they be under the Government of Christ in his Church; and that when grown up and qualified, they have Baptism for their Children." Increase left his position on membership unstated in the biography, employing instead a strategy of using the example of Richard's life to inspire his readers to discover the grace and salvation that would make the issue irrelevant.

However, soon after he composed the biography, Increase recognized the wisdom of his father's compromise, and he altered his position. Thus, it appears the act of writing the biography served several purposes for Increase:

it helped him to clarify for himself and his readers the role of the later generations in relation to the founders, it softened his heart toward those of his own generation who lacked the spiritual confidence that had enabled him to confront the Lord, and it released some of the guilt he felt over his division with his father. The central theme of the work is that each successive generation must carry on the founders' mission by reviving the original zeal. Richard Mather's plea for spiritual continuity joins with that of every other first-generation minister in calling for all the Puritan progeny to take up the challenge of the sacred mission.

Continuing the family tradition fifty-four years later, Cotton Mather published a biography of Increase, *Parentator* (1724). Whereas Increase's biography of Richard appeared at the beginning of the watershed decade of the 1670s and is a model of the genre, Cotton's work illustrates the secularization that occurred during the five decades after Richard's death. Although he followed the general guidelines of Puritan hagiography, Cotton filled his text (several times longer than his father's work) with copious details of daily life. It is ironic that Cotton's biography of Increase stands as blatant testimony to the failure of Increase's generation to meet the challenge that Richard and the collective fathers had foreseen.

In *Parentator*, Cotton takes a defensive and self-centered posture, and his envy of his father, who had taken the reins of leadership when Puritanism was still powerful in New England, is barely masked. In Cotton's view, *Parentator* was a minor but necessary "appendix," as he called it, to his *Magnalia Christi Americana* (1702), in which he had celebrated the lives of the founders and of several of Increase's contemporaries who had already died (see Chapter 5). Cotton praises Increase's efforts but laments the decline of the spirit that Increase proved unable to prevent. Unlike Increase's celebratory narrative of Richard's life, Cotton's *Parentator*, for all of Cotton's protests to the contrary, is implicitly a study of early success and ultimate failure.

The first formal history of Puritan New England began in 1630 when William Bradford began composing the manuscript that he called *Of Plimoth Plantation*, which would not be published until 1856, when it was given the title *History of Plymouth Plantation*. Bradford was born in Austerfield, England, in 1590, into the family of fairly comfortable yeoman parents. The deaths of his parents during his early years resulted in frequent moves from one relative to another. These disturbing events and a long illness led him as a boy to much private reading of the Bible and of John Foxe's *Book of Martyrs*, which prepared him for the message of the nonconformist minister Richard Clyfton, whose church in neighboring Scrooby he joined. Influenced by other congregationalists like William Brewster and later the separatist John Robinson, Bradford moved with the church in 1608 to

Amsterdam and then Leyden. There he married Dorothy May, with whom he had a son, John. Dorothy and John accompanied William to Plymouth in 1620, but Dorothy drowned off Cape Cod a few days after the landing and before the passengers had disembarked. Because Bradford fails to mention this event in his history, some have speculated that the shock of the sight of the bleak winter coastline of New England drove her to suicide. Bradford soon married Alice Carpenter Southworth and had three other children: William, Mercy, and Joseph.

In his first year of writing the history, Bradford produced about one-fourth of the final work, covering the years of preparation and departure for America. During the next fifteen years, he appears to have kept a journal or diary from which he then composed a second book in 1646 covering the years between 1630 and 1646. The first book was copied into the Plymouth church records and was thereby preserved, but the second book was lost after the American Revolution and was not discovered again until 1856, when the entire work was published for the first time. Since then, it has come to be recognized not only as an important historical source but as one of the major literary texts of early New England literature. Bradford's plain-style eloquence, his vivid descriptions, his sensitivity to human nature, and the structuring of his material reflect his acute literary sensibility.

Bradford was familiar with the ancient historians such as Herodotus, Thucydides, and Tacitus, but the more important models for his Puritan conceptions of history were the two branches of historiography that emerged in the Middle Ages: the universal history inspired by Augustine's *City of God* and the genre of the chronicle. In universal history, the historian tried to discern some larger pattern of God's plan in the recorded events; the chronicle tended to be a straightforward account of details. During the Crusades, biography was blended with history to add human drama and enable the writer to group seemingly unrelated events around a life. The Puritan historians inherited these available models and added to them what they called a "spiritualized," or providential, dimension – that is, they sought to discover in past events possible divine meanings, just as a minister tried to discern the hidden truths of biblical passages. Some later Puritan historians such as Edward Johnson and Cotton Mather went further and compared current events directly with Old and New Testament types, discovering parallels that elucidated how the scriptures were being fulfilled daily.

Because Bradford did not often make such overt comparisons, discussions of his history turn upon the question of how consciously he reshaped events, selected details, and colored his textual construction to bring it subtly into alignment with implicit providential or typological patterns others would interpret. In the first book of Bradford's text, God leads his people out of a corrupt land into a new one and shields them against trials and hardships until they prosper and multiply. Though more fragmented, the chronicle form of the second book enforces the biblical pattern with the depiction of the deaths of the first-generation patriarchs, the spread of sin, and the weakening of the church. No doubt Bradford was aware that his account parallels the experiences of the ancient Hebrews. From another perspective, the entire work appears structured upon alternations between success and failure. This cyclical dimension undercuts the more apocalyptic ending by suggesting that, with God's help, His chosen may go forward again.

Although Bradford was a pious believer in divine Providence and trusted in God's protection, he was also a pragmatic leader. His repeated reelection to the governorship of Plymouth demonstrates the faith others had in his good sense, and some scholars have read the two parts of his history in relation to his practical nature. The differences in the tone and structure from the first book of the history to the second, written sixteen years later, may be the result of the very different political contexts for each writing. With the arrival of the much larger Massachusetts Bay Colony in 1630, the Plymouth Colony faced one of the greatest challenges to its existence. Bradford knew that the invading thousands of nonseparatists might swallow up, persecute, or even expel the separationists. The subsequent intolerance of the Massachusetts Bay theocracy toward the views of Roger Williams and Anne Hutchinson would demonstrate that Bradford was right to be wary. Bradford's choice of this moment to begin to record Plymouth's history surely sprang, to some degree, from the clear geographical and political threat that the Winthrop colony represented. His strong emphasis upon the Pilgrims' rationale for their emigration, the foundations of their beliefs, and the role of Providence in their survival and success functions as both a self-definition of the colony and a defense against outside criticism. Once time had assured the Bradford colony of its autonomy, he could look back upon the years following 1630 differently. As he took up his pen again in 1645, his text did not need typology to support his argument justifying the Plymouth way; rather, it could be a practical man's sober accounting of the trials, pressures, and even fractures the colony had experienced. After all, with all of Boston's troubles over those years, Bradford's candid account of Plymouth's trials was no proof that Plymouth was less divinely favored.

Aboard the *Arbella*, John Winthrop began the journal that would eventually become *The History of New England from 1630 to 1649*, first published in this form in 1825–26. An earlier version, entitled *A Journal of the Transactions and Occurrences in the Settlement of Massachusetts and the Other New England Colonies from the Year 1630 to 1644*, was published in 1790. Unlike Bradford, Winthrop never attempted to turn his journal into a true history, but over the years his entries became longer and richer in their depiction of characters and circumstances, and his summaries of his own views and feelings became more revealing so that the final product is both a diary and a chronicle. Winthrop himself called his work a history; although giving no name to the first volume, he called the other two *A Continuation of the History of New England*. A striking difference between Winthrop's and Bradford's chronicles is that Bradford kept himself very much out of the account, even referring to himself in the third person, whereas Winthrop is a fully active character. Indeed, at times it seems that Winthrop's principal desire in the journal is to justify, either to himself or to posterity, his decisions and actions, especially those against his opponents.

Although the status of Winthrop's history as a literary work has never been fully settled, literary scholars are still drawn to it because of the author's personality, which alone inscribes the work with a narrative unity, and because of the unique perspective it provides on critical events. Deeply religious, Winthrop was always cognizant of the divine presence in every aspect of the New England experiment: "It is useful to observe as we go along, such especial providences of God as were manifested for the good of these plantations." Particularly suggestive are those passages in which he reflects upon the ways that the very success of the colony brought on new problems and made it harder for him and the ministers to control the people: "As people increased, so sin abounded and especially the sin of uncleanness, and still the providence of God found them out." Though Winthrop sometimes feared that the experiment was destined to fail, he never doubted that the outcome would ultimately fulfill God's plan.

Although Winthrop never found a solution to this problem of the growing population and the accompanying moral pollution, he did have occasion several times during his years as governor to sharpen the definitions and applications of New England federal theology. One of the most famous passages in his *Journal* was recorded on July 3, 1645, after he had been acquitted of the charge of exceeding his authority in office. In response to this challenge, he delivered to the General Court what has come to be called his "Little Speech on Liberty," which he later recorded in the *Journal*. With a combination of general humility and total self-assurance about specifics, Winthrop provided a concise summary of the structure of authority in a theocracy. Interestingly, his use of the analogy of marriage and the submission of the wife to her husband to illustrate the nature of civil authority casts as much light on the Puritan view of gender relations as it does on political order:

> The great questions that have troubled the country are about the authority of the magistrates and the liberty of the people. It is yourselves who have called us to this office, and being called by you, we have our authority from God. For the other point concerning liberty, I observe a great mistake in the country about that. There is a two-fold liberty, natural

(I mean as our nature is now corrupt) and civil or federal. The first is
common to man with wild beasts and other creatures.... It is a liberty to
evil as well as to good. This liberty is incompatible and inconsistent with
authority... This is that great enemy of truth and peace, that wild beast
which all the ordinances of God are bent against.... The other kind of
liberty I call civil or federal, it may also be termed moral.... This liberty is
the proper end and object of authority.... This liberty is maintained and
exercised in a way of subjection to authority.... The woman's own choice
makes such a man her husband; yet being so chosen, he is her lord, and
she is to be subject to him, yet in a way of liberty, nor of bondage; and a
true wife accounts her subjection her honor and freedom, and would nor
think her condition safe and free, but in her subjection to her husband's
authority. Such is the liberty of the church under the authority of Christ,
her king and husband.... Even so it will be between you and your
magistrates.

Given Winthrop's interpretation here, it is not surprising that he found the
rebellion of Anne Hutchinson to be so unnatural. Moreover, it demonstrates
the way in which Puritan gender relations were ultimately prefigured by the
permanence of Puritan typology.

Because neither Bradford's nor Winthrop's histories were published during the seventeenth century, three other printed works provided several
generations with the only coherent record of the English settlement of
New England. The first, entitled *Mourt's Relation* (1622), was composed by
a G. Mourt, which may have been a pseudonym for a person still unknown
or a misprint for George Morton, who was instrumental in the work's publication and a member of one of the Leyden groups of separatists who later
landed at Plymouth. Another opinion is that at least part of the work was
that of Edward Winslow, with substantial contributions (perhaps two-thirds)
by William Bradford, but the real identity of the author remains a mystery.
Composed in the form of a history, the text is really a tract to encourage
emigration, and its publication in England in 1622 was directed to prospective colonists seeking information about Plymouth. Unlike the promotional
tracts of John Smith and of the Virginia colonies, *Mourt's Relation* provides
a straightforward, uninflated, and undisguised account of the realities of life
in New England.

Another published account of the early years of the Plymouth Colony
was Nathaniel Morton's (1613–85) *New England's Memorial* (1669). Morton
was one of the early settlers who arrived from Leyden on the ship *Anne* in
1623. He lived for a time in the home of William Bradford and served as
his secretary before he went on to be the keeper of records for the colony
from 1647 to 1685. He became one of the wealthiest men in Plymouth
and drafted most of the town laws. In 1669, Morton published his history,
which remained the major account of the colony's settlement until Bradford's

history was discovered in the nineteenth century. In the early 1670s, Morton worked on a more complete history, which was destroyed in a fire in 1676. He then wrote another version, which was published in 1680. Morton's history is distinct from *Mourt's Relation* in being a much fuller account imbued with strongly didactic and providential elements. Even after the discovery of Bradford's history, Morton's work remains critically valuable, for it supplies certain details missing from Bradford, such as a list of the signers of the Mayflower Compact and the name of the ship that departed with the *Mayflower* but had to turn back – the *Speedwell*.

A third history published in the century is the highly controversial *A History of New England* (1654) of Edward Johnson (1598–1672). Johnson was born in England, the son of a parish clerk, and he managed to acquire land in Canterbury and to rise in the military to the rank of captain. In 1630, he visited New England, perhaps on the *Arbella* with Winthrop, and he was admitted as a freeman in 1631 but chose to return to England. In 1636, he and his wife, the former Susan Munnter, and their seven children moved to Boston, but later they settled on land he purchased in nearby Charlestown. In 1640, he was invited to participate in the building of a new community at Woburn, where he remained active in community affairs for the rest of his life, holding a variety of positions such as selectman and militia captain. Neither a clergyman nor university trained, Johnson was an unusual Puritan author.

Running to nearly 300 pages in modern printings, Johnson's *History* stands out as the most complete and coherent report on the first twenty-five years of the colony before Cotton Mather's monumental *Magnalia Christi Americana* of 1702. Johnson considered his title to be *The Wonder-Working Providence of Zion's Saviour in New England*, which was used in the running heads, repeated in the text, and appeared on the title page of subsequent editions. Evidence suggests that he began composing the work in 1649 and that he completed it in 1651. Unified in style, tone, and voice, it is divided into three books, each of which covers a seven-year period: 1630–37, 1637–44, and 1644–51. In a lively and energetic style, Johnson's brisk narration and colorful personality convey his own enthusiasm for the Puritan experiment and his profound religious convictions. Johnson's writing and opinions have not been received with unmixed praise, however, for in his own time, and still today, some have found his work crude, strained, and unnecessarily biased. His swagger and occasional bombast sound in stark contrast to the reserve of Bradford and the subtlety of Winthrop. Puritan literary scholarship of the last twenty-five years has considered Johnson's most important contribution to be his liberal use of biblical typology to support his arguments and vision. From his perspective, New England was the New Zion, and its people's progress was the fulfillment of the divine will. Evidently, by the time

Johnson was composing his work in the late 1640s, the myths and images of a divine mission were firmly enough established in the Puritan imagination that Johnson accepted them unquestioned. Guided by his prophetic sense of sacred history, Johnson gave his work an epic grandeur: the Puritans are imagined as a mighty army commissioned by Christ to battle the Antichrist and prepare a place for Christ's triumphant return to the world in New England. Forecasting the spirit of independence that would eventually inspire the American Revolution, Johnson's rhetoric explored a paradigm that would be repeated by many American presidents to come: "Here the Reader is desired to take notice of the wonderful providence of the most high God toward these his new-planted Churches, such as were never heard of . . . that in ten or twelve years there should be such wonderful alteration, a Nation born in a day, a Commonwealth orderly brought forth from a few fugitives."

In addition to articulating the Puritan vision of America, the work provides insights into more mundane attitudes of the Puritans that his "common-man" viewpoint reveals. His opinions on relations with the Indians are particularly interesting. Although he frequently expresses compassion for Native Americans, Johnson also reiterates the accepted Puritan view, found in Winthrop, that Christ had prepared the way for His chosen by divinely causing the smallpox epidemic that devastated several tribes and weakened those potential warriors who did survive. Similarly, his account of the Pequot War describes, with sadness, the brutal killing of hundreds of native women and children, while also expressing a self-righteous pride in exercising the will of the Lord.

Correspondingly, those passages of the *History* that deal with the antinomian crisis expose a typical Puritan male's attitude toward Anne Hutchinson as a woman. An orthodox supporter of the clergy and magistrates, Johnson had deep concerns about any movements or individuals that threatened order and discipline in the colony. He had no sympathy for Hutchinson, and his descriptions of her reflect his impatience with all "erronists." For him, it made no sense for people to risk all, to transport their families across an ocean to practice their faith, and then to be caught up in dissension: "stopped and startled in their course by a kennel of devouring wolves" like those from which they fled. Of Hutchinson herself, whose name he never mentions, he says that:

> the weaker Sex prevailed so far that they set up a Priest of their own Profession and Sex, which was much thronged after, abominably wresting the Scriptures to their own destruction: this Master-piece of Women's wit, drew many Disciples after her . . . being much backed with the Sorcery of a second, who had much converse with the Devil. . . . This woman was wonted to give drinks to other Women to cause them to conceive . . . but sure there were Monsters born not long after.

These passages of misogynistic stereotyping of Hutchinson and her supporters are surrounded by others that reveal the social context in which to better understand how a man like Johnson had come to such positions. More candid than the guarded expressions of the elite, Johnson's persona provides insights into the attitudes of the average, devout, but untrained layman. Besides providing a useful overview of events in early New England, Johnson's work is a prime example of spiritualized, typologized history. Johnson's *History* is the most self-consciously political history in the first fifty years of the Puritan settlements, but it would not be the last. Indeed, historiography became the subject of open public controversy in the 1670s when Increase Mather and William Hubbard (c. 1621–1704) produced two quite different kinds of histories of King Philip's War.

In February 1674, Increase Mather preached one of the sermons that would establish him as the leading minister of his generation. In a jeremiad entitled *The Day of Trouble is Near*, Mather warned his congregation that the saints were soon to pay for their sins and backsliding, for a great trial was coming that would precede the Apocalypse. Quoting Matthew, he predicted, "Ye shall hear of wars and the rumors of wars." Mather was presumably thinking of troubles in Europe and how these might affect Massachusetts, but very soon his words took on unexpected prophetic resonances. Lamenting the time that men were spending on profits instead of on family prayer – "*On this world, the World* undoeth many a man" – he envisioned a "cloud of blood . . . over our heads which begins to drop upon us." In the very next year, 1675, the devastating King Philip's War erupted. Under the leadership of the resourceful Chief Sachem Metacomet of the Wampanoags, several Native-American tribes joined in what they perceived to be their last chance to stop the whites from pushing them completely out of their homelands. During the eighteen months of fighting, both sides suffered high casualties, and the economy of the English colony underwent a complete disruption. As people fled farming villages and distant communities, Boston and other coastal towns perforce overflowed with homeless refugees. Some historians believe that this social and economic calamity, more than shifts in religious attitudes or the actions of the English Crown, was primarily responsible for dismantling the Puritan social, political, and economic structures.

From the standpoint of literary history, the war also had immediate and perhaps longer-range consequences. All that Increase Mather's *Day of Trouble* had predicted and worse had happened, and Mather repeatedly referred to the fulfillment of his prophecy. The governor of Massachusetts, John Leverett, and his deputies and military commanders understood the Indians' motives and the machinations of the war in practical, political, and financial terms, but Mather placed himself in opposition to them in a struggle for the moral and spiritual leadership of the Puritan colonies in time of peril. From the outset of the war, Mather began preaching and publishing about the real causes of the war, which he perceived to be the many sins of the English, especially of young people: disobedience to parents and ministers, drunkenness, profligacy, wantonness, swearing, Sabbath-breaking, new fashions in dress and new hairstyles, sleeping during sermons, and leaving services early. For him, the best defense against the Indians would be more fast days, stricter laws governing moral behavior, and covenant renewals in the churches. New England's sins were the "provoking evils" that God was punishing with his cloud of blood.

The governor and the members of the General Court did not agree with Mather but saw no harm in increased discipline among the English during wartime. They recognized that following Mather's proposals would at least not hurt the war effort even if they did not really believe that God would destroy the Indians if the saints repented. As a result, Mather appeared to gain political power and position during the war, influence that he built upon in the following decade. The truth was, however, that Leverett and his fellow magistrates felt little sympathy for Mather's position.

As the war seemed to go against the English, the men of Leverett's generation – twenty years older than Mather – grew weary of Mather's unrelenting accusations that they were responsible for the losses because they failed to legislate behavior more strictly. When it came time to select a preacher for the election day sermon for May 1676, the deputies and magistrates selected William Hubbard, who, twenty years Mather's senior, was his known opponent and had a reputation for good sense. Hubbard was an orthodox minister who basically shared Mather's providential view of history, but he also agreed with his pragmatic-minded brethren that other, natural factors entered into events. Hubbard was a reasonable Puritan who was skeptical of Mather's exhortations and intolerance, and his sermon that day constituted a dispassionate assessment of the crisis. He found hope in the rising generation and insisted that whatever spiritual problems existed, they could be rooted out with neither "civil nor ecclesiastic censures." Arguing that God deals with His people as individuals rather than as communities, Hubbard thereby shifted the blame for the war from the group and their leaders. For Hubbard, public events such as wars were not necessarily the direct results of divine intervention, and thus he spoke of the war more in secular than in providential terms. Entitled *The Happiness of a People in the Wisdom of their Rulers*, Hubbard's sermon looks forward to an approaching peace to be achieved more expeditiously through the people's quiet obedience to their leaders than through lamentations and fast days. When the sermon was published at the expense of the General Court, Hubbard dedicated it to Governor Leverett.

Responding to the challenge, Increase Mather countered with an essay called *An Earnest Exhortation to the Inhabitants of New England*, which argues that the people should look to the scriptures and the experience of "Israel of old" for the causes of the present war. Mather quotes the original charter of the colony, which asserts conversion of the Indians rather than land acquisition as their covenanted mission. He thereby exposes one of the most sensitive areas of their communal conscience: the communal failure to put more resources into the conversion of the Indians. As a final reminder of how far the present leadership had strayed from the aims of the founders, Mather included a woodcut of the original Massachusetts seal, which shows an Indian entreating his white brothers across the ocean to "Come over and help us."

Meanwhile, it became apparent in the summer of 1676 that the English were winning the war, especially after Metacomet was killed in August. In an act of brutal vengeance, the English dismembered his body and displayed his head on a pike in Plymouth and his hands in Boston. Such horrific displays of aggression and power were to become paradigmatic expressions of triumph and superiority in racial conflicts in the American West, and later English and American texts such as Aphra Behn's *Oroonoko* (1688), Herman Melville's "Benito Cereno" (1856), and W. E. B. Du Bois' *Autobiography* (1968) describe similar horrendous acts. Within a few weeks after Metacomet's death, Mather rushed to complete his *A Brief History of the War with the Indians in New England*, a spiritualized history that used typology to impose Mather's own interpretation upon the war. Mather's history appeared that fall in Boston and London, but he had not yet heard the last on this subject from Hubbard.

During the winter of 1676–77, Hubbard finished his own history, *A Relation of the Troubles Which Have Happened in New England, By Reason of the Indians There* (1677). Hubbard's argument is not extraordinarily different from Mather's – for him too the war resulted from God's displeasure with the Puritans – but Hubbard's handling of many particulars differ in important ways. In making such remarks as "Time and Chance hath strangely interposed to the prolonging of our Miseries," Hubbard asserts a scientific notion of natural causes and effects that is quite contrary to Mather's spiritualized account. Hubbard's tendency to use reason and to strive for a degree of objectivity in his assessment of events looked toward a new historical methodology that would characterize later works such as Thomas Prince's *A Chronological History of New England in the Form of Annals* (1736).

The General Court was so pleased with Hubbard's more rational version of the war that they commissioned him to write a "General History of New England," which he completed in 1680. This history was not published, however, until the early nineteenth century. Historians are not certain why Hubbard's history was left unpublished for so long; most speculate that Mather blocked the work directly or indirectly. During the years following the war, Mather was busy denouncing the apostasy of the younger generation and predicting further disasters, and by the early 1680s he managed to gain control of the Boston press by becoming a member of the Board of Printers' Licensers. During the 1680s, with the political autonomy of Massachusetts under attack from England, Mather censored works that he deemed dangerous to the colony's interests. He believed that it was harmful for people to think that events occurred for natural reasons rather than by God's design because such modern notions would weaken the Puritan cause. Secularism and scientific ideas of natural causes had to be quelled, for if God's plan were called into question, even Puritan property rights were at stake. Although Hubbard's manuscript was damaged and sections were lost during the eighteenth century, it became a source for several later historians, including Cotton Mather, and was finally published in 1815. The likely suppression of Hubbard's work indicates, however, that by the latter half of the seventeenth century, the writing of history had become a highly politicized activity and that the battle between the myths of the past – which some called spiritualized history and others were beginning to call fictions – and efforts at accurate documentary was a contentious one.

In the course of fifty years, the writing of Puritan history and biography had developed from the tentative jottings of Bradford and Winthrop in their personal journals and the elaborately typologized and spiritualized narratives of Edward Johnson to become the site of academic and philosophical disputes over the processes of knowing the past and present, the legitimate methods of recording and reporting events, and the authority to reveal or conceal competing interpretations of experience. For Puritans like the Mathers, flawed human reason and memory necessarily undermined the authenticity of representations of experience and ensured the indeterminacy of history. This fallen human condition required that the inspired interpreter of the past construct narratives of events, like renderings of the scriptures, in ways that would yield the greatest spiritual benefits for the progress of God's chosen toward their temporal and heavenly callings.

Chapter Five

Poetry

Because the New England Puritans radically distrusted the senses and the imagination and were highly suspicious of all forms of art, most literary scholars either have ignored their poems or have treated them as curiosities. The advocates of Anne Bradstreet continue to construct an image of her as a cultural rebel who produced poetry in spite of the religious and social forces against her as a woman and as a Puritan. Similarly, when the poems of Edward Taylor were discovered and published in the late 1930s, many literary historians explained that his self-conscious artistry violated Puritan doctrines and that his poetic impulses suggested that he was by temperament more Catholic or Anglican than Puritan. The long disappearance of his work prompted a conclusion that he had feared exposure of his artistry and thereby enjoined his heirs to suppress his poetry. Not only, in this view, did theology prevail against Puritan art but the harsh physical conditions of New England life left no time for aesthetic indulgences. Bradstreet's productions were attributed to the leisure available to a woman of her high social standing and Taylor's to the quiet life in his wilderness parish of Westfield, Massachusetts.

To be sure, there are many valid historical reasons for assuming the term "Puritan poetry" to be an oxymoron. In England from the late sixteenth century, Puritan theologians and ministers had warned that the senses were unreliable, that appeals to the imagination were dangerous, and that the use of figurative, imagistic, or symbolic language bordered upon idolatry. Reasoning that God had inscribed all the truth that humanity needed in the scriptures, they held that plain and direct discussion of His word was the only truly legitimate and humble mode of verbal expression. The Catholics' and Anglicans' use of graven images, emphasis on pulpit eloquence, appeals to congregations through music, and ornate vestments were further proof to the Puritans that artistry invited idolatry. The Puritans' iconoclastic destruction of religious statuary during the Civil War, their closing of the theaters, the plainness of their own churches, and their official statements condemning ornate speech and dress strongly support a view that Puritan art and poetry were all but impossible. Puritan doctrines generally forbade the use of any figurative language except for religious instruction. With all of these obvious barriers to poetic art, most scholars of the Puritans assumed that practice followed theory.

Indeed, Puritan leaders and clergy made their condemnation of literary artistry quite explicit. In 1640 a group of American Puritan clergy produced their own translation of the Psalms, *The Whole Book of Psalms Faithfully Translated into English Meter* (commonly known as *The Bay Psalm Book*), to replace what they viewed as the overly poetic translation of Thomas Sternhold and John Hopkins used by the Anglicans. John Cotton provided a preface often cited as evidence of the Puritans' firm rejection of verbal artifice:

> Neither let any think, that for the meter's sake we have taken liberty or poetical license to depart from the true and proper sense of David's words in the Hebrew verses, no; but it hath been one part of our religious care and faithful endeavor to keep close to the original text.... If therefore the verses are not always so smooth and elegant as some may desire or expect; let them consider that God's Altar needs not our polishings.

Cotton's widely quoted assertion of Puritan literalism and plainness appears to rule out further discussion of Puritan artistry.

Yet, from the 1940s through 1960s, scholars continued to discover and publish considerable numbers of Puritan poems, many of which contain provocatively striking figurative language and allusions not only to the Bible but to classical models such as Ovid, Cicero, Virgil, Horace, and Livy. Numerous poems also contain intertextual references to the work of contemporary poets, among them Spenser, Sidney, Shakespeare, Herbert, Vaughan, and Quarles. Such evidence of an apparent gap between Puritan theory and poetic practice continues to appear. For example, one discovery revealed that at Harvard in the 1640s two sons of ministers, Seaborn Cotton and Elnathan Chauncy, copied into their commonplace books various love poems of John Cleveland as well as Robert Herrick's "Gather ye rosebuds" and Francis Beaumont's "Psyche: or Loves' Mysteries." Archives have yielded a wide variety of poems: formal elegies, lyrics, hymns, ballads, dialogues, and witty anagrams, acrostics, and epigrams. Their authors were sea captains, housewives, military men, and judges, as well as the clergy themselves. The increasing recognition of Edward Taylor's literary sophistication has led some scholars to question the relationship between narrow dogma and expressed aesthetic theory and the Puritan poetic discourse itself.

One reconsideration seeks to interrogate the artistic and imaginative inclinations of Puritans themselves as people. Those who emigrated to New England had been, after all, heirs to a rich literary tradition, and many must have cherished the beauty of the language and treasured eloquent expression in spite of religious scruples. Eventually the ministers expanded their doctrines or discovered new complexities within them that allowed an increase in the number and quality of artistic expressions. By 1650, a major shift had become evident authorizing writers to use sensual imagery more freely and even to strive consciously for eloquence. A notable sign of this change was the revised translation of *The Bay Psalm Book* undertaken in 1651 by President Henry Dunster of Harvard and Richard Lyon, who said they had "a special eye" for the "sweetness of the verse." Cotton Mather later said of this edition that "it was thought that a little more of Art was to be employed upon the verses."

This movement toward verbal artistry received its strongest official endorsement from the eminent English Puritan Richard Baxter (1615–91) in his highly popular *The Saint's Everlasting Rest* (1650). A military chaplain in the Puritan army during the Civil War and a respected antipapist, Baxter could be trusted to deal safely with such sensitive matters as the relation of meditation to conversion and salvation and the uses of the senses, imagination, and language in the meditative or poetic processes. Intended primarily as a handbook for tracking the stages of the saint's spiritual journey, Baxter's work also had important implications for legitimizing literary invention because he endorsed sensual appeals to the imagination.

Several centuries of learned debates over the meditation process and its function in religious experience had preceded Baxter's work. In fact, in England in 1632 Thomas Hooker (1586–1647) had elaborated upon the meditative process in his *The Soul's Preparation for Christ* and justified the use of the senses, imagination, and affections for making spiritual truth more compelling to the understanding. Even John Cotton, who most feared the idolatry that could result from placing sensual images between the saints and God, said that a person "may lawfully in his meditations make use of diverse Creatures or Things, that are apt and fit to represent Spiritual things unto him." Still, such a qualification as Cotton's implies that the more pious the believer, the less the need to use such "diverse Creatures."

At a key moment then in the development of New England Puritanism, the endorsement of Baxter, a poet himself, of the use of metaphor as a positive act, even a spiritual duty, was a significant event. Baxter argued that God gave humanity figurative language in order to enhance people's abilities to perceive His truths. Highlighting the many uses of figures in the Bible, he proposed that "these with most other descriptions of our Glory are expressed as if it were the very flesh and sense, which though they are all improper and figurative, yet doubtless if such expressions had not been best, and to us necessary, the Holy Ghost would not have so frequently used them." Not only is it permissible for the saints to use such metaphors in meditation, Baxter submitted, but people are obliged to use this God-given system and to take delight in the world of the senses, which is itself a metaphor, a vehicle of God's instruction. Although Baxter still cautioned that the meditating saint or poet must make certain that the image or figure remained a channel to the divine and not become an earthly shadow eclipsing God, he encouraged a broad range of metaphorical experimentation and even playfulness in language. Thus, the act of signification became a roving, rather than fixed, enterprise. Language became a vehicle, no longer a revealed truth.

The other developing component of Puritan thought that served to certify a Puritan poetics was the more liberal employment of biblical typology. The routine clerical explications of the fulfillment of Old Testament types in the New Testament antitypes had established a mode of symbolic expression. In the early decades of the settlements, some clergy, such as Roger Williams, warned against the extension of this hermeneutic method, but, over time, the creative impulses of Puritan ministers and other writers and the inviting vision of New England as the New Zion led to a most liberal use of typology, opening the system toward more elaborate constructs integrating biblical types with historical events, moral formulations, and even the characters of well-known individuals. Present-day reappraisals of Puritan poetry have served to reconfigure conceptions of Puritan poetics. With a new awareness that it was very possible for a Puritan poet to strive consciously for artfulness, readers have been less inclined to dismiss newly discovered productions and more open to recognizing aesthetic achievement.

Inconsistency and contradiction between Puritan aesthetic theory and poetic practice appear in the case of Roger Williams. As discussed earlier, Williams adhered to the most conservative use of types, and he displayed stubborn convictions about what he perceived as the misuse of biblical types when applied to current events in New England. But in his poetry, Williams broke with convention in significant ways. In *A Key into the Language of America* (1643), he described the characters of the Native Americans he knew and taught, and he critiqued the English, often in scathing terms, particularly in regard to their mistreatment of the natives. At the end of each chapter, he placed a poem to function as a terse summary of his prose remarks. In these poems, usually of twelve lines divided into three numbered stanzas, Williams created powerful images carefully linked to religious and moral precepts. His language is plain and direct, and his images are often homey and earthy. The rhyme is uneven and the iambic meter is rough, but the images are nonetheless remarkably effective.

In some poems, the speaker addresses his English readers directly (roman and italic type as in the original edition):

> *Boast not proud English of thy birth and blood.*
> *Thy brother Indian is by birth as Good.*
> *Alone blood God made Him, and Thee and All,*
> *As wise, as faire, as strong, as personall.*

Although Williams believed that Indians could be converted and could receive saving grace, he felt that the English had a great advantage because their education and cultural heritage taught them how to prepare their hearts for grace. He preached in his poems that being so favored the English have a special obligation to have "*thy second birth, else thou shalt see, /Heaven open to* Indians *wild, but shut to thee.*" In other poems, Williams used aspects of indigenous appearance or customs to form an apparent contrast to the English, which he sometimes reversed:

> *Truth is a Native, naked Beauty; but*
>   *Lying Inventions are but Indian Paints,*
> *Dissembling hearts their Beautie's but a Lye*
>   *Truth is the proper Beauty of Gods Saints.*

Here truth and the "native" exist in tandem, and the Indian's innocent application of decorative paints is far less dissembling than the false hearts of the English hypocrites. The next stanza asserts that the hair and paint of the Indian may appear "*Fowle*" to the English, but the clean faces and groomed hair of the inwardly corrupted English hypocrites look even "*More fowle*" to Christ when he sees "*such Faces in Israel.*" This substitution of the biblical Israel for New England would appear to contradict Williams's position on typology, but apparently in poetry he felt types could be employed more liberally. In the final stanza, the Indians appear disordered but still genuinely innocent; in contrast, images of fire, storms, and tears depict the fate awaiting those English sinners who do not repent before Judgment:

> *Paints will not bide Christs washing Flames of fire,*
>   *Pained Inventions will not bide such stormes:*
> *O that we may prevent him, that betimes,*
>   *Repentance Tears may wash of all such Formes.*

In several of these poems, Williams suggests that, though lacking saving grace, the Indians are morally superior to many of the English. In one, he contrasts the serene culture of the Indians with the empty and disruptive pastimes of the English, who relentlessly violate the peace that had characterized Indian territories: "*What noise and tumults in our owne, /And eke in* Pagan lands?*" And in one of the earliest proclamations by an English settler that the wilderness could be a source of comfort instead of threat, the speaker comments: "*Yet I have found lesse noyse, more peace /In wilde* America.*" This poem concludes its contrast of cultures with the obligatory religious point that, in regard to grace, both the natives and the English must remain spiritually passive "till God's call." In another poem, Williams contrasts the superior morals and laws of the Indians with those of the English. The speaker asserts that the natives firmly punish such crimes as adultery, murder, and theft, whereas the English treat the same crimes more lightly. When the natives learn of the English leniency, they express shock and disdain:

> *We weare no Cloths, have many Gods,*
> *And yet our sinnes are less:*
> *You are Barbarians, Pagans wild,*
> *Your Land's the Wilderness.*

Because Williams consistently asserted the spiritual equality of Native Americans, he may not have realized how using them as a metaphor for the "other," even when his images of them were positive, would function to reinforce the racial division and antagonism of the English toward them. It is likely, however, that Williams was the first English writer in English America to use the idealized image of the native, in what would become a persistent tradition, in order to berate his fellow whites to emulate more humane principles.

Writers like Williams, Edward Taylor, and John Cotton adhered to the Puritan principle of poetic didacticism, but there were other Puritans who recorded personal observations in secular verse. William Wood's (1606–post–1637) promotional work *New England's Prospect* (1634) describes the natural setting of New England and urges the English to establish trading and exploring companies in America. Little is known about Wood, but it is believed that he was a member of John Endecott's group and that he settled in Salem in 1631. Throughout the pages of his prose narrative, Wood included verses depicting his new surroundings.

Another Puritan author who wrote secular prose and poetry about America was John Josselyn (1610-post–1692). After a brief visit in 1637 to Massachusetts, where he met John Winthrop and John Cotton, he returned in 1663 and stayed until 1671. During his extended residence, he became disillusioned with the New England Way and severely criticized it in his *An Account of Two Voyages to New England* (1674). His earlier book, *New England's Rarities Discovered* (1672), describes the natural beauty and wildlife of America in prose full of wonder and some exaggeration. Interspersed among his observations are some verses on a sea storm and on springtime in New England as well as an unusual poem describing a Native-American woman.

The poem "Verses made sometime since upon the Picture of a young and handsome Gypsie, not improperly transferred upon the Indian Squaw" sets up an internal debate over whether women of fair or dark complexion are more beautiful. Anticipating the complex ways gender and race will intersect in numerous later American texts, this poem explores the erotic power of the exotic. A curious ethnic ambiguity is created by the speaker's switch to the word "Red" near the end of the poem after he had been describing the woman as "Black." This shift may indicate Josselyn's linking of all people of color into a generalized "other."

The poem's organizational principle is borrowed from the Petrarchan model, which examines a woman's charms using each of the senses in turn:

> Whether White or Black be best
> Call your Senses to the quest;
> And your touch shall quickly tell
> The Black in softness doth excel,
> And in smoothness.

With an implicit admission in the words "softness" and "smoothness" that the speaker has had physical contact with the woman, he initially mixes the senses of sight and touch in these lines. Then, he proceeds to the sense of hearing and to the quality of her mind that he can detect in her conversation:

> but the Ear,
> What, can that a Colour hear?
> No, but 'tis your Black ones Wit
> That doth catch, and captive it.

Because introducing the sense of taste would perhaps be too risqué, Josselyn's speaker both evades and underscores that omission with a pun: "Nor can ought so please the tast /As what's brown and lovely drest." This image provocatively evokes the picture of the woman in the nude since her "dress" may be brown skin. Acknowledging that the debate over complexion and beauty is endless – "Maugre then all that can be sed / In flattery of White and Red" – he then gives his own preference for darker women:

> Those flatterers themselves must say
> That darkness was before the Day;
> And such perfection here appears
> It neither Wind nor Sun-shine fears.

Although this text may be an early example of one English author's attempts to challenge racial and ethnic stereotypes regarding Native Americans and Africans, as well as "Gypsies," another possibility is presented by the recent discovery of a comic form that attained a degree of popularity in seventeenth-century English verse: the parody of the Petrarchan love sonnet. In works such as John Collop's "On an Ethiopian beauty, M.S." and his "Of the black Lady with grey eyes and white teeth," the poet mocks the extravagant praises of standard love poetry by constructing what the poet presumes to be an absurd situation in which the white male speaker expresses passion for a black woman. Since there is ample evidence of physical attraction, romantic love, and sexual relations among Native Americans, Europeans, and Africans in early America, and since little else is known of Josselyn's personal views on race and gender, the issue of the author's intention in this poem remains open to speculation.

As the broad range of Puritan poetry has come to light, one of the surprises has been the discovery of so many poems about love and desire, which seems to contrast with the popular image of Puritan reserve and restraint. The most prolific author of love poems was John Saffin (1626–1710), a prominent lawyer and judge and a member of the church at Boston. In 1665, he began his commonplace book, published in 1928 as *John Saffin, His Book*, which he continued until two years before his death. The work consists of scientific notes, philosophical contemplations, summaries of his reading, and poetry, which includes satires, elegies, characters, occasional verse, and love poems. Saffin also recorded views on the requirements of good poetry that differ rather drastically from those of most Puritan clergy: "He that would write well in verse must observe these rules...that it be elegant, emphatical, metaphorical, and historical; running in a fluent, and smooth channel." No mention here of the dangers of figurative language or the need for religious precepts. His "Sayle Gentle Pinnace," written during his courtship of Martha Willett, has been praised as one of the finest poems of seventeenth-century America. One of Saffin's favorite types of poem was the acrostic, which requires that the first letter of each line when read downward spell out the name of the person who is the subject of the poem. The poet also must use as many words as possible formed from the person's name. Saffin has the distinction of having written the first valentine poem in America: "On Presenting a rare Book to Madame Hull Senior: his Vallintine."

Although Saffin may have had success in his friendships with women, he had frequent disputes with male colleagues. Judge Samuel Sewall of Boston, famous for his *Diary* and for his early antislavery tract *The Selling of Joseph* (1700), was moved by an action of Saffin's to compose a poetic barb. Saffin had argued a case for reenslaving Adam, his black slave, after he had officially obtained his freedom. Sewall, who considered slavery "the most atrocious of capital Crimes," wrote in his poem "To John Saffin":

> Superanuated Squier, wigg'd and powder'd with pretence,
> Much beguiles the just Assembly by his lying Impudence.
> None being by, his sworn Attorneys push it on with
>   might and main
> By which means poor simple Adam sinks to slavery again.

It is not known whether Sewall ever presented his poem to Saffin or whether he kept it where it was eventually discovered, in the privacy of his diary.

Given the hardships of their frontier society, the Puritans had frequent occasions to compose elegies. Rather formulaic and varying greatly in quality, elegies were mainly given to family members and circulated only in limited copies, although a few, composed on prominent figures, became popular as broadsides. Usually elegies focused upon the events and accomplishments of the deceased's life, stressing the signs of grace operating in the person's character and actions. Many elegies also emphasized the bond between the individual saint and the covenanted community, first expressing regret over the group's loss and then consolation and assurance that the saint is at peace with God and His chosen. During the early decades of the colony, all of the elegies preserved were written by men about men, but beginning in the 1680s and then with greater frequency into the eighteenth century, elegies celebrating the lives of women appear as well.

The most admired Puritan elegy was produced by the Reverend Urian Oakes (1631–81) on the occasion of the death of Thomas Shepard, Jr. (1634–77), a minister and son of the first-generation Shepard. Educated at Harvard, Oakes went to England, where he was a teacher and minister for seventeen years before returning to New England in 1671. He served as president of Harvard from 1675 until his death. Composed of fifty-two stanzas of six lines each, his elegy on Shepard is one of the longest of the period. The poem's opening lines make it clear that the attitudes of ministers toward poetic artistry had changed since the 1630s, for Oakes's first seven stanzas lament his inadequacy of "Art and Fancy" to pay Shepard a fitting tribute. Beginning by proclaiming "Oh! that I were a Poet now in grain!" he restated this desire in several ways:

> Now could I wish (if wishing could obtain)
> The sprightli'est Efforts of Poetic Rage;
> . . . .
> And could my Pen ingeniously distill
>   The purest Spirits of a sparkling wit
> In rare conceits, the quintessence of skill
> In *Elegiack Strains*; none like to it:
> . . . .
> Could I take highest Flights of Fancy, soar
> Aloft; If Wits Monopoly were mine:
> All would be much too low, too light, too poor
> To pay due tribute to this great Divine.
> Ah! Wits avails not, when the Heart's like to break,
> Great griefs are Toung-ti'ed, when the lesser speak.

Besides elaborating upon Shepard's qualities and his successful ministry, Oakes reads the untimely death as a possible sign of God's anger with New England: "Lord! is thy Treaty with *New-England* come / To an end? And is War in thy Heart?" Near the end of the poem, Oakes explicitly places the blame for Shepard's death upon the people: "Our sins have slain our

Shepard! we have bought / And dearly paid for our Enormities." Frequently,
Puritan elegies, especially those by clergy, also became sermons, as in this
case: "*New England* know that Heart-plague [for] / *With him New England
fell!*" In spite of these formulas, the language also makes evident the strong
personal friendship that existed between Oakes and Shepard. This personal
element enables the poem to transcend the conventions and the preaching,
as in the poignant final stanza:

> My Dearest, Inmost, Bosome-Friend is Gone!
> Gone is my sweet Companion, Soul's delight!
> Now in a Huddling Croud I'm all alone,
> And almost could bid all the World *Goodnight*:
>   Blest be my Rock! God lives: Oh let him be,
>   As He is All, so All in All to me.

The most prolific producer of elegies in seventeenth-century Massachusetts was Benjamin Tompson (1642–1714), whose gravestone in Roxbury
bears the epitaph: "the renowned poet of New England." The son of a
minister, a Harvard graduate, and a schoolmaster by profession, Tompson
was the first American-born Puritan to publish a volume of poetry about
the country. He composed his best-known poem, "New England's Crisis,"
in 1676 during King Philip's War. Like Oakes's elegy, this verse jeremiad
cites backsliding as the cause of war and war itself as God's chastisement.
The poem begins by recalling the early days of settlement: the "golden
times (too fortunate to hold)," which "were quickly sin' d away for love of
gold." Now that the people are interested only in imported chocolate and
French wines, God is reducing them "so that the mirror of the Christian
world / Lyes burnt to heaps." Since at the time of composition, Tompson
could not know the war's outcome, he concluded that either God would
destroy the Puritan experiment or else He would use the war to humble
and chasten the colony and thereby prepare it for a new beginning.

Though humor is rare in Puritan poetry, Tompson also produced a small
mock-epic, "On a Fortification at Boston Begun by Women" (1676), which
presents a satirical, yet rather admiring, portrait of Boston women who
erected a barricade around the city to defend it against native attack until
the Englishmen returned from patrol:

> A Grand attempt some Amazonian Dames
> Contrive whereby to glorify their names,
> A Ruff for *Boston* Neck of mud and turfe,
> Reaching from side to side from surfe to surfe,
> Their nimble hands spin up like Christmas pyes,
> Their pastry by degres on high doth rise.

Although his domestic imagery defines women's "proper" sphere, it is note-worthy that, as an occasional public poet, Tompson did acknowledge their efforts and felt that they deserved a kind of formal, though begrudging, memorial.

Scholars generally agree that the three most productive and important poets in seventeenth-century New England were Anne Bradstreet, Michael Wigglesworth, and Edward Taylor. Anne Bradstreet's (c. 1612–72) *The Tenth Muse, Lately Sprung Up in America*, published in London in 1650, remains the first extant book of poetry by an inhabitant of the Americas. Born in Northampton, England, Bradstreet was educated by her father, Thomas Dudley, steward to the Earl of Lincoln, in the earl's library, where father and daughter read extensively in the classics as well as in the writ-ers of the English Renaissance. She was especially fond of Joshua Sylvester's 1605 translation of the French poet Guillaume du Bartas's *Divine Weekes and Workes*. Dudley, a devout Puritan, saw no contradiction between his reli-gious beliefs and the enjoyment of good literature, and he was exceptional among Puritan men in advocating the philosophical and literary education of young women. Around 1628, Anne Dudley married her father's assistant, Simon Bradstreet, and both families made plans to emigrate to America.

Sailing aboard the *Arbella* with John Winthrop in 1630, the Bradstreets and Dudleys experienced great hardships on the three-month journey, which continued during their first years in New England. Shocked at the difficult living conditions in Massachusetts and by the high rate of sickness and death among the colonists, Anne confided to her diary that she missed the comforts of England and that her "heart rose" with resistance to the "New World and new manners" of America. Bradstreet was always a devoted and dutiful Christian, but she often questioned and privately rebelled against certain dogmas of Puritanism and the strong patriarchal authority in New England. At one point, she wondered: "why may not the Popish Religion be the right? They have the same God, the same Christ, the same word: they only interpret it one way, we another." Such doubts infuse many of her poems with an enlivening tension that troubles the otherwise orthodox expression.

One source of personal frustration for Bradstreet and a context for il-luminating certain subtleties of her poetry is the situation of women in seventeenth-century New England and England. From medieval times, the church and state had systematically subordinated women through both cus-tom and law, and the Protestant revolt was especially male-centered, as demonstrated by the rejection of the Catholics' emphasis on the importance of the Virgin Mary. Most Protestant theology stressed that within the family the husband-father was the representative of God and his word was absolute, subject to neither discussion nor question. Laws in America proclaimed that wives must submit themselves to their husbands and that the husband had total authority over the family and servants. If the social and economic aspects of the Puritan revolution had provided any opportunity for women to gain in social and political status in Massachusetts, that opportunity was dashed with the antinomian affair in the 1630s, for Anne Hutchinson became a symbol for decades after of the dangers of a woman's intellectual and verbal powers. For example, in 1645 John Winthrop was certainly mindful of Hutchinson's perceived transgressions when he recorded the case of Anne Yale Hopkins in his journal:

> April 13, 1645. Mr. Hopkins, the governor of Hartford upon Connecticut, came to Boston and brought his wife with him, (a goodly young woman, and of special parts) who was fallen into a sad infirmity, the loss of her understanding and reason, which had been growing upon her divers years, by occasion of her giving herself wholly to reading and writing, and had written many books. Her husband, being very loving and tender of her, was loath to grieve her; but he saw his error, when it was too late. For if she had attended her household affairs, and such things as belong to women, and nor gone our of her way and calling to meddle in such things as are proper for men, whose minds are stronger, etc., she had kept her wits . . . in the place God set her.

Similar opinions about the necessarily finite role of women remained fixed well into the end of the century and found frequent expression during the Salem witchcraft trials. Given this limiting context, it is remarkable that Bradstreet was able to write poetry, have it published, and be revered for her talent during her lifetime. Perhaps her unusual degree of freedom was the ironic result of having two influential male political figures in her immediate family: her father and her husband.

After their first years of struggle in America, the Bradstreets and Dudleys began to achieve what eventually became considerable financial and social success. After several relocations, they settled in 1645 at Andover, where Thomas Dudley prospered and became the wealthiest man in Roxbury and, for a period, governor of Massachusetts. Anne's husband, Simon, became a judge, legislator, royal councillor, and finally also governor of the colony. Between 1633 and 1652, Anne had eight children, ran the household, and educated her progeny. Although it seems probable that her wealth and her servants did allow her more time for intellectual pursuits than other women had, it also seems indisputable that the many exigencies faced by an active woman in a wilderness community still put great demands on her time and energies.

As Puritans were taught to do, Bradstreet frequently examined her conscience to discover her sins and shortcomings. When she did not have a child between 1630 and 1633, she was convinced that her own spiritual failings had caused God to make her barren. Throughout her life, she frequently recorded such feelings of inadequacy: "I have often been perplexed as that I have not found that constant Joy in my Pilgrimage and refreshing which I supposed most of the servants of God have." As a highly intelligent and somewhat rebellious woman, Bradstreet by inclination frequently questioned her spiritual situation.

What is clear in her poetry, however, is a frequent tension between a passion for the material world – natural beauty, books, home, and family and the countervailing Christian dictum that the world is corrupt and vile and vastly incomparable to the love of Christ. This textual anxiety is explicit in her poem "Contemplations":

> Then higher on the glistering Sun I gaz'd,
> Whose beams was shaded by the leavie Tree,
> The more I look'd, the more I grew amaz'd,
> And softly said, what glory's like to thee?
> Soul of this World, this Universal Eye,
> No wonder, some made thee a Deity:
> Had I not better known, (alas) the same had I.

Although she follows the convention of Puritan poetry by making a religious, even doctrinal, point, the tone of wonder and the vivid natural images suggest a competition between the love of this world and the doctrine of divine sovereignty.

Bradstreet composed her first known poem in New Town in 1632 at age nineteen, and in 1645 she first collected her poetry into an informal volume, which she dedicated to her father. These early poems tend toward a rather formulaic and dutiful presentation of religious themes. When the family moved to Andover in 1645, however, Bradstreet began to produce more mature works in which her personal voice gains strength and poetic resonance. In 1647, her brother-in-law, John Woodbridge, went to England with a copy of her poems, which he had published without her knowledge as *The Tenth Muse*. Though warmly received in London, the volume actually contained none of the poems on which Bradstreet's current reputation depends. She composed her more complex poetry over the next two decades, and these works were collected six years after her death in a volume entitled *Several Poems* (1678).

The first section of *The Tenth Muse* includes four long poems known as the quaternions and titled "The Four Elements," "The Four Humors of Man," "The Ages of Man," and "The Four Seasons." Demonstrating Bradstreet's broad learning, these works engage a range of historical and philosophical discourses and include elaborations on anatomy, astronomy, cosmology, physiology, and Greek metaphysics. As these poems graphically illustrate, Bradstreet drew upon her own personal experiences for images and illustrations to buttress her arguments. For example, in her analysis of the ages of man, she recalled her own childhood illnesses:

> What grips of wind my infancy did pain,
> What tortures I in breeding teeth sustain?
> What crudityes my stomach cold has bred,
> When vomits, fits, and worms have issued?

Although the quaternions display her erudition, the rhymed couplets, which she herself called "lanke" and "weary," sometimes become a mechanical vehicle for her learning. Indeed, she herself may have found this exercise tedious because she stopped writing before finishing the second part of the second section, called "The Four Monarchies."

In the third section, "Dialogue between Old England and New," Bradstreet adhered less to older models and allowed her own voice to emerge more forcefully. The poem presents a dialogue between Mother England and her daughter, New England, on the subject of the English political turmoil and the Civil War. Granting superior status to Old England, the speaker asserts that the survival of New England depends upon the stability of the mother country. The speaker expresses a strong attachment to England:

> O pity me in this sad perturbation,
> My plundered Towers, my houses devastation
> My weeping virgins and my young men slain;
> My wealthy trading fallen, my dearth of grain.

Bradstreet's writing as a whole suggests that she never really felt comfortable in America and that she often yearned for the land of her birth.

Bradstreet's positions on the issue of women's status in society and on her own role as a woman writer are more ambiguous. At times, her work expresses acquiescence to women's subordination, as in the "Prologue" to her book, where the speaker says:

> Let Greeks be Greeks, and women what they are
> Men have precedency and still excell,
> It is but vain unjustly to wage warre;
> Men can do best, and women know it well
> Preheminence in all and each is yours;
> Yet grant some small acknowledgement of ours.

Even as these lines appear to express the requisite acceptance of secondary status, they also imply that men are not only dominant but are parsimonious and lack the magnanimity that should accompany power. At the same time, in the stanza preceding this apologia, Bradstreet's speaker takes a more assertive position and castigates those who held that a woman should not be a poet: "I am obnoxious to each carping tongue / Who says my hand a needle better fits." Moreover, she complains of those who, assuming that women cannot be writers, will "say it's stoln, or else it was by chance." In the final stanza, she presents an ironic and ambiguous conclusion in which she tells male poets who find her poetry worthy of laurels, "Give [me a] Thyme or Parsley wreath, I ask no bayes." In requesting domestic herbs from the kitchen instead of laurels, she seems to be subordinating herself once more, but her last two lines undercut that self-effacement with a broad hint of sarcasm when she suggests that blinding male pride must be appeased: "This mean and unrefined ure of mine / Will make your glistering gold, but more to shine." Bradstreet's choice here of the wreath of "Thyme or Parsley" may also suggest her awareness of her doubly humble status as a colonial, American woman in a land devoid of the more ornate foreign or classical rewards.

In her 1642 poem on Queen Elizabeth, "In Honor of that High and Mighty Princess Queen Elizabeth," the persona makes a more direct claim that women are the intellectual equals of men. Drawing for support upon the power that Elizabeth's memory had for nearly all the English, the speaker strongly protests male condescension:

> Nay Masculines, you have thus taxt us long,
> But she, though dead, will vindicate our wrong,
> Let such as say our Sex is void of Reason,
> Know tis Slander now, but once was Treason.

Later in the poem, the speaker praises Elizabeth for her wisdom and strength, adding "millions can testify that this is true." Emboldened by Elizabeth's example, the speaker argues that her precedent, as well as the poet's present example, should provide continuing evidence of the intellectual powers of women: "She has wip'd off th' aspersion of her Sex, / That women wisdome lack to play the Rex." Evidence suggests that both Bradstreet's father and her husband accepted her intelligence and feminist inclinations, but other families, even within the Bradstreet–Dudley circle, were less tolerant of intellectual women: Anne's sister, Sarah Cain, was rejected by her husband and finally excommunicated for prophecying and for "gross immorality." This episode is an emblematic reminder of the vulnerable position women held in the society and the great personal risk that Bradstreet knew she was taking with a poem as bold as "Mighty Princess Queen Elizabeth."

The second and expanded edition of her works, *Several Poems* (1678), provided the first publication of what have become Bradstreet's best-known poems. Although she died before this book was published, she was able to correct many errors that had appeared in those works first published in the hastily produced *Tenth Muse*, and she added a new opening, "The Author to her Book." In this poem, the speaker is a poet-mother whose children are her book and her poems. She apologizes for the fact that her child had been taken from her and sent into the world before she had a chance to prepare her properly and teach her to run with "even feet." The poem serves as an apt and witty introduction to this new book because domestic imagery is a strong component of many of the new poems, which are much more personal than the stiffer, more formal and academic works of the first edition. Further, these references to the domestic are ironic because they both embody "feminine" discourse and serve as a vehicle to transcend that limited discursive field.

In *Several Poems*, there are verses relating to her personal illnesses, elegies on the deaths of her grandchildren and daughter-in-law, love poems to her husband, and a poem on the burning of her house. These are the works that are most often anthologized, for critics consider them to be far superior to Bradstreet's earlier work because of their candor about her religious experiences, their lyrical language, and their insistence on the primacy of personal experience. For example, in "Before the Birth of One of her Children," the speaker expresses her fear that she might not survive childbirth, and she admits that she is afraid to die. Addressing her husband directly in the poem, she implores him to continue to love her after her death and prevent any harm from being done to her children by the future stepmother they are sure to have: "Love thy dead, who long lay in thine arms / . . . look to my babes my dear remains / . . . These O protect from step Dames injury."

As the century progressed, Puritan poets strayed from the didactic imperative, and Bradstreet's later poems reflect this development. Her love poems to her husband are, in fact, completely free of religious instruction and frankly acknowledge her desire for him when he is abroad: for example, "I wish my Sun may never set, but burn / Within the Cancer of my glowing breast," and in another, "I, with many a deep sad groan / Bewail my turtle true . . . Return my Dear, my joy, my only Love / . . . Let's still remain but one, till death divide." She signs this poem "Thy loving Love and Dearest Dear / At home, abroad, and every where."

Many of Bradstreet's later poems also reveal the tension and anxiety she felt when she had to accept with pious resignation the tragedy of the death of a loved one or the loss of her property. Her sense of resentment toward God is barely concealed in some of these poems, although her speaker always becomes reconciled to divine justice in the end. The poem she wrote after her house burned down in 1666 reveals most clearly the conflict between human attachment to the things of this world and the indifference required by Puritan doctrine. Upon being awakened by the flames and first seeing the catastrophic destruction of the dwelling, the textual voice stoically displays the proper Christian attitude: "I blest his Name that gave and took / . . . It was his own: it was not mine." Yet she goes on to say that later, whenever she passed the ruins, she could not help thinking of the things that she had cherished:

> Here stood that Trunk, and there that chest;
> There lay that store I counted best:
> My pleasant things in ashes lye,
> And them behold no more shall I.

She also laments that no guests will be able to visit there again, where tales could be told and pleasures relived. Grief intrudes upon the textual inscription of doctrine. Drifting off into a near reverie, she speaks to the ruins, "Adeiu, Adeiu" [sic], but then she quickly reminds herself that "All's vanity." She chastises herself for placing such store in material existence and reassures herself that a better home awaits her with Christ. Yet the ritualistic closing – "The world no longer let me Love, / My hope and Treasure lyes Above" – is not sufficiently convincing to elude the previously expressed longing for material trappings. The reader cannot help but suspect that the next time the speaker passes the ruins she will dream again of the times and treasures she had "loved." In her meditations, Bradstreet correspondingly reflected on her difficulty in rejecting the physical world, concluding that only the knowledge of death rather than religious doctrine compels people to look forward to eternity: "for were earthly comforts permanent, who would look for heavenly?" Bradstreet often contemplated her own mortality, but until the last years of her illness, it had always been with noticeable reluctance that she anticipated her eternal peace.

In 1669, three years before her death, Bradstreet wrote what may have been her last poem, "As Weary Pilgrim, now at Rest"; the disease of her last years may have prevented her from writing more works. Here, the speaker thinks not of worldly pleasures but instead reviews life's trials: the "dangers past, and travailes done," the "bryars and thornes," "hungry wolves," "erring paths," "rugged stones," "the earth perplext / With sinns with cares and sorrows vext / By age and pain brought to decay." Longing to be "at rest / And soare high among the blest," she calls out to Christ: "Lord make me ready for that day / Then Come deare bridgrome Come away." For all of Bradstreet's personal strengths and her desire to see women on a more equal basis with men, her textual voice finally succumbs here to the dominant gender imagery of the scriptures. She imagines herself a dependent bride in the arms of the divine bridegroom. All her life she had contemplated and explored the socially restricting implications of such language, and her use of this image in her last poem seems to constitute a final, self-conscious act of submission to God, church, and her culture.

Unlike Bradstreet, the preacher-poet Michael Wigglesworth (1631–1705) abided strictly by the rules of the Puritan aesthetic, writing always in the plain style and with a didactic message. After Bradstreet and Taylor, Wigglesworth was the third most prolific and important poet of the period. Although he was popular in his own time and even into the nineteenth century for his sermonic, orthodox *The Day of Doom* (1662) and his *Meat Out of the Eater* (1670), he has received relatively little critical attention in the twentieth century. Although biographers have been able to discover many facts of Wigglesworth's public life, they remain divided over the nature of his inner life (for biographical details, see Chapter 3). Focusing primarily on dry doctrines and Last Days, his diary and other writings present him as the stereotypical gloomy Puritan. His self-acknowledged lack of feeling regarding his father's death and his seemingly cold, but properly Puritan, reaction to the death of his first wife reinforce that image. However, sympathetic biographers suggest that his efforts to adhere dutifully to Puritan doctrines may have led to self-destructive repression and even depression, which appear to modern readers of his works as cold indifference rather than contained personal suffering.

In spite of his private turmoil, Wigglesworth's public persona and poetry project an image of the grim Puritan, and his work has often been cited as typical of Puritan verse. America's first "best-seller," *The Day of Doom* was primarily intended to teach children several doctrinal truths. Written in the ballad form with a meter of seven-foot "fourteeners," the poem consists of 224 eight-line stanzas. Presented as a narrative, the action is set on Judgment Day, when, with sudden fury, Christ gathers the righteous sheep at His right hand and the sinful goats at His left. After a catalogue of the various types of sinners to be punished, the goats are allowed to plead their pitiful cases for mercy. Through this device, Wigglesworth presents the errors of doctrine and fallacious reasoning that sinners employ to justify their sins, and he illustrates how God and His righteous will demolish such false arguments and punish the wicked.

This theological instruction constitutes the thematic center of the poem, but the elements that gave the work its popular appeal are the vivid and dramatic descriptions of the shock of doom and the casting of the sinners into hell's fire. These passages appear primarily in the opening and closing stanzas. Suddenly "at midnight brake forth a Light, / Which turn'd night to day," and when Christ appears, "Skies are rent asunder," and the people hear "a mighty voice, and hideous noise, / More terrible than Thunder." As they realize that they have been caught in sin, some "do not spare their flesh to tear / Through horrible despair" while others "hide themselves in Caves." Tombs open and "Dead Bodies all rise at his call," and those whose crimes are seemingly minor, "Scoffers at Purity," are gathered together with the vilest villains: "Children flagitious, / And Parents who did them undo / by Nurture vicious" are grouped with "Murd'rers, and Men of blood / Witches, Inchanters, and Ale-house haunters." Children hearing this poem for the first time would long remember this scene and the dragons, serpents, and "Legions of Sprights unclean, / And hellish Fiends." The images at the end of the poem also seem especially designed to terrify children when they depict pious mothers and fathers rejecting their sinful offspring, who are then cast upon the burning lake for eternity.

In addition to this "verse catechism," as Cotton Mather called *The Day of Doom*, Wigglesworth also produced a verse jeremiad, *God's Controversy with New England*. Written in 1662 in the midst of a major drought, this poem warns readers that they are weakening in their commitment to their divine mission and that God's anger is evident. Joining a growing chorus of communal lamentations that would continue for the next thirty-five years, Wigglesworth mourned the loss of the zeal of the founders and the laxity of the younger generation:

> Such, O New-England, was thy first,
>   Such was thy best estate:
> But, Loe! a strange and suddain change
> ....
> The brightest of our morning stars
>   Did wholly disappeare:
> And those that tarried behind
>   With sack-cloth covered were.

Then, for the next 400 lines, the poem describes the forms of present backsliding, the various expected punishments, and finally a formula for returning to God and hearing again His assurances for New England.

Wigglesworth also wrote several poems, and in 1670 he published his last major work, *Meat Out of the Eater*, which went to its fourth edition in 1689. More personal in tone than his others, it seems based upon his own experiences during a lengthy illness. The main purpose of the work is to console those who have endured suffering by reminding them of the goodness of Christ and the compensations of a holy life. Some of the poems in this collection suggest that Wigglesworth possessed a gift for writing poetry that would be appealing to contemporary tastes but that his usual rigorous adherence to official Puritan poetics led him to suppress his natural talents.

Usually considered the most gifted English poet in America before the nineteenth century, Edward Taylor was born in Sketchley, Leicestershire, England, probably in 1642. He grew up on a farm, was educated at a nonconformist school, and developed strong anti-Anglican and anti-Catholic opinions. After his mother's death in 1657 and his father's in 1658, Taylor became a teacher, but the Restoration government eventually threatened to bar him from teaching unless he signed the Act of Uniformity of 1662, requiring loyalty to the Church of England. He refused, and after several years of persecution, he departed for Massachusetts in 1668. Graduating from Harvard in 1671 at the unusually advanced age of twenty-nine, Taylor accepted a post in the remote village of Westfield, where he was pastor and town physician. In 1674, he married Elizabeth Pitch and together they had eight children, five of whom died in infancy. "Upon Wedlock, & Death of Children," one of his most moving poems, expresses his suffering over these losses. In 1692, Elizabeth died, and three years later Taylor married Ruth Wyllys, who raised Elizabeth's three surviving children and the six others she herself bore. Because King Philip's War raged around Westfield in the mid-1670s, Taylor's ordination was delayed until 1679.

Once established, however, he preached tirelessly at Westfield until a few years before his death at the age of eighty-seven in 1729, and he made only a few visits to Boston and other New England towns. Over sixty of his sermons are extant, as is a long theological treatise, *The Harmony of the Gospels* (published in 1983). He completed the poems that make up *God's Determinations Touching His Elect* around 1682, and he wrote the poetry included in his *Preparatory Meditations* between 1682 and 1725. Theologically, Taylor was a pious conservative congregationalist, and over the course of his career, he engaged in several heated religious disputes with various other ministers, most notably Solomon Stoddard at nearby Northampton. Strongly opposed to innovations in church polity, Taylor composed a series of sermons attacking Stoddard's decision to open the sacrament of communion to all members of his congregation whether or not they considered themselves regenerate. Taylor argued that those awaiting grace should not fall prey to Satan's (and Stoddard's) trick of inviting them to the Lord's table while they remained in doubt. Taylor's solution was to assist the faithful to perceive more clearly the signs of their own conversions, which would likely occur for the patient.

Even Taylor's most sympathetic biographers admit that he could be a "grave, severe, stubborn, and stiff-necked" disciplinarian in his public life; for example, when his congregation built a new meeting house in 1721–22, Taylor refused to preach there. At the time, Stephen Williams, pastor of Longmeadow Church, recorded in his diary that "Mr. Taylor is very fond of his own thoughts and I am afraid will make a very great difficulty and division in the town." Taylor was then nearing eighty years old, but this event seems representative of a life in which compromise was a rarity. Taylor's positions were always based upon his sincere convictions regarding the individual's relation to God, and no one in Puritan New England was more certain that the form of congregational Protestantism practiced in Massachusetts in the 1630s and 1640s was the one true religion.

Taylor's poetry is distinguished from that of his fellow Puritans by a strain of mysticism that infused his spiritual vision and led him to a more complex understanding of metaphor. Taylor felt a strong personal relation to God and believed that Christ was immediately present in the sacrament of communion. This mystical, or imaginative, side allowed him to conceive of language and metaphor as the bridge between the human mind and God and to perceive of death metaphorically as a glorious moment of union between this world and the next. These ideas were quite in keeping with the positions of earlier Puritan theologians such as Baxter, but Taylor embraced them with a fervor and devoted to them an abundance of rhetorical elaboration that exceeded that of his colleagues. His faith in the symbolic meaning invested in the physical universe empowered his poetic and interpretive gifts: "natural things are not unsuitable to illustrate supernaturals by. For Christ in his parables doth illustrate supernatural things by natural, and if it were not thus, we could arrive at no knowledge of supernatural things, for we are not able to see above naturals."

Taylor's critics generally hold that he wrote poetry primarily as a form of meditation as he prepared himself to preach or that he used the composition process to put himself in the proper mental and spiritual state for receiving and administering communion. Although he may never have intended his poems for publication, he did carefully preserve them in a quarto of 400 pages in a leather binding that was passed down from his grandson Ezra Stiles (1727–95), president of Yale, and deposited in the college library in 1883, where it was discovered by Thomas H. Johnson in 1937. Many of his preparatory meditations are directly linked to his sermons by biblical passages that serve as titles to sermons on the same texts that he preached around the time that he composed the poems. Other poems, especially the miscellaneous ones, seem to have been inspired by his observations of things in nature or daily life. It may be that he used the exercise of writing these poems to prepare himself for pastoral instruction, for often these verses use metaphors, images, and analogies based in the ordinary life of simple country folk.

Taylor's literary style and poetic techniques link his work to that of John Donne and the English metaphysicals, and he clearly knew and admired the poetry of George Herbert and probably Richard Crashaw. Yet, because he left England in 1668, he remained untouched by developments in post-Restoration English poetry. Some of Taylor's early critics observed that his meter and rhymes are often rough and awkward, but scholars later recognized these features to be the likely result of Taylor's conscious attempts to have the roughness in his language reflect and express the strenuous and often painful nature of religious experience and conversion. Similarly, many of Taylor's poems are difficult to read aloud, thereby suggesting that the reader must recognize that certain complex matters exceed the range of human speech. In these aspects, his techniques may be compared to attempts by modernist writers to give voice to the inarticulate. Other examples of his poetry are characterized by verbal wit and by inventive play upon biblical types and figures. He was especially fond of using sensuous images from the love poetry of the biblical Song of Songs, where images of the body, often quite erotic, function for interpreters as religious symbols, and he was also drawn to the astonishing depictions of heavenly beauty and earthly destruction in Revelation. Combining such biblical language with imagery from farm and town life, he created startling, sometimes incongruous metaphors that are in the baroque tradition of the metaphysical conceit.

What is most compelling about Taylor's poetry for modern readers is that his works repeatedly depict the conflicts between, on the one hand, human will, desire, and love of this world and, on the other, Puritan doctrine, especially of divine sovereignty and retribution. To resist temptations to doubt God's goodness, Taylor repeatedly put himself through the same spiritual and psychological process in his meditations. His poems most often duplicate the spiritual exercise: the speaker creates a metaphor as a device for understanding God's purposes and then exposes the metaphor as inadequate to this awesome task; then, as the speaker approaches the point of despair, he struggles to find a new way to rationalize the divine purpose, only to end up resigned to submitting in faith to God's will, although this acceptance is often mixed with subtle hints of continued future resistance and struggle. Taylor repeated this pattern so often that some biographers have questioned his spiritual sincerity, but for Taylor, as for Thomas Shepard, spiritual peace was only a momentary hiatus in a lifelong process of painful soul-searching and conflict. He seems to have understood this human struggle as a permanent process and to have accepted it as something the mind could engage not only with genuine devotion but also with wit, play, and humor.

Taylor's *God's Determinations Touching His Elect* has been compared in form and design to Milton's *Paradise Lost* and Dante's *Divine Comedy* as an epic of salvation and conversion. The work also shares features of a medieval morality play, an Ignatian spiritual meditation, and a Puritan sermon. Rhetorical in style, it appears directed to those church members who had not yet experienced conversion and who feared that they would never be touched by grace. Analyzing the psychic operations provoked by Satan to drive the soul to despair, Taylor proposes that grace awaits those who are able to cast off the Devil's temptations of melancholia and to prepare their hearts for Christ. The remainder of the poem's full title provides an outline of its three-part structure: *The Elect's Combat in their Conversion and Coming up to God in*

Christ together with the Comfortable Effects thereof. Simply put, the message is fight Satan, pray to Christ, and receive God's grace and peace.

Perhaps for modern readers, the most singular aspect of Taylor's major work is that, orthodox Puritan though he was, he saw the individual saint's position in the world as fundamentally comic. God had already determined each soul's spiritual fate, and yet He allowed the saint to be caught up in a dramatic struggle of hope, doubt, anxiety, and ultimate joy. Taylor may not have believed that God sported with people, but he certainly suggested that from the human perspective, at least, that was how the situation sometimes appeared.

Thus, by beginning *God's Determinations* with a parody of the ways that people have tried to imagine God and His dealings with them, Taylor infused his epic of salvation with a strong element of the comic. "The Preface" sets forth in miniature the entire spiritual process that the rest of the work details. The first word, "Infinity," underscores the enormous distance between God's power and being and the finite world where humans labor futilely to grasp His nature or purpose. Although all human understanding of the supernatural is necessarily through metaphors, these vehicles are ultimately inadequate devices for imagining God, "for we are not able to see above naturals." In the first two lines, the speaker recalls that the universe is an oxymoron, an infinity of nothingness: "Infinity, when all things it beheld / In Nothing, and of Nothing all did build." Later he will return to play more upon the idea of something from nothing, but here he is setting up a list of metaphysical questions that he develops through a series of witty images. In them, the speaker uses "naturals" to try to project the idea of God. The images depict God as carpenter, blacksmith, builder, seamster, weaver, sportsman, and home decorator: the speaker asks who could make the "Globe" of the world upon his "Lath"; who "Moulds" planets in his "Furnace Vast"; who "Lac'de and Fillitted the earth" with "Rivers like green Ribbons"; and who "Spread the Canopy" of the heavens and "Curtains Spun" for the skies? Then, in case the absurdity of such inadequate human projections of the divine has been lost on his audience, he asks, "Who in this Bowling Alley bowld the Sun?"

Such feeble constructions may fail, but they do have the spiritual benefit of reducing the terror of being subject to such power. While reminding himself that the Almighty "can half buy looks / Root up the rocks and rock the hills by th'roots," Taylor's speaker adds consolingly that this is a loving God whose intentions for humanity, if mysterious, are generous and merciful. Undue fear can block the soul from His saving grace and love. Thus, in the final ten lines, the speaker returns to the image of nothing and speculates about why God bothered to create the universe and humankind at all:

Which All from Nothing fet, from Nothing, All:
Hath All on Nothing set, lets Nothing fall.
Gave all to nothing Man indeed, whereby
Through Nothing then imbosst the brightest Gem
More pretious than all pretiousness in them.

For all of His infinite power then, God seems not only to have generously
given insignificant humans all of the universe to enjoy but to have engaged
Himself in a kind of game with humanity: by making the most valuable
thing in creation the human soul and giving one of these gems to each
individual, God invites each to perform freely, like an actor, for His approval
or disapproval. At present, the people of New England have "thrown down
all by sin" and "darkened that lightsome Gem" so that "now his Brightst
Diamond is grown / Darker by far than any Coalpit Stone." Although souls
in this darkened state have reason to fear God's wrath, Taylor's imagery
and logic lead to the conclusion that a loving God is ready to smile upon
his creatures again if they can manage to restore the "Coalpit Stone" to
a "Diamond." Many of Taylor's colleagues would have termed his use of
humor blasphemous, but the poet's ludicrous portraits of God in various
human occupations – sporting with people and as an audience for human
performances – function to reduce the incommensurability between God
and His people. The entire poetic sequence making up this book seems
designed to empower the discouraged and wayward soul to return to a
worthy state and to prepare for grace in the hope that against all human
reason, an omnipotent God loves His people.

Consisting of 217 numbered poems written over forty-three years,
Taylor's other work, the *Preparatory Meditations*, is divided into two series,
the first written between 1682 and the end of 1692 and the second from
1693 until 1725. The full title describes them as a collection of verbal exer-
cises, each Preparatory Meditation composed *before my Approach to the Lord's
Supper. Chiefly upon the Doctrine preached upon the Day of administration.* These
poems vary greatly in language, tone, and subject matter, but they all appear
to have the same basic purpose: to allow Taylor an opportunity to focus upon
his unworthiness so that he would approach the communion table humbly.
He used the meditation ritual to imagine new situations for himself and
to generate new metaphors enabling him to recall that without God he is
insignificant; in his "Prologue" to the first series, his speaker is a "Crumb
of Dust." The first twelve poems of the first series are concerned with the
spiritual pleasures of the Lord's Supper and the attraction of Christ as savior.
Taylor drew upon the Song of Songs for erotic imagery to describe the love
of Christ, and he used abundant imagery of food and drink to heighten the
appeal of the communion table for sense-bound fallen creatures.

The frequently anthologized "Meditation Eight" illustrates effectively the poetic method of these works. As in "The Preface" of *God's Determinations*, Taylor opens this poem with images that suggest God's inaccessibility. He observes that neither the "Astronomy Divine" of theology nor his poetic metaphors can bridge the distance between God and people: "A Golden Path my Pensill cannot line, / From that bright Throne unto my Thresholdly." But while he is having "puzzled thoughts about it," he suddenly discovers that God has intervened in the natural world by putting "the Bread of Life in't at my door." Here, Taylor joins the Old Testament type of manna with the New Testament antitype of Christ as the new bread of life. The futility of human efforts to earn salvation is assuaged by God's gift of grace and eternal happiness.

The second stanza presents the image of the soul as a "Bird of Paradise put in / This Wicker Cage (my Corps)," which "in golden days" foolishly "peckt the Fruite forbad: and so did fling / Away its food." Through Original Sin, the speaker's soul is born into him already corrupt and starving from the "Celestial Famine sore" begun with the loss of Eden. Speaking to his own soul, the persona expresses his plight in being unable to get "soul bread" either from the natural world or from the angels, who show him only "An Empty Barrell" where grain for spiritual bread might normally be found. In language typical of the psychic nadir in the meditation process, the speaker cries out, "Alas! alas! Poore Bird, what wilt thou doe?" The point, clearly, is that he can do nothing. Then, in the last three stanzas, the speaker discovers God's mercy: "In this sad state, Gods Tender Bowells run / Out streams of Grace." Although the word "bowels" in the seventeenth century referred to the center of the body, which included the heart and the stomach and was considered the seat of the emotions, Taylor's digestive imagery nevertheless renders the passage rather eccentric for depicting the flow of grace. One way of viewing this imagery is that the grinding of the wheat for communion bread is like a digestive process within the body of the person who consumes it. Such a human form of dispersion and absorption, though an incongruous metaphor, is an apt and memorable emblem for people to imagine the way that God provides his grace to the starving soul.

Mixing images of liquid and solid forms to convey the conflict of grace embodied in communion bread and wine, the speaker next creates an elaborate conceit in which God rakes the "Purest Wheat in Heaven, his deare-dear Son," and transforms Him into the "Bread of Life." He "Grinds, and kneads up" Christ and has him "Disht on thy Table up by Angells Hands." The speaker then asks incredulously if it is really true that God loves His people so much as to announce: "Come Bate thy fill . . . Its Heaven's Sugar Cake." Finally, in the last stanza the speaker reminds himself that "souls are but petty things" in comparison to the glory of God's grace; but even as he laments his insignificance, the speaker receives Christ and the promise of eternal life: "This bread of Life dropt in thy mouth, doth Cry. / Bate, Bate me, Soul, and thou shalt never dy. "Swallowed alive and speaking, Christ becomes apart of the speaker's own body and soul.

Although Taylor's personal piety, humility, and gratitude for God's grace and communion shine through the language of his meditations, it is in many of his miscellaneous poems that particular personal experiences give the speaker's voice greater individual distinction. One of his most popular, and subtle, poems is "Upon a Spider Catching a Fly" (undated). Upon first reading, this poem appears to contain only simple, didactic moral instruction. The speaker addresses a spider as it spins its web and catches a wasp and a fly, and he observes that the spider does not attempt to kill the wasp immediately for fear of its sting and that it carefully strokes and calms the wasp lest its thrashing tear the web. In contrast, when a fly is ensnared, the spider hastily bites it dead. The speaker then elaborates the moral: just as a creature in nature avoids a direct confrontation with another of greater strength, so too should humans avoid battle with "Hells Spider," who sets his nets to "tangle Adams race," for God will send His "Grace to breake the Cord." Thus, the point seems to be that the saints should try to elude Satan's web and should pray for God's grace.

In the final stanza, however, the persona shifts oddly to a different image, that of a nightingale singing "on high / In Glories Cage . . . for joy," and this new figure throws the apparent lesson into question. The speaker claims that one lesson is that creatures in nature know better than to challenge those stronger than themselves, but his illustration really does not make that point. The fly did not seek to encounter the spider but instead flew accidentally into its web. Although the spider avoids a direct attack upon the wasp, the fate of the wasp still appears to be a certain, if slow, death. If the fly represents a regenerate Christian awaiting grace, then the analogy fails, for it dies without redemption. If the fly is an unregenerate soul predestined to hell, then there is nothing to be learned from its example except that the fate of the damned is hell. Perhaps then it is the wasp that symbolizes the regenerate Christian, but in that case, the reader must ask: if the venom that saves the wasp from instant death symbolizes God's grace and if the wasp's struggling in the net represents a saint's exertions against Satan, why does God let the wasp die after prolonged agony? The speaker who pretends to explain the allegory has presented a deceptively inadequate explication.

It appears, then, that the speaker is playing a game with his imagined reader – or with himself; if so, the real lesson appears to be a warning against thoughtless acceptance of the type of simple moral instruction the poem seems to present. The student must use his or her wits to look at all sides of an analogy. The speaker himself might be the spider here, who has laid a verbal net to "tangle Adams race" by lulling readers into a false sense of confidence about the easy way to heaven only to trick them into realizing that they are "foppish" wasps who have the power of grace to "fret" Satan's net but who are too easily stroked into passivity. If the nightingale singing to God represents the poet controlling the speaker, the method of this poem is not unlike John Donne's use of the unreliable persona in many of his songs and sonnets. Like a teacher who says something absurd in order to provoke complacent students, the poet attempts to awaken readers to their own casual acceptance of easy answers or their own mistaken assumptions. Such a reading may trouble those who assume that Taylor was writing only for himself; from that standpoint, the poem could be a private exercise, a literary self-entertainment of a brilliant mind in a remote New England village.

Although Taylor's poetry usually abides by the Puritan aesthetics established early in the century and liberalized somewhat by Richard Baxter in 1649, Puritan poetry written in Boston and along the seaboard from about 1680 into the eighteenth century came under the secular influences of the Restoration and the Augustan movement in England. Clergymen such as John Danforth (1660–1730), Cotton Mather (1663–1728), Benjamin Colman (1673–1747), and Mather Byles (1707–88), as well as devoted laymen like Samuel Sewall (1652–1730), Richard Steere (1643–1721), and Roger Wolcott (1679–1767), adopted more public modes of expression and composed many poems that had no obvious religious themes and even some that seemed to defy Puritan precepts. For example, Steere, a defender of the congregational way in his religious practice and author of anti-Catholic satire, also wrote the only Nativity poem in seventeenth-century America, thereby violating the Puritan rules against the practice of "Christmaskeeping," long considered a form of Catholic idolatry.

In 1712, Cotton Mather remarked that women "have wrote such things as have been very valuable; especially relating to their own experiences." He had Anne Bradstreet specifically in mind, but he also was aware of several other women writers of Puritan New England, whose works have only recently been discovered. No seventeenth-century Puritan women voluntarily published their writing, probably for fear of incurring a fate like that of the "insane" Anne Yale Hopkins, but several did write poetry, and in the early eighteenth century some New England women did publish their works. Those who have been recently rediscovered are Anna Hayden (1648–c. 1720), who left two elegies; Sarah Kemble Knight (1666–1727), who wrote six poems that she included in her well-known *Journal*; Mary English (c. 1652–94), who wrote an acrostic poem on her own name; Sarah Goodhue (1641–81), who wrote a poem included in a book of her writings, *Valedictory and Monitory Writing*, published in Cambridge at the time of her death; Grace Smith (c. 1685–1740), whose *The Dying Mother's Legacy* (1712) contains some poetry; and Mercy Wheeler (1706–96), who also wrote a didactic deathbed work, *An Address to Young People, Or... Warning from the Death* (1733), which contains some lines of verse. Single poems have survived from two other Puritan women: Susanna Rogers (b. c. 1711), who wrote an elegy for her fiancé after he was killed by Native Americans in 1725; and Mary French (c. 1685–1730), who was taken captive by Native Americans in 1703 in a raid on Deerfield, Massachusetts, and wrote a poem to her sister from captivity.

The daughters of the Reverend Benjamin Colman, Jane Colman Turell (1708–35) and Abigail (Celia) Colman Dennie (1715–45), were also poets. They were educated by their father, who himself wrote poetry. Abigail, who ran away from her parents' home in 1733 until financial need forced her to return, wrote a poem to her sister revealing her suffering:

> To you alone I venture to complain;
> From others hourly strive to hid my pain.
> But Celia's face dissembles what she feels,
> Affected looks her inward pain conceal.
> She sings, she dresses and she talks and smiles,
> But these are all spectators to beguile.

Besides Anne Bradstreet, however, the only Puritan woman to leave a substantial body of poetry appears to be Jane Colman Turell. Despite having four children and enduring the childhood deaths of each, Turell managed to keep writing regularly during her troubled twenty-seven years. Most of her prose and poetry was devoted to religious subjects, but she also wrote, in the words of her husband, Ebenezer, "pieces of wit and humor, which if publish'd would give a brighter idea of her to some of [her] readers." In addition to experimenting with the pastoral and neoclassical techniques, Turell wrote a poem at the age of seventeen in which her poetic persona expresses a desire to transcend the limitations that Puritanism placed upon all aspiring poets:

> O let me burn with Sappho's noble fire,
> But not like her for faithless man expire.
> ....
> Go lead the way, my muse, nor must you stop,
> 'Til we have gain'd Parnassus shady top:
> 'Till I have view'd those fragrant soft retreats,
> ....
> And so be worthy of a poet's name.

At her death, when her father selected some of her works to publish in *Memoirs of the Life and Death of... Mrs. Jane Turell*, he did not include her more humorous or rebellious works.

All Puritans with literary aspirations were aware that their religion did not encourage literary ambitions, but women of literary talent were especially stifled. Given the limitations of doctrine and the difficult living conditions, it is remarkable, however, that so many Puritans wrote poetry at all and that among their texts are some that still speak to modern readers with intensity and passion. Although Bradstreet and Taylor far surpassed others in their skill and energy, the works of many Puritan poets express the enduring will to articulate desire, conflict, uncertainty, and longing even in a highly controlled society.

Chapter Six

The Jeremiad

By the time of the Restoration of Charles II in England in 1660, Puritan New England had developed into a relatively prosperous, stable, and independent colony. Some who had left for England during the Protectorate returned to New England after 1660, and other English Puritans, like Edward Taylor, fled to America to escape renewed Anglican persecution. With the native tribes still traumatized by the violence of the Pequot War in the late 1630s, Puritan villages proliferated, and different local governments, customs, and economies replicated the various peasant cultures of places such as Yorkshire, Kent, East Anglia, and the West Country of England. On the whole, travelers in New England in the 1650s described flourishing agricultural communities of pious, hardworking families where the churches and the state appeared to cooperate in governance.

In larger cities such as Boston and Salem, there arose a merchant class based upon manufacturing, the fishing industry, and foreign trade, while the rural villages remained dependent upon farming. Open-field farming continued in some areas until the late seventeenth century, but most land was converted to small individual holdings. Because congregationalism encouraged village independence, forms of government were quite varied, with selectmen sometimes possessing broad powers, and in many the influence of the ministers upon civil decisions was diminishing.

This slow process of secularization was hastened and became more dramatic when two serious difficulties arose that would precipitate drastic changes in the social and religious order between 1660 and 1690: a land shortage and growing religious uncertainties among the young. Word of the prosperity of the early colonists attracted to New England growing numbers of less pious immigrants who primarily sought financial opportunities. These new arrivals pressured village governments to apportion land to them at the very time that established members had begun to desire more property for their own, often numerous, adult children. The newcomers were often denied church membership and thus land by selectmen who accused them of being opportunistic hypocrites. As church and congregational power expanded, those seeking admission had to testify publicly about their conversion experiences, and in some cases their spiritual relations had to conform to a complicated morphology of conversion established by the clergy. Such tests discouraged applicants, though perhaps not by design. This linking of language, sainthood, property ownership, and political franchise became troublesome for the established Puritans as well, however, when increasing numbers of their own adult children also failed to have or recount the requisite conversion and become full church members. The original colonists doubted that their children and grandchildren were as reprobate and deserving of exclusion as the new immigrants, and they urged authorities to find a means of distinguishing between unconverted outsiders and their spiritually inhibited offspring.

Events in the town of Sudbury in the early 1650s illustrate this crisis especially sharply. When the town had been founded, the original members set aside land for expansion, but no land was ever granted to new immigrants. By 1650, there were twenty-six adult sons of founders seeking land from the reluctant selectmen. Dissension raged for five years, and the minister Thomas Brown joined the side of the elders and preached against the degeneracy and immorality of the unconverted youths. In 1655, the frustrated young people proclaimed: "If you oppress the poor, they will cry out; if you persecute us in one city, we must fly to another." John Ruddock, an elder who supported the sons, presented a formal declaration of exodus: "God has been pleased to increase our children, which are grown to men's estates. [Their fathers] should be glad to see them settled before the Lord take us away from hence. . . . Some of us having taken some pains to view the country, we have found a place which lyeth westward." A short time later, the young people became among the first Anglo-Americans to migrate westward when they moved fifteen miles to found the town of Marlborough.

During the 1650s, a group of ministers led by Richard Mather and James Allin explored ways of modifying membership policies to respond to the problem of the unconverted children of the saints. In the 1630s, the clergy had decided that the children of the saints could be baptized in infancy on the assumption that, as children of the elect, they would surely experience conversion and become full church members. When many did not, there was the new problem of whether to baptize their children in turn. By the original rules of the 1630s, offspring of unconverted second-generation members could not be baptized. Mather and Allin argued that the grandchildren of the elect should be baptized, whereas other clergy and elders, initially including Richard's son Increase, held out fiercely for preserving the old policy. In 1662, a rancorous synod resulted in a revised doctrine, mockingly labeled the Half-Way Covenant by its opponents (see Chapter 3), that allowed the grandchildren of the founders to be baptized but still did not solve the problem of the unconverted parents. Frustration and dismay over this spiritual paralysis, whatever its cause, persisted among the elect and the clergy throughout the 1670s and 1680s.

These same conflicts recurred throughout New England during the second half of the century, and the themes of Thomas Brown's preaching against the "rising generations" were repeated in sermons now called Puritan jeremiads. Taking their texts from Jeremiah and Isaiah, these orations followed – and reinscribed – a rhetorical formula that included recalling the courage and piety of the founders, lamenting recent and present ills, and crying out for a return to the original conduct and zeal. In current scholarship, the term "jeremiad" has expanded to include not only sermons but also other texts that rehearse the familiar tropes of the formula such as captivity narratives, letters, covenant renewals, as well as some histories and biographies.

In addition to the persistent problems of landownership, several natural disasters and larger political problems between 1660 and 1690 caused the Massachusetts Bay communities to undergo a series of traumas, for which the jeremiad became the ritual response. Natural events, including fires, floods, droughts, earthquakes, and the appearances of comets; internal conflicts such as renewed fighting with the Indians, increasing occurrences of satanic possession and witchcraft, and growing secularism and materialism; external intrusions like the arrival of numbers of Quakers and Anglicans, the revocation of the Massachusetts Bay charter in 1684 by the London Court of Chancery, and finally the installation in 1686 of the Anglican royal governor, Edmund Andros – gradually, insistently, these events and the internal tensions present from the 1630s unraveled the Puritan community. Andros exacerbated the tense situation of 1686 by proceeding to nullify all land titles and to meddle in religious affairs, which sparked further lamentations over the decline of piety that, in the minds of many, had provoked God's anger and resulted in all their trials.

Whether an actual decline of religious commitment and zeal among the Puritans in these decades did occur remains one of the most debated issues in Puritan scholarship. Church membership records suggest that the decline in membership may have been a myth born of the jeremiad ritual and the compulsion to place blame for what seemed otherwise to be inexplicable disasters. Yet a shared perception of moral deterioration accrued social and political force and inspired many of the colony's most interesting literary texts, and indeed, the trope of decay or decline became central to later Puritan expressions.

The tradition of opening the annual General Court in May with an election sermon began in Boston in 1634 and continued until 1834. Most of the best-known ministers in New England gave at least one election sermon, and beginning in 1667, the sermons were printed yearly with few exceptions. When the king revoked the Massachusetts Bay charter in 1684, he banned elections and appointed Governor Edward Randolph. In defiance, the clergy stopped preaching election sermons until 1691, when the new charter formulated under William and Mary allowed for the election of a body of councillors to advise the appointed governor.

From the beginning, the content of the election sermons was expected to integrate the theory of Puritan society and the current social and religious practices. The pattern created a familiar ritual: the minister summarized the larger historical picture, took stock of the past and present, and articulated a prophecy for the future, designed to inspire the people and leaders to pursue their heavenly as well as their earthly callings. The election sermon followed the standard three-part division used for most sermons. It opened with a biblical text, followed by an "Explication," which closely examined the meaning of each of the words of the text. Often the preacher would review the biblical events that foreshadowed the text, and his audience knew to look for typological parallels to the current New England situation, which the preacher would make explicit in the later "Application." In the second part of the sermon, the "Doctrine," the preacher announced the general laws and lessons that he perceived to be the basis of the text and then divided those larger principles into "Propositions" and "Reasons." The third section, the "Application," demonstrated how the Doctrine and Proposition pertained to contemporary New England. Here, the preacher expounded upon several "Uses" of the analogy between the biblical past and recent experiences. Finally, election sermons often concluded with the preacher's addressing the various groups in the audience directly: the governor, the current representatives, those standing for election, the voters, and the clergy. He might refer to former election sermons and to times of similar conditions, using the past to formulate a prophecy of what might follow, especially if the people were so foolish as to ignore his warnings.

From the late 1660s through the early 1690s, gloomy prospects and catastrophic fears of the imminent failure of the holy experiment led most ministers to construct their jeremiads as mournful dirges. In the early decades of the century, the major themes of election sermons had been the nature of good leadership, the limits of liberty and authority, the biblical roots of Puritan ideas of government, and the proper relationships between the governor and the deputies, between all leaders and the people, and between civil and ecclesiastical powers. To these themes, the jeremiads added anxiety over recent apostasy, over possible connections between tragic current events and God's design for New England, and over the danger that God would abandon his saints forever. Overall, the jeremiads had a complicated, seemingly contradictory, communal function. On the one hand, they were designed to awaken a lethargic people. On the other hand, in their repetitive and ritualistic nature, they functioned as a form of reassurance, reinscribing proof that the saints were still a coherent body who ruled New England in covenant with God under His sometimes chastising and yet ultimately protective hand. The tension between these competing, yet finally reconciled, purposes gives the jeremiads their literary complexity and power.

Often held to be the prototype of the form is Samuel Danforth's (1626–74) *A Brief Recognition of New England's Errand into the Wilderness*, which was preached in 1670 and published the following year. Born in Framlingham, Suffolk, England, Danforth had lost his mother when he was three and came with his father to New England in 1634, when he was eight. He graduated from Harvard in 1643 and accepted a post as minister in Roxbury in 1650, where he served with John Eliot, whose missionary work among the Indians left Danforth to perform the major duties of the parish. In 1651, Danforth married Mary Wilson of Boston, and they had twelve children, several of whom died young.

Although he took his text for his famous jeremiad from Matthew 11:7–9 and not Jeremiah, Danforth announced in his preface that his theme was the "loss of first love . . . being a radical disease too tremendously growing upon us," and he declared that the "observation of that declension [was] justly calling for so meet an antidote." From a literary perspective, Danforth's project is particularly notable for its imaginative evocation of wilderness imagery and its incorporation, in the final pages, of a dramatic dialogue between Danforth and a community of fearful listeners. The text thus can be read as resonant with Christ's ironic dialogue with the followers of John the Baptist upon John's return from the desert where he began his ministry. The Doctrine that Danforth draws from the text forms a typological connection between John and the Puritan founders: both are "such as have sometimes left their pleasant cities and habitations to enjoy the pure worship of God in a wilderness." Like those who followed John and eventually lost interest in his preaching, some Puritans "are apt in time to abate and cool in their affection." At which point, "the Lord calls upon them seriously and thoroughly to examine themselves, which it was that drew them into the wilderness." Elaborating the several instances in biblical history in which the Jews forayed into the desert only to lose their fervor, Danforth introduces the prophet Jeremiah, who, "that he might reduce the people for their backslidings, cries in the ears of Jerusalem," just as Danforth himself does at the present critical moment.

In the Application, Danforth expands upon the metaphor of the wilderness. First, he recalls the journey of the first settlers "over the vast ocean into this waste and howling wilderness." Depicting their spiritual progress in terms of transforming the harsh wilderness into a fruitful garden, he recalls the times when they "Gleaned day by day in the field of God's ordinances, even among the sheaves, gathering up handfuls." In comparison, the churches today are best described in Proverbs 24:31: "the vineyard is all overgrown with thorns, and nettles cover the face thereof, and the stone wall is broken down," which is a "certain sign of calamity approaching." Instead of a fruitful vineyard, the wilderness becomes once more a threatening space where some "fall into the coal pit," others are "swallowed up alive [in] the lime pit," and "some split upon the rock of affected ostentation." Recalling that they had forsaken the pomp and riches of England for the purity of a simple pious life in the wilderness, he charges that now many, especially the "ladies of Zion," have begun to affect courtly manners and fancy dress, which are "very unsuitable to a wilderness." Linking the external physical wilderness to the internal spiritual wilderness that evil has fostered, he expands the natural imagery: "Why hast the Lord smitten us with blasting and mildew now seven years together, adding sometimes severe drought, sometimes great tempests, floods, and sweeping rains . . . blazing stars, earthquakes, dreadful thunders and lightings, fearful burnings?" In the context of his representation of New England as an enclosed garden circumscribed by wilderness, he asks why it is that so many of the founders and great ministers have died recently: "such burning and shining lights out of the candlesticks; the principal stakes of our hedges; the cornerstones of our walls? . . . breaking down our defensed cities, iron pillars?" He speculates that, like comets, the deaths too are omens: "Is it now a sign that God is making a way for his wrath?"

In his final pages, Danforth adopts a dialogue technique recalling the exchange in Matthew 12:9–13, in which Christ heals a man with a withered hand. Like this man who sought help in near despair, the people of New England should be crying out to Christ, "Alas, we are feeble and impotent; our hands are withered and our strength dried up." In a crescendo of metaphors, Danforth proclaims that the people should deplore and confess their "wound grievous," because their prejudiced hearts have provoked the "sea tempestuous," their empty fields, and the "machinations and contrivances" of their "many adversaries. "For each affliction discussed, Danforth gives evidence from scripture of Christ's power and readiness to calm the waters, feed His chosen, and "restrain the rage and fury of adversaries." The key to restoring the community to the blessed state in which it was first established is "diligent attention to the ministry of the Gospel." Through this dialogic structure, Danforth suggests that the leaders of the colony recognize that in assuming their political and social tasks they must also acknowledge the central role of religion in their work, for if they do not and the tragedies continue, Danforth and the other clergy will know who to blame most severely. The citizens hear that in their spiritual lives they must strive for grace and salvation without discouragement, for the corporate survival depends upon the piety of each living soul.

Throughout the 1670s and in the early 1680s especially, preachers used election days, fast days, funerals, executions, and any special events to perform the jeremiad ritual, and more often than not the younger, or "rising," generation was the chosen target. Increase Mather proved masterful in his exploitation of the form, and with four such sermons each, he and his son Cotton preached more election sermons than any other ministers. In addition to his *Day of Trouble is Near* (1674; see Chapter 3), Increase's jeremiads included: *A Renewal of Covenant the Great Duty Incumbent on Decaying and Distressed Churches* (1677), *Pray for the Rising Generation* (1678), and *A Call from Heaven to the Present and Succeeding Generations* (1679). A few other titles of famous jeremiads convey a sense of the consistency of theme: William Adams's *The Necessity of Pouring Out of the Spirit from on High Upon a Sinning Apostatizing People* (1679), Samuel Hooker's *Righteousness Rained from Heaven* (1677), Jonathan Mitchell's *Nehemiah on the Wall in Troublbed Times* (1671), Urian Oakes's *New England Pleaded With* (1673), Thomas Shepard, Jr.'s *Eye-Salve, or a Watch-Word . . . To Take Heed of Apostasy* (1673), Thomas Walley's *Balm in Gilead to Heal Zion's Wounds* (1669), and Samuel Willard's *The Firey Trial No Strange Thing* (1682). Many of the ministers favored imagery of sickness to characterize the corrosive and dangerous condition of apostasy, and some of the most vivid use of such imagery appears in two jeremiads by Samuel Torrey (1632–1707). In *Exhortation Unto Reformation* (1674), he depicted New England laboring under a "heavy aggravation" that had drained "the internal, spiritual power and purity of the people," and he proposed that "if we do not speedily recover we shall let go and lose all and bury ourselves in our own ruins." Particularly vulnerable to "ill-worship" and other pernicious disorders were young people: "The sins of the Youth (which are many of them some of the most flagitious sins of the Times) are become the sins of the Churches." In *A Plea for the Life of Dying Religion* (1683), Torrey describes the "*vital decay, a decay upon the very Vitals* of Religion," which had led God to smite "us with a deadly destruction: The killing sword, a moral Contagion." And again, he pointed to the "carelessness, slothfulness, unfaithfulness" of the young, who had allowed the religion of their parents and grandparents to "decay, languish, and die away."

Whether the clergy continued to preach jeremiads in the middle to late 1680s at the rate they did in the 1670s is not certain, but fewer such sermons were printed in those years. The sermons that were published were on the whole more reassuring, less occupied with the young and with the decline of religion. Perhaps the specter of perceived external enemies in the form of the Indians and the royal governors with their Anglican brethren served to unify the congregationalists and shift blame to external scapegoats. During and after King Philip's War, most Puritan writings about Native Americans depicted them as children of Satan lurking in the wilderness, the site of evil and corruption. Then, when Governor Andros occupied the churches and insisted that Old South Church be shared with Anglican worshippers, the unfamiliar sound of hymns pouring from the Old South may have been objectionable enough to reconcile the differences among several political factions that had formed among the New Englanders in the 1670s.

There is also evidence that some churches, although they did not go as far as Solomon Stoddard, who opened the communion table to the unconverted, did reduce the psychological pressures upon potential full members by eliminating the necessity of public confession and allowing people to give their testimony to the minister privately or simply to report that they now believed they were saved. The content of the sermons published during the late 1680s indicates that the clergy were approaching their congregations with more assurance and discussing the accessibility of communion. Even the titles convey more hopeful messages: John Bailey's *Man's Chief End to Glorify God* (1689), Ezekiel Carre's *The Charitable Samaritan* (1689), Cotton Mather's *The Call of the Gospel* (1686), Increase Mather's *Some Important Truths Concerning Conversion* (1684), Joshua Moodey's *A Practical Discourse Concerning the Choice Benefit of Communion with God in His House* (1685), Richard Standfast's *A Little Handful of Cordial Comforts for a Fainting Soul* (1690), John Whiting's *The Way of Israel's Welfare* (1686), and Samuel Willard's *Covenant-Keeping the Way to Blessedness* (1682), *A Child's Portion: or the Unseen Glory* (1684*)*, *Mercy Magnified on a Penitent Prodigal* (1684), and *Heavenly Merchandise; or the Purchasing of Truth Recommended and the Selling of It Dissuaded* (1686). In this last sermon, Willard baldly appealed to motivations linked to the increasingly materialistic attitudes that most clergy had only recently berated. During this decade, Edward Taylor preached his series of sermons on Christ as savior (collected and published as *Christographia*, 1962) partly in reply to Stoddard; Taylor believed it was proper to prepare souls for conversion by preaching of the beauty and generosity of Christ rather than by using communion as an instrument of conversion. For Taylor, language itself was a means of salvation, a bridge from the heart of the saint to grace, rather than – as it had been previously – merely a vehicle for externalizing the internal spiritual stirrings that were the signs of the presence of the spirit.

As increasing numbers of younger people became full church members in the 1680s, the clergy may have recognized that what they had perceived to be a decline in piety was more likely a myth, an appearance generated by youthful humility and spiritual temerity and by community need for internal reasons to explain difficult times. After the witchcraft delusion in the 1690s, the number of jeremiads increased again but not to the level of frequency of the earlier period or with the emphasis on the failures of the young. Indeed, one of the most notable jeremiads of the 1690s was seventy-eight-year-old Joshua Scottow's (1615–98) *Old Men's Tears for Their Own*

Declensions (1693), in which he places the blame for the secularization of New England not upon the young but upon his own generation for having lost their original zeal and sense of purpose.

Although jeremiad preaching never returned to the fury of the 1670s, the ritualistic form had become firmly established in the culture, and groups of immigrants coming to America in the centuries to follow would rehearse the familiar sequence – idealism and dreams of success followed years later by feelings of disillusionment, loss, and disappointment, especially with complacent children – thereby keeping the jeremiad resonant within the American imagination. Thus, even today on every Fourth of July, speakers across the country hail the "Founding Fathers," assail present failures, and urge audiences to revive original ideals so that America can fulfill its manifest destiny. From presidential addresses to works of literary artists, the jeremiad appears as a fundamental structure in American expression. *Moby-Dick, The Narrative of the Life of Frederick Douglass, Life in the Iron Mills, Walden, The Great Gatsby, The Grapes of Wrath, Gravity's Rainbow* – these works and many others have all been called jeremiads because they seem to call for a return to a former innocence and moral strength that has been lost.

In the seventeenth century and to the present time, the jeremiad themes and structure characterize not only sermons but other writings as well. Captivity narratives usually follow the jeremiad design, with the victim reflecting upon the period of his or her life preceding the capture and discovering personal faults that had brought on God's punishment. During the time of captivity, the repentant victim searches within the self and vows to return to earlier piety, a decision that appears to be rewarded when the captive is freed. Mary White Rowlandson's captivity narrative, the first and most famous, can be read as such a jeremiad.

Mary White was born about 1637 in South Petherton, Somerset, England. Her father, John White, emigrated to Salem, Massachusetts, in 1638 and sent for the rest of the family in the following year. The family eventually moved to Lancaster, where her father, a wealthy landowner, was one of the founders. She married Reverend Joseph Rowlandson, pastor of the church at Lancaster, and the Rowlandsons had four children, one of whom died in infancy. On February 10, 1676, during King Philip's War, a Wampanoag raiding party attacked Lancaster, killing twelve citizens, including members of the Rowlandson family, burning their homes, and taking Mary and others captive. Mary's brother-in-law, eldest sister, and her sister's son were killed, and Mary's youngest daughter, Sarah, whom she held in her arms, was fatally wounded by a bullet that first passed through Mary's side. Twenty-four were taken captive, and the parents were separated from their children. Rowlandson carried her six-year-old Sarah with her until she died on February 18. Her other two children, ten-year-old Mary and thirteen-year-old Joseph, were held apart from Mary, but as she reports, she did see them briefly a few times during her captivity. All were eventually ransomed, with Mary's release coming on May 2, 1676. During her months in captivity, Mary lived with and was the servant of Weetamoo of the Pocassets and her husband, Quanopen, a chief of the Narragansets and one of the leaders of the attack on Lancaster. After her release, the Rowlandsons lived in Boston for a year before her husband became minister to the church in Wethersfield, Connecticut. Rowlandson began her narrative in either 1677 or 1678. Her husband died in November of 1678, and the last public record of her as Mary Rowlandson occurs in 1679 when she was awarded a pension and a sum for his funeral. Until very recently, historians assumed that she probably died before her narrative was published in 1682, but new evidence indicates that she married Captain Samuel Talcott on August 6, 1679, and lived in Wethersfield, Connecticut, until January 5, 1711, when she died at the age of seventy-three.

Creating, perhaps, what would become the formula for the captivity narrative, Rowlandson declares that she was moved to write of her experience because it was evident to her that God had used her for His purpose and that she wanted to convey the spiritual meaning of her experience to others. Despite this religious motive, it was a bold act for a woman to undertake a major prose work in seventeenth-century New England, and her text is the only lengthy piece of prose by a woman published in seventeenth-century America. It is likely that she was strongly encouraged to write it by Increase Mather, who had helped her husband during the ransom negotiations. Mather wrote a preface to the narrative, in which he provided the official Puritan interpretation of Mary's ordeal and of her narrative. Mather was very concerned after King Philip's War that people in New England and leaders in England should understand the reasons and meaning of the catastrophe of the war in providential terms. The war had devastated the population and the financial resources of New England at the very time that King Charles was looking for a reason to intervene in the prosperous colony's affairs. Mather's history of the war, his sermons, and Rowlandson's narrative all inscribe a "spiritualized" construction over the brutal reality of the war and allow Mather to assert that New England had been redeemed; thereby, it seemed, the colonies acquired a divine reprieve to be left politically independent.

The first part of Rowlandson's title, usually dropped in modern editions, demonstrates how her personal experience is to be subordinated to religious precepts. The full title is *The Sovereignty and Goodness of God, Together with the Faithfulness of His Promises Displayed; Being a Narrative of the Captivity and Restoration of Mrs. Mary Rowlandson, Commended by her to all that Desire to Know the Lord's Doings to, and Dealings with Her. Especially to her Dear Children and Relations.* The words pertaining to her actual experience are virtually surrounded by, contained within, and outnumbered by others that are to transform her suffering into a sign of God's "Goodness." The horror of the divine wrath presented in the text is erased in the title by God's "Faithfulness" to Mary and New England. As a Puritan and a minister's wife writing under the gaze and likely guidance of Mather and her husband, Rowlandson was certainly aware of the communal function of her narrative. To complete the holy packaging of the first publication, the text of Rowlandson's narrative was bracketed by Mather's preface and by a sermonic afterword on the war by Joseph Rowlandson. But, in spite of these devices of control and containment, Rowlandson's grief refuses to be reconstructed into an acceptance of divine will, and the emotional power of her experiences emerges through the discursive structure of the jeremiad rhetoric.

With personal feelings and Puritan rhetoric competing to control the text, the work is characterized by an internal tension resulting from the author's effort to reconstitute painful personal experiences in language and at the same time to construct her narrative in accordance with the religious expectations and demands of Mather and her fellow Puritans. In order to justify the angry God who sent the Indians into battle, Rowlandson therefore must discover in herself the signs of the failures for which God punished her, just as all of the Puritans were having to do to understand why their numbers and wealth had been so drastically diminished. She reports that on the first Sabbath of her captivity she began to recall her sins: "I then remembered how careless I had been of God's holy time, how many Sabbaths I had lost and misspent, and how evilly I had walked in God's sight." Later, she reveals, she remembered her wicked desire for smoking. For these faults, she considers that she really deserved to be killed, but that in His mercy, God had spared her: "how righteous it was with God to cut off the thread of my life and cast me out of His presence forever. Yet the Lord still showed mercy to me and upheld me; and as He wounded me with one hand, so He healed me with the other." The economic and political reasons for the attacks are either not apparent to Rowlandson or are simply perceived as irrelevant. Even the converted natives, the "Praying Indians," are dehumanized; because some of them betrayed whites during the fighting, Rowlandson concludes that no Native American can be trusted. If it ever occurred to Rowlandson that her punishment was rather harsh for her offenses or that the Native Americans had their own reasons for attacking, the pressure to narrate events in accord with Puritan ideology probably kept her from expressing those thoughts in her text.

As represented in *The Sovereignty and Goodness of God*, the captivity period thus becomes the opportunity for Mary to prepare her heart for grace, to search out the corruption in her nature, and to rediscover the glory of God in His scriptures. As it happens, a warrior who had taken a Bible during another raid gave it to Rowlandson. At first, when she attempted to read it, her spiritual torpor caused the words to seem distant and vague, but grace gradually enabled her to feel the joy of God's words again. Rowlandson conveys that the most frightening part of her experience was neither the physical suffering nor the mental anguish over her children but her lonely metaphysical passage through the dark night of her soul, during which she feared that God had abandoned her. Rowlandson thus becomes an emblematic public example or type – a New England Job – reflecting the entire community's endurance of the war. She preaches the need to remember that only things and creatures of this corrupt world were lost, to accept God's just and wise punishment, and to thank Him for His cleansing fires, deliverance, and reconciliation.

In spite of the standard rhetoric and perhaps in spite of herself, Rowlandson does manage to convey aspects of her personal experience, and where she does so, the text is most compelling for modern readers. The most passionate sections express her feelings about the loss of her loved ones and her near despair. For example, when Sarah died in the middle of the night, Mary did not tell her captors that she was dead for fear that they would discard the body in the forest without a proper burial. In her narrative she recalled how, as she kept the corpse by her through the night, she was overcome with thoughts of suicide:

> I cannot but take notice how at another time I could not bear to be in the room where any dead person was; but now the case is changed – I must and could lie down by my dead babe, side by side, all night together. I have thought since of the wonderful goodness of God to me, in preserving me in the use of my reason and senses in that distressed time, [so] that I did not use wicked and violent means to end my own miserable life.

Such passages, even with the gloss of inserted religious precepts, impart the depth of Rowlandson's suffering and the degree to which her own individual narrative resists the narrative tropes of Puritan ideology.

Most interesting in this dialogue between Rowlandson's spiritualized depictions and her reports of actual, unreconstructed reactions are those passages in which she describes her interactions and experiences with the Native-American people. At the outset, she casts her narrative in the language of racist stereotypes that characterized white attitudes especially during and after the war. She describes the Indians as "atheistical, proud, wild, cruel, barbarous, brutish (in one word) diabolical creatures." Her early reactions to Algonkian culture were typical of English and European conceptions of native life. She did not recognize the people as having culture at all and saw them simply as living in senseless chaos. Soon, however, her accounts shift away from the stereotypes. The Indians cease to be merely "others" and become individuals with whom she engages in commerce and civilities. Rowlandson learns that she can use her sewing skills to make clothing and then barter for things she needs, especially food. In the text, these exchanges deconstruct Rowlandson's preconceptions and indicate implicitly that the Indians are people much like herself with different traits and temperaments. Rowlandson comes to understand savagery as a consciously constructed concept, and she even recognizes that the Indian may view her as savage. This idea finds particular emphasis when Rowlandson earns a piece of bear meat for making a shirt and a quart of peas for knitting a pair of stockings. She cooks the two foods together and offers to share her meal with an Indian couple, but the woman refuses to eat because she is repulsed to see meat and vegetables cooked together. Then, when Rowlandson returns to the wigwam of her master and tells this story, he and his wife are angry that she embarrassed them by visiting the home of another and letting it appear that she did not receive enough to eat from her master.

Perhaps Rowlandson's most striking reversal of racist stereotyping occurs in her representation of Metacomet, the hated "King Philip," who was regularly portrayed in Puritan writings as a beast of Satan. Rowlandson recounts her conversations with Metacomet, which include his request that she make a shirt for his son, his offer of a pipe of tobacco to her in friendship, and his concern about her appearance: "He asked me, When I washed me? I told him not this month, then he fetched me some water himself, and bid me wash, and gave me the glass to see how I looked." The "glass," which frequently in frontier writings reveals the savage "other," ironically here references the savagery of the intruding colonist. Contrary to Mary's and her readers' expectations, Metacomet seems more concerned with grooming and civility than she does, for she seems to have degenerated into a "primitive" state.

Within the postwar atmosphere of 1676, Rowlandson could certainly not assert that she found the Indians and their leaders to be more like herself than she expected, but her account nonetheless demonstrates the subversive subtext of her narrative. This narrative is rare because of its willingness to humanize the Native American, who speaks words of human concern, self-assertion, and compassion.

Samuel Sewall (1652–1730) was surely an avid reader of Rowlandson and one who thought more seriously about questions of race and justice in his society than most. Best known as the author of the richest American Puritan diary, a major source of New England social history from 1674 to 1729, Sewall also wrote works that might be called secular jeremiads. Born in 1652 to wealthy, merchant-class parents, Henry and Jane Sewall, in Bishop Stoke, Hampshire, England, Samuel was brought to America at age nine. He attended Harvard; for two years he was the roommate of Edward Taylor, who remained a close lifelong friend. He graduated in 1673 but remained at Harvard as a tutor and took an MA in 1674. In 1675, Sewall married Hannah Hull, the daughter of John Hull, the colonial treasurer, master of the mint, and the wealthiest man in Boston. The Sewalls had fourteen children before Hannah died in 1717. Sewall remarried twice, in 1719 to Abigail Tilley (d. 1720) and in 1722 to Mary Gibbs. His record of his futile courtship of the widow Katherine Winthrop is the most amusing (though unintentionally so) and the most frequently anthologized section of his diary.

Although Sewall trained for the ministry, his first marriage led him to a calling in a business. He was a merchant, banker, judge, and important leader in the church and government; his diary suggests that he never doubted that his opinions were important to the community as a whole. He was elected to various political offices and was the only person to accompany Increase Mather on the crucial mission to England in 1688 to try to have the charter restored and Edmund Andros recalled. Elected to the council that was authorized to advise the governor under the new charter in 1692, Sewall served in this leading role until he retired from the position in 1725. As a friend of Governor William Phips, he was also appointed to be one of the nine judges of the Salem witchcraft trials. Although he joined in prosecuting the victims, Sewall made very few entries in his diary about the trials, perhaps feeling some anxiety about their justice. In 1697, when Samuel Willard preached that the trials had been misguided, Sewall stood up in his pew, passionately confessed his errors and guilt, and begged forgiveness from the congregation. That afternoon, he wrote a formal statement admitting his mistakes, which he gave to Willard and recorded in his diary.

In that same year, Sewall published his first book, *Phaenomena quaedam Apocalyptica Ad Aspectum Novi Orbus Configurata. Or, some few Lines towards a Description of the New Heaven, As It makes [sic] to those who stand upon the New Earth*, a text of sixty pages explicating the Book of Revelation as a forecast of the history of New England. At a time when some Puritan clergy were beginning to recognize that the population of New England was becoming religiously diverse and that the ideas of the city on a hill and the divine errand would remain unfulfilled dreams of a previous generation, Sewall argued strenuously that New England was still the New Heaven and New Jerusalem. In his enthusiasm, he included two prefaces reasserting this vision, one addressed to Lieutenant Governor William Stoughton, and he went throughout Boston giving copies of his book to important leaders. In this work, he recounts the history of the Protestant Reformation and the persecution of the Huguenots, and he insists that the Puritans had converted many Indians – a point attested to by the signatures of eighteen fellow citizens. With energy and eloquence not so evident in his diary, Sewall buttresses his typological arguments with natural evidence. He asserts that the physical beauty of New England, as well as biblical prophecies, proves that New England is the New Zion. His description of an island off the coast of Massachusetts is for modern readers one of the most aesthetically appealing passages in all of Puritan writing:

> As long as Plum Island shall faithfully keep the command post, notwithstanding all the hectoring words and hard blows of the proud and boisterous ocean; as long as any salmon or sturgeon shall swim in the streams of the Merrimack or any perch or pickerel in Crane Pond; as long as the sea-fowl shall know the time of their coming, and not neglect seasonably to visit the places of their acquaintance; as long as any cattle shall be fed with the grass growing in the meadows, which do humbly bow down themselves before Turkey-Hill; as long as any sheep shall walk upon Old-Town Hill; and shall from thence pleasantly look down upon the River Parker, and the fruitful marshes lying beneath; as long as any free and harmless doves shall find white oak or other tree within the township, to perch, or feed, or build a careless nest upon, and shall voluntarily present themselves to perform the office of gleaners after barley harvest; as long as Nature shall not grow old and dote, but shall constantly remember to give the rows of Indian corn their education by pairs; so long shall Christians be born there, and being first made meet, shall from thence be translated to be made partakers of the inheritance of the saints in light.

The shift from the focus upon food and nature to the spiritual reaping reveals verbal skills that are not apparent in the more pedestrian writing of Sewall's diary.

It is frequently said of Sewall's diary that it reveals the gradual transformation of a staunch seventeenth-century Puritan into an eighteenth-century cosmopolitan Yankee, but even as he adapted to change in some ways, Sewall embraced religious orthodoxy until his death. However, his anti-slavery tract, *The Selling of Joseph* (1700), reveals a mind poised between two worlds: Sewall's Puritan tendencies toward constant introspection and scrutiny of biblical passages to support his arguments are blended with the thought of John Locke and other Enlightenment figures whose work would dominate eighteenth-century Anglo-American philosophy and ideas. The three-part structure of the argument demonstrates this fusing of modes of thought. In the first section, he depends heavily upon the scriptures to propose that whites and blacks are all children of Adam and Eve and thereby benefit equally from the contract that God made with humankind after the Fall granting them liberty. Because of this contract, the selling of Joseph by his brothers was "the most atrocious of capital Crimes." In the second part, Sewall provides a more pragmatic gloss by suggesting that the system of using indentured servants is superior to slavery because the servants are looking forward to their freedom and are thus more motivated to work hard than slaves, whose "continual aspiring after their forbidden liberty renders them unwilling servants." In the third part, he combines scriptural and pragmatic arguments in an effort to answer the objections of some that the Bible approved of slavery and that the Africans, as descendants of "Cham" (refers to Canaan, son of Ham, in Gen. 9:25–7), were condemned in the Bible to be slaves. He also replies to the thesis that because the slaves brought to America had been taken prisoner in African wars and made slaves there, they consequently may lawfully remain slaves in America. Finally, he returns to his original biblical argument and concludes that "these Ethiopians, as black as they are, seeing they are the sons and daughters of the first Adam, the brethren and sisters of the last Adam, the offspring of God; they ought to be treated with a respect agreeable."

Although Sewall is to be admired for writing the first antislavery work in New England, it must be recognized that many of his arguments are structured by cultural stereotypes. He opposes the inhumane practice of slavery but does not advocate racial integration. Rather, he urges stopping the flow of Africans into America. He argues that Africans should be kept out because "they can seldom use their freedom well" when they are free and because with the large number of African men and few African women in the community, the whites might be "obliged to find them wives." Already, he regrets, there are so many black men in the militia that "the places [are] taken up of [white] men that might make husbands of our daughters." He also argues that the Africans are a burden on the legal system and the economy: "It seems to be practically pleaded that they might be lawless; 'tis thought much of, that the law should have satisfaction for their thefts, and other immoralities." Sewall's observations necessarily reflected white racism – and white culture's inability to accept difference and the sovereign humanity of the Africans – but at least he did have the courage to take the unpopular position of denouncing slavery itself as "the most atrocious of capital Crimes."

Cotton Mather (1663–1728) was the author of the grandest, indeed epic, jeremiad and the most controversial figure of late Puritan New England. Born in Boston in 1663, the first child of Increase and Maria Cotton Mather and the grandson of the eminent founders Richard Mather and John Cotton, third-generation Cotton was practically destined from birth to go to Harvard (AB 1678, MA 1681) and to become a leading minister. Today, he is the best-known Puritan minister partly because of his prolific authorship of over 400 publications and because of the persistent, though unjustified, myth that he was the most severe and self-righteous of Puritans. During his lifetime, however, he remained in the shadow of his father, Increase. Cotton served as the teacher of Old North Church under Increase's pastorship from Cotton's ordination in 1685 until Increase's death in 1723 at the age of eighty-four. Cotton led the church for only four years before he died in 1728. Because he tried desperately to uphold the old New England Way during the waning decades of Puritanism and because his writing style often tends toward the hyperbolic, pedantic, and shrill, many of his texts support the worst images of him as overbearing and self-righteous. He is most identified with his works on witchcraft: *Memorable Providences, Relating to Witchcrafts and Possessions (1689)* and *The Wonders of the Invisible World. Observations as well Historical as Theological, upon the Nature, the Number, and the Operations of the Devils* (1693). Even though he appears less inflamed than most of his contemporaries during the episode, Mather is remembered as the preeminent witch hunter. Recent biographers, however, have stressed other sides of his personality and have substantially revised the stereotype into a complex portrait of a brilliant and, in many ways, enlightened thinker. Some scholars have sympathetically depicted him as a victim of the familial, social, and historical circumstances that tormented him and made him appear less tolerant and rational than he actually was.

With the burden of upholding the reputations of the two most prominent clerical families of New England, precocious Cotton was a pious and studious, but unhappy, youth who mastered Latin and Greek well enough by the age of eleven to pass Harvard's entrance exam. During Cotton's childhood years, his father was cold and preoccupied, caught up in the political turmoil of the Boston Synod of 1662 and the Half-Way Covenant that divided him from his own father and led to a split in the congregation of Old North Church. Convinced that God was abandoning New England, Increase recorded in his diary his emotional distress brought on by problems with the churches, his marriage, his doubts about his own calling, and his longing to live in England. From 1669, when Richard died, to 1671, Increase experienced physical incapacities, nightmares, and depression, and he feared he was dying or going insane. Perhaps it was during this traumatic period that Cotton, who was six when Richard died, developed a stammer, about which Increase confided to his diary that he worried "lest the Hesitancy in his [Cotton's] speech should make him incapable of improvement in the work of the ministry, whereunto I had designed him." When Cotton entered Harvard, he suffered "some discouragement" as a young freshman, perhaps because of his stuttering and his inclination to correct the mistakes of others, including his older classmates. His father perfunctorily removed him from school and educated him at home that year. Cotton seems to have been abused again in his second year, but this time he stayed on to graduate.

At Cotton's graduation when he was only fifteen, President Urian Oakes praised him for his learning and declared the hope of all Puritans that he would rise to restore the churches to the happy state they had enjoyed under his forefathers: "in this youth COTTON and MATHER shall in fact as in name coalesce and revive." In Cotton's impassioned efforts to live out this charge to reverse the social, political, and intellectual forces that saw New England moving rapidly away from the world of his grandfathers, Cotton embodied the many tensions and ambiguities of late Puritanism as it fragmented around him, in the storm of ideological change. With visitations of angels to inspire him and a consciousness of divine purpose to drive him, Cotton frantically wrote, preached, ministered, prayed, wept, fretted, counseled, taught, and campaigned for various causes throughout his life, winning the admiration of some and the enmity of others. For all of his seemingly ceaseless and frenetic activity, he always felt that his deeds were inadequate and that his performance failed to fulfill the promise of his name.

Although Mather did bring many hardships upon himself through his dogmatism and his sense of superiority, he also endured many unexpected personal sufferings. His first wife, Abigail Phillips, whom he married in 1686, died in 1702; and his second wife, Elizabeth Clark Hubbard, whom he married in 1703, died in 1713. In 1715, he married Lydia Lee George, but her descent into apparent mental illness caused him much worry and embarrassment; she also brought debts to the marriage incurred by her former husband, and for these Mather was nearly arrested. In 1718, he wrote in his diary that he felt "a continual Anguish of Expectation that my poor Wife, by exposing her Madness, would bring a Ruin on my Ministry." After several turbulent years together, Lydia left Mather in 1723. He also buried nine of his thirteen children, four of them and his wife Elizabeth within a few days during a measles epidemic in 1713. Always financially troubled, he supported three sisters whose husbands had died.

Though Mather is often thought of as one of the harshest and most ideologically rigid of Puritan theologians, he was actually somewhat liberal and opposed his father's conservatism on many issues. For example, while his father persistently ranted against the sins of the rising generation, Cotton convened study groups to instruct young people on Christ's free grace and to encourage their assurance of salvation. Although he was certainly orthodox and preached against sin and backsliding, he also offered many comforting sermons on New Testament texts. In a *Companion for Communicants* (1690), Mather almost approached Stoddard's radical position on open communion when he said, "Assurance is not Absolutely Necessary in order to a *worthy Coming* unto the Holy Supper." He urged uncertain members to "come with all your involuntary and unavoidable Infirmities . . . with all your Hated and your loathed Plagues . . . you shall be welcome here though you have but Faith enough to say with Tears, Lord, help *my unbelief!*"

Indeed, ambivalence and ambiguity characterized Mather's positions on many subjects. For example, he recognized and praised the contributions of women to the churches, to the education of children, and to the civilizing of society. In funeral sermons for Mary Brown, *Eureka: The Virtuous Woman Found* (1711), and for Sarah Leverett, *Monica America: Female Piety Exemplified* (1721), and in a sermon on the ideal Puritan wife, *Ornaments for the Daughters of Zion* (1692), he lauded not only these individuals but women in general. In *Ornaments*, he wrote: "There are far more *Godly Women* in the world than there are *Godly men* . . . It seems that the *Curse* in the Difficulties both of *Subjection* and of *Childbearing*, which the *Female Sex* is doom'd unto, has been turned into a *Blessing* . . . [for] God . . . makes the *Tenderness* of their Disposition a further *Occasion* of Serious Devotion in them." In his biography of Anne Bradstreet, he warmly praised her intelligence, talent, and piety. At the same time, however, in many of Mather's texts there is evidence of possible ambivalence and anxiety regarding women. He was especially disturbed by impious women and was particularly venomous toward the memory of Anne Hutchinson. Also, he often invoked imagery of the female body negatively in discussions of sin and error; doctrinal adultery, wombs of misconception, monstrous fetuses of heresy, and similar tropes appear throughout his works. These figures were common enough in Puritan sermons, but Mather's frequent employment of them may indicate an unconscious fear and disdain of women that his conscious pronouncements functioned to mask.

Certain contradictions also exist in Mather's life and writings in regard to matters involving Africans and Native Americans. Mather often publicly denounced the cruelty of the African slave trade. With Sewall, Mather recognized blacks to be equal to whites as human beings, and in his sermon *The Negro Christianized* (1706), he argued that Africans should receive a Christian education and be allowed to join the church. In spite of his financial problems, he used his own money to pay a schoolmistress to teach local Africans to read, and he entertained the religious society of blacks of his church in his home. However, he also congenially accepted a black slave, named Onesimus, given to him by his congregation. He taught the young man to read and converted him to Christianity, but his negative comments about him as being superstitious and having a "thievish Aspect" suggest that he shared the racial prejudices of his fellow whites. In regard to Native Americans, Mather learned the Iroquois language (in addition to his six other foreign languages), and he worked to integrate the local Indians into white society; of course, he did not recognize that this very process demonstrated a lack of respect for the native cultures.

Inconsistencies and contradictions also appear in many of Mather's writings on science and nature. He firmly believed that every natural event resulted from divine providence, but he saw no conflict in doing scientific research and altering nature to improve living conditions. He consistently demonstrated a desire to be a member of the international scientific community and always felt that he was intellectually confined living in provincial New England. For many years, he wrote remarkably detailed descriptions of the plants, animals, and birds of America, which he sent to the Royal Society in London. Perhaps because he hoped to impress the society's members, these letters contain some of his most evocative prose, often alternating between expressions of pride in being a New Englander and of frustration in being "in an infant country entirely destitute of philosophers." Mather also wrote the first general book on science in America, which he sent in manuscript to the society in 1714 and had published as *The Christian Philosopher* in 1721, followed in 1722 by his important medical text *The Angel of Bethesda . . . An Essay upon the Common Maladies of Mankind . . . and direction for the Preservation of Health*. His research work was admired throughout Europe, and he was elected to the Royal Society.

Perhaps Mather's most important contribution to science came in the field of medicine, a subject he pursued avidly all of his life. In 1721, during one of the smallpox epidemics that ravaged New England about every twelve years, Mather recommended the use of inoculation, which he knew was being tried in other parts of the world. For this proposal, Mather was widely attacked (including an actual assassination attempt); some of the most virulent criticism came from young Benjamin Franklin and his brother James in their newspaper, *The New England Courant*. When other ministers such as Benjamin Colman, Solomon Stoddard, and John Wise supported Mather, the public outcry against inoculation contributed to a growing anticlericalism in New England that hastened the decline of the ministry's influence in the 1720s. Mather stood firm, and successful inoculation was eventually instituted, ultimately making him a hero in the history of eighteenth-century American medicine.

Apart from the many harsh insults he received during the inoculation controversy, Mather suffered other painful professional setbacks. Throughout his life he remained hopeful that he would one day be elected president of Harvard as his father had been, but repeatedly he was passed over for less qualified men. This obvious snub was very likely the direct result of the Mathers' persistent political conflicts with Governor Joseph Dudley. Also, although Mather's role in the witchcraft trials was not more significant than that of many others who supported the court, his publications on the subject were attacked by Robert Calef (1648–1719) in his devastating rebuttal *More Wonders of the Invisible World* (1700); as a result Mather became the scapegoat of the affair. Perhaps his greatest public humiliation came, however, in 1712 when he managed to convert success into embarrassing failure. Partly because of his liberal admission policies, the congregation of Old North Church expanded, and Mather had pews built for new parishioners. This action impinged upon the presumed privileges of many established members, who felt that the newcomers did not deserve such status. A faction of Mather's leading members split from his church in protest, elected their own minister, and built New North Church three blocks away, much reducing the size of Mathers' congregation and diminishing his influence in the city. In addition to these discouragements, Mather also complained bitterly in his diary of his failure, despite three decades of trying, to find a publisher for his twelve volume biblical translation and commentary, "Biblia Americana," which he compiled over twenty years and which he viewed as his magnum opus. It has yet to appear in print.

Of Mather's many publications, the one that has generated the greatest number of modern interpretations is his *Magnalia Christi Americana; Or, The Ecclesiastical History of New England, from Its First Planting in the Year 1620, unto the Year of our Lord, 1698*. Written between 1694 and 1698 and published in 1702 in London, the work fulfilled his father's long-standing charge that "the memory of the great things the Lord hath done for us be transmitted to posterity." Running to over 800 pages, the complex work is divided into seven books: the settlement of New England; the lives of the governors; the lives of the leading ministers; Harvard College and the lives of its important graduates; Puritan church polity; "Remarkable Divine Providences"; and problems that arose with heretics, Indians, Satan, Edmund Andros, and others. It also contains several poems, notably elegies by such writers as Benjamin Tompson. In spite of this seeming fragmentation, the overall effect of the work is as a unified, epic jeremiad. In the text, Mather glorifies the Puritan founders, inflates the events of the early years, and laments the decline of fervor and purpose in the recent past. His aim, he proclaims, is to keep "*Alive*, as far as this poor *Essay* may contribute thereunto, the Interests of *Dying Religion* in our Churches."

As with so many Puritan writings, however, the *Magnalia Christi Americana* is marked by an internal tension, which doubtless arises from Mather's conflicting double motive: to celebrate the heroism of the founders in creating a New Zion and to reconcile the Puritan churches of his own time with the English Crown and with fellow English Protestants. Thus, at the outset, Mather proclaims in epic style the glories of the sacred New World: "I WRITE *the wonders* of the CHRISTIAN RELIGION, flying from the Deprivations of *Europe*, to the *American Strand*." Here, as in other textual performances, Mather embraced a chiliastic notion that Christ would soon return to earth to begin a millennium of His rule based in His chosen New England. In preparation for this event, New England must recapture the spirit of the first generation: "The *First Age* was the *Golden Age*: To return unto *that*, will make a Man a *Protestant*, and I may say, a *Puritan.*" Yet in contrast to this emphasis on New England's uniqueness, Mather repeatedly stresses throughout the text that the founders of Massachusetts Bay were not separatists who had scornfully fled England; they had always loved their mother country and only sought to reform their own Anglican church: "the First Planters of *New England*, at their first coming over, did in a Public and a Printed Address, call the Church of *England*, their *Dear Mother.*" In fact, Mather declares that many would have returned if only the Anglicans had removed the trappings of Catholicism. He also stresses that religious freedom was presently the rule in New England, where they "dare make no Difference between a *Presbyterian*, a *Congregational*, an *Episcopalian*, and an Anti *paedo-baptist*, where their *Visible Piety*, makes it probable, that the Lord Jesus Christ has received them." Nonetheless, given the intolerance toward Anglicans and Quakers demonstrated as late as the 1680s, some scholars read Mather's position as a disingenuous and self-serving attempt to garner political favor abroad and thereby to compensate for his own diminished influence at home.

In fairness, however, it seems necessary to remember the cultural context from which Mather produced his texts: he was born into a world of orthodox governors elected under the old charter and yet he soon found himself with a royal governor, surrounded by Anglicans, and under a new charter; in the 1690s he was himself trying to reconcile in his own mind the inherited myth of the New Jerusalem with contemporary realities. Thus, the *Magnalia Christi Americana* can be read as inscribing the myth of the New Zion upon the New England imagination while also reinterpreting it so that the present would seem to have unfolded teleologically. As his father had tried through narrative to reconstruct the devastations of King Philip's War as spiritual victory, Mather similarly attempted to mystify the shattering of the Puritan synthesis, which never really existed, as the ordained fulfillment of sacred history. Thus, he can be quite sincere in his conviction that God brought His chosen to America not to set them permanently apart from their English compatriots but rather, "*By* them, [to] give a *Specimen* of many Good Things, which He would have His Churches elsewhere aspire and arise unto." In Mather's view, providential history consists of many repeated cycles of such pious beginnings, declines of fervor, and restorations of faith. He considered his present moment in Boston to be one of the lapses, to be followed soon by the "dawning of that day" of religious revival.

This Janus-faced dimension of the *Magnalia Christi-Americana* is quite apparent in the biography of Governor Phips, who was royally appointed. In the early 1680s, Phips had been arrested in Boston for commanding a debauched ship's crew; he was known for his swearing and cursing, and at his trial he defied Governor Bradstreet. Then, a decade later, when Phips was appointed governor, Mather praised him as though his accession followed providentially from Bradford, Winthrop, Bradstreet, and other pious Puritan governors. The Phips biography stands in subtle contrast, however, to those on Bradford, Eliot, and the early leaders, for whereas Mather praises them for their piety, he lauds Phips's industry and business abilities. The Phips biography anticipates Benjamin Franklin's *Autobiography*, the Horatio Alger stories, and later fictions engaged in American self-fashioning. Moreover, it suggestively illustrates how Mather and his *Magnalia Christi Americana* performed at the intersection between two conflicting visions of America – one spiritual and one materialistic – that he was attempting to reconcile, while recognizing that each mythology threatened to dismantle the other.

Although Benjamin Franklin had attacked Mather during the smallpox epidemic, he later praised him in a famous passage of his *Autobiography* for having inspired him to live a life of moral righteousness, hard work, and good deeds. Like Franklin, Mather desperately conceived himself to be a person whose mission in life was to be of service to others. Indeed, as his son Samuel said of him: "the Ambition and Character of my Father's life was Serviceableness." This motivation correspondingly finds thematic resonance with one of Mather's most enduring works, his *Bonifacius, an Essay Upon the Good* (1710). Of all of Mather's writing, this was the text that most inspired Franklin. It also displays the liminality of Mather's intellectual situation as he slipped into an eighteenth-century mentality, recommending good works for their practical worldly value and proposing common sense as the way to salvation and wealth. This interpretive gloss appears to have been Franklin's, and the mediating subtext can easily be formulated through selective quotation from the multivalenced language of the text. Close and comprehensive reading, however, reveals Mather still to be steeped in the traditional Puritan theology that privileged grace and conversion as the only means of salvation and that commended the spiritual over the material world. Yet surrounded by wealthy merchants in a flourishing and increasingly secular society that was coming under the intellectual influences of the European Enlightenment, Mather must have been conscious of using his words in ways that permit both a conservative doctrinal reading and a more practical moral application. He may very well have felt tormented that he had to employ such terms in order to reach his generation. The New England world of 1710 was a very different one from that of 1678, when Mather had graduated from Harvard, and there was probably no other person in 1710 who wanted so much to be able "To return unto *that* [Golden Age that] will make a Man a *Protestant*, and I may say, a *Puritan*."

Mather's accomplishments and his voluminous writings testify to the persistent power of Puritan modalities of thought and of the dominating narrative of the American errand. Although Mather did not live to witness the Great Awakening of fervor that he always believed was coming, his texts suggest that he recognized that graduating from Harvard and Yale in the early 1720s were indeed several *"Excellent Young Men"* who "Study and Resolve their Duty," and are the *"Rain-bows* of our Churches." Mather passed on to these very men the Puritan dream he had struggled to keep alive, and in 1727, just a year before Mather died, Jonathan Edwards, the grandson of the Mathers' old antagonist Solomon Stoddard, was ordained pastor of the church at Northampton. There, Edwards would lead the spiritual renewal that the Mathers had prayed for and anticipated for five decades.

Chapter Seven

Reason and revivalism

Beginning in the 1650s, the growing number of merchants in Boston, Salem, Cambridge, Newtown, and other large towns along the seaboard began to discover themselves to be a special class. Unlike farmers, who were threatened by new immigrants seeking land, the merchants favored the growth and development of new products and international trade. During the Half-Way Covenant controversy of the 1660s, powerful merchants such as John Hull embraced those Pauline aspects of Puritan doctrines that had originally favored expansion of the fellowship, and they sided with those who supported more liberal membership standards. As disputes raged within First Church, Boston, in the 1660s, a coalition made up mainly of merchants split off to found Third Church, later known as the Old South. Under the leadership of Thomas Thatcher until 1678 and of Samuel Willard from then until his death in 1707, the Old South maintained quite lenient membership requirements.

One critical text confronting the issue of church membership was Giles Firmin's *The Real Christian* (1670). A prolific contributor to the parliamentary debates under Cromwell, Firmin lived in New England in the 1630s and 1640s and then returned to England during the Protectorate. Firmin had criticized his former New England colleagues Thomas Hooker and Thomas Shepard for being too rigid in their schematic accounts of preparation and for their discouragingly high standards for proving conversion. Firmin tried to persuade his English colleagues to advocate more tolerance, to understand "self-love" as natural, and to recognize God to be merciful and reasonable. His work found wide circulation in Boston in the 1670s, and its republication in Boston in 1742 demonstrates that the debates over conversion and church membership still continued seventy years later.

During the tumultuous 1670s and 1680s, membership issues divided old friends and often entire congregations. As a member of the Old South, Samuel Sewall noted that "one might gather by Mr. Willard's speech that there was some Animosity in him toward Mr. [Increase] Mather," and Sewall, who respected the Mathers, worried about whether he was correct to be in Willard's congregation: "I have been exceedingly tormented in my mind sometimes lest the Third Church should not be in God's way in breaking off from the old." Yet, despite their differences, the New Englanders remained bonded together during the greater part of the century by their mutual interest in resisting the intrusions of the English government. After the witchcraft delusion and the establishment of the new charter in 1692, attention on external enemies temporarily waned, and internal divisions arose again in the late 1690s, resulting this time in serious and permanent fragmentation.

People began to define ministers categorically as either "conservative" or "liberal." Those termed "liberals" were usually opposed to formal narrations of the conversion experience, reassuring about the likelihood of salvation, tolerant of other denominations, and supportive of union between the congregationalists and the Church of England. They also practiced a more florid and eloquent preaching style, were inclined to attend an Anglican celebration service on Christmas Day, were approving of the Lord's Prayer, and were unopposed to such previously transgressive pursuits as card playing, drinking alcohol for health reasons, and the wearing of periwigs. Conservatives were likely to require public confessions of the conversion experience, emphasize a just and wrathful God, worry over hypocrites entering the churches, disapprove of decadent new fashions as corrupting morals, stress New England's decline in religious fervor, and resist Anglican presence and European influences.

These conceptual divergences became most apparent in 1699 when a group of Boston merchants and ministers, including John Leverett, Simon Bradstreet, and William and Thomas Brattle, became so frustrated with the old order controlled by the Mathers and Willard that they broke from the established churches and built the Brattle Street Church, which they passionately committed to the most liberal of theological trends. They invited the brilliant and personally appealing young Benjamin Colman (1673–1747), who had graduated from Harvard in 1695 and had traveled abroad and joined the Dissenters in England, to return to Boston and assume the pulpit of the new church. Knowing he would face stiff opposition from the Mathers and others, Colman had himself ordained by the Presbyterians in London and returned to Boston importing English credentials and European cosmopolitanism and elegance.

With Thomas Brattle and other reformers, Colman produced the polemical *Manifesto* (1699) and *The Gospel Order Revived* (1700), which introduced many progressive innovations into religious practice such as offering baptism to all children, giving communion to any who claimed to be justified, electing ministers by the vote of the entire membership, including women, and adopting the Anglican practice of reading the scriptures in church without comment. In general during these dynamic years, the roles of women in the churches became increasingly important. The number of published funeral sermons on women increased, and these frequently expressed admiration for the woman's intelligent conversation, her intellectual stimulation of her husband, and her wise counsel within the church and community. For example, accompanying the publication of Nathaniel Appleton's funeral sermon on Mrs. Martha Gerrish are several of her letters, which he said had guided her many correspondents and which he asserts had been as influential as many sermons. It is not surprising that many women tended to favor those ministers who gave them more encouragement and respect, and those clergy were usually among those referred to as "modern" or "liberal."

Although Colman basically adhered to Calvinist doctrines, he and his friends challenged many established rules of church polity and liturgy. Within a few months of Colman's *The Gospel Order Revived*, Increase Mather published a seventy-page treatise, *The Order of the Gospel* (1700), steadfastly defending the old ways. In response, some members of the Brattle church wrote a satirical parody of Mather's work that they called *Gospel Order Revised* (1700). Despite Mather's efforts, Colman enjoyed immediate, strong popularity, and his tolerance and peacemaking abilities soon enabled him to repair the breach with the Mathers, in whose church he had been reared and whom he admired. Cotton Mather, who liked to fancy himself a "modernist," must have helped to persuade his father to bend with the times, although Increase, who saw New England slipping toward hell, vented his distress in his most scathing jeremiad, *Ichabod. Or, a Discourse, Showing What Cause There is to Fear that the Glory of the Lord is Departing from New England* (1702). The establishment of Brattle Street Church signaled a new phase in the evolution of Puritanism that would gradually yet inexorably push the Mathers and their supporters to the margins of early eighteenth-century history.

One of the most significant developments at the turn of the century that contributed to the liberal movement was the shift in the control of the Board of Overseers of Harvard College and the establishment of Yale College in 1701. Complicated manipulations of local politics involving members of Brattle Street Church resulted in Increase Mather's resigning the Harvard presidency in 1701 and in the interim appointment of Samuel Willard. For six years, Willard, who sympathized with the Mathers but supported the Brattles, and Governor Dudley, who disliked the Mathers, laid the groundwork for the appointment of John Leverett of the Brattle Street faction to the Harvard presidency. As Harvard came increasingly under the control of the liberal faction, students of the ministry emulated Colman's discursive style and embraced the progressive ideology of those who called themselves "moderns" or "modernists." These included such influential figures as Joseph Sewall (1688–1769; Harvard, 1707), Thomas Prince (1687–1758; Harvard, 1707), and Charles Chauncy (1705–87; Harvard, 1721). In Connecticut, religious disputes and a reluctance to depend upon Harvard for their ministers led a conservative group who shared many of the positions of the Mathers to found Yale College, from which Jonathan Edwards (1703–58) graduated in 1720. Most scholars agree that, with many qualifications over finer points of theology, a line of theological tradition can be traced from Leverett's liberal Harvard through the Universalism of Chauncy to the Unitarianism of William Ellery Channing and the Transcendentalism of Ralph Waldo Emerson. On the other side, from Edwards's Yale, an opposing evangelical, and eventually fundamentalist, tradition evolved, which can be traced down to Timothy Dwight and Lyman Beecher in the nineteenth century and to many kinds of religious enthusiasts in the twentieth.

While squabbling among themselves, the clergy of the new century soon recognized that ministers of every party were losing favor. The leaders of all factions realized the need to act to prevent religion from becoming increasingly inconsequential for the busy, prospering colonists and to prevent the clergy from becoming so weak as to be at the mercy of the civil authorities and lay people. The clergy reacted in two ways: they coalesced in associations and councils in an effort to strengthen their political stature and to pass legislation controlling ordination and ministerial credentials; and they preached numerous sermons stressing the importance of a trained clergy and respect for learning and scholars.

In 1704, Benjamin Colman led the Cambridge-Boston association of ministers in a convention that drafted several proposals designed to reempower the clergy. Although the Anglican governor Joseph Dudley refused to enact their resolutions into law, the meeting of the association did embolden individual ministers to lead their congregations more firmly. In 1708, the Connecticut clergy formed the Saybrook Platform, which served the same purpose. Both conventions stirred great ferment among congregations and ministers, some of whom saw this consolidation as creating an unnecessary division between the clergy and the people by fostering clerical elitism, self-importance, and worldliness. Increase Mather opposed the association movement and held to the traditional view that the clergy possessed no more authority than laymen in ecclesiastical matters. As he saw it, the forming of associations involved "the very same path the church of Rome walked in . . . [for] their beginning was a taking of the power of privilege from the brethren."

Another result of the efforts of the clergy to regain status and influence was the emergence of special privileges and advantages for the wealthy in matters pertaining to religion and education, and such favoritism was increasingly evident in the colleges. Between 1700 and 1720, admission to the New England colleges became conspicuously dependent upon the social position of parents rather than on the piety and ability of the sons, and as a result, the quality and seriousness of the students declined. In 1722, young

Benjamin Franklin wrote a scathing attack upon Harvard, where, he said, students "were little better than Dunces and Blockheads" because parents "consulted their own purses instead of their Children's Capacities." Indeed, at both Harvard and Yale in these decades, the intelligent and pious young men who would become famous ministers, such as John Cleveland, Joseph Sewall, Thomas Prince, Charles Chauncy, and Ebenezer Pemberton, formed religious clubs that were havens of serious study within the increasingly secular and often raucous settings. The growing class division between those from monied backgrounds who attended college and became ministers and the average church members resulted in increased scorn toward the clergy in general.

The congregational clergy also suffered attacks from the Anglicans, who questioned their very credentials to be ministers. The Anglicans contended that if the New England clergy considered themselves members of the Church of England, as they claimed, then they should be ordained within the English church. The rumored weaknesses of the colleges and the general clerical Anglophilia that increased in the new century led many American ministers to doubt the legitimacy of their own ordinations. In 1723, a "Great Apostasy" occurred when President Samuel Johnson of Yale and six tutors declared their intentions to be ordained again in England by Anglican bishops. Shortly thereafter, the simple congregational ordinations were replaced by more elaborate and polished ceremonies that were more like those of the Anglicans.

In spite of all the clergy's efforts at consolidating their power and improving their collective image within the shifting culture, clericalism failed. The many bitter disputes over ministers' salaries and the rise in laypeople's insistence on their equal religious authority suggest that many congregations ultimately came to resent clerical elitism. For decades, the clergy had been calling for a renewal of piety and zeal and some had heard of "awakenings" in New Jersey, but ironically, when the revival came to New England, it served to further disempower the clergy. Beginning in the early 1720s, some small revivals in Stoddard's Connecticut River domain were held, and the movement gained momentum on October 29, 1728, when a major earthquake disrupted the province with "a most violent clap of Thunder" sounding like "a sudden and sharp crack like firing a gun." The earthquake and its many aftershocks damaged homes and businesses and left many expecting to see "the Great Day of the Son of man's appearing." For weeks, ministers reported a decline in civil contentiousness and an increase in attention to sermons. Then in 1734, a larger religious revival began in Jonathan Edwards's parish in Northampton, from which it would sweep through the Connecticut River Valley. Edwards's report on these revivals, *A Faithful Narrative of the Surprising Work of God in the Conversion of Many Hundred Souls* (1737), was widely circulated and helped prepare for the Great Awakening a few years later.

In the fall of 1740, the evangelical minister Reverend George Whitefield arrived from England and embarked upon a preaching tour of the colonies. Upon hearing of his success in the middle colonies, Colman was particularly anxious to have him preach in New England. Although some ministers were dubious about whether the passions Whitefield aroused represented genuine religious zeal, those clergy who felt that religion and clerical power were languishing looked to him for help. Colman invited Whitefield to Boston, where his success prompted dozens of New England churches to welcome him. Whitefield was soon followed by the Presbyterian revivalist from New Jersey, Gilbert Tennent, and then by dozens of other itinerant evangelicals. As many local ministers also generated their own awakenings, the spirit spread across the land, and for the first time in years, people, men in particular, urgently sought answers to religious questions. Ministers called for a reestablishment of family orders, and during the revivals men were converted in far greater numbers than women. This regenerated concern caused "awakened parishioners" to read and interpret the Bible for hours on end and to attempt to establish firmer discipline in both home and community.

At first, the ministers supported and led the revivals, but soon the people began to take control of the phenomenon by proclaiming visions, preaching spontaneously to congregations, and carrying on religious discussions in the absence of the minister, as Anne Hutchinson had done a hundred years before. Many clergy quickly saw that instead of buttressing their authority, the revivals were undermining it. Once again, the concept of perceived truth was an issue; the debate hinged on who was empowered to proclaim-speak – certain divine truths. Some ministers began to preach against the itinerant clergy and the effects of the movement, which was called the Great Awakening. Former alliances were destroyed, and a new division formed between the "New Lights," or "New Side," clergy, who supported evangelism, and the "Old Lights," or "Old Siders," who opposed the movement. Some of the New Lights, such as Colman, were theological liberals, and some of the Old Lights, like John Barnard, were conservatives; on the other hand, the liberal Charles Chauncy strongly opposed revivalism, and Jonathan Edwards was a conservative New Light Calvinist.

Despite all these upheavals, however, the general movement of the clergy during the first half of the eighteenth century, with some notable exceptions, was away from strict Calvinism and toward the liberal ideas of what would come to be called the Euro-American Enlightenment. Adhering to the old school and perhaps recognizing that congregations were reacting against clerical elitism, some ministers such as John Barnard (1681–1770), pastor at Marblehead from 1717 until 1770, spurned the modern ways. Barnard's image was that of the humble, unpretentious, country parson who labored on a small salary in equal social standing with his parishioners. His ministerial style stood in sharp contrast to the model of Benjamin Colman, and he represented the kind of clergyman to be found more often in country villages as opposed to the urban centers, where periwigs and English fashions dominated.

A friend of the Mathers, though he outlived them by four decades, Barnard helped to preserve and extend the seventeenth-century Puritan vision into the era of the American Revolution. Barnard is known today because he published several books and because his verbose, gossipy autobiography appeared in 1836. Others like him are not so well remembered, but their parishes dotted the countryside of New England. When Thomas Paine, Thomas Jefferson, John Adams, and Benjamin Franklin invoked the discourse of the jeremiad and the rituals of fast days to arouse the passions of Americans against King George, the English Antichrist, in the 1770s, they were touching emotional chords that had remained sensitive throughout the colonies due to the work of "Old Calvinists" like Barnard rather than to the moderns such as Colman and Chauncy.

Precocious in linguistics and mathematics as a youngster, Barnard had been a pupil at Boston Latin School, where he studied under the renowned schoolmaster Ezekiel Cheever, whose extraordinarily popular *A Short History of the Latin Tongue* (1709) endured as the standard text in America well into the eighteenth century. Barnard graduated from Harvard in 1700 just before the sea change to liberalism there under the Brattles and Leverett. Shortly after arriving at Marblehead, he married Anna Woodbury; the couple had no children. Like William Hubbard before him, Barnard adhered to the early Calvinist spirit but also gave substantial place to the role of reason in all affairs except conversion. A "sweet reasonableness" was the central characteristic of his sermon style. A carpenter and shipbuilder in his spare time, Barnard was a keen observer of the economic conditions in his town, and his recommendations for improving the efficiency of the fishing and shipping industries of Marblehead contributed to its notable prosperity.

When Barnard first began to preach in Boston after his graduation, the Mathers heard in his sermons too much emphasis on works and accused him of Arminianism, but they later saw their error. Although his sermons always stressed reason and diligence, he never lost sight of divine sovereignty. In his election sermon of 1734, *The Throne Established by Righteousness*, Barnard used his plain and direct style to project his nostalgic vision of a promised land of hard work, morality, and salvation. With the type of religious–economic argument that would lead Max Weber to formulate a theory about the bond between Calvinism and the rise of capitalism, Barnard proposed that government should facilitate prosperity by "due encouragement of labor and industry, by proper premiums for serviceable manufactures, by suppressing all that tends to promote idleness and prodigal wasting and consuming of estates, by a due testimony against all fraud and deceit and unrighteousness in dealings, by cultivating frugality and good husbandry." If the government does its part, Barnard reasoned, God will fulfill His sacred promise to New England still. Barnard's holy economics was good for business and for religion. When the enthusiasm of the Great Awakening affected his congregation, he brought his parishioners to a balance of fervor and reason in his *A Zeal for Good Works, Excited and Directed* (1742), recommending a "zeal guided by knowledge, tempered with prudence, and accomplished with charity."

Another representative of these country preachers is the Reverend John Wise (1652–1725), who has been called the most original prose writer in colonial America and an early American Puritan democrat. Wise too was a conservative Calvinist and a supporter of congregational church government, but he often appealed to natural law and reason. Operating within what was already identified in Europe as a tradition of American discourse – modest, folksy, and seemingly without guile – he employed a language of homey metaphors, country humor, and commonsense examples. He was born in Roxbury, Massachusetts, to a former indentured servant, and probably would not have qualified socially to attend Harvard had he been born thirty years later. After his graduation in 1673, he served as a military chaplain during King Philip's War. From 1677 to 1682, he was pastor at Hatfield; there he married Abigail Gardner, with whom he had seven children. From Hatfield, he was called to the new Chebacco parish in Ipswich, where he became famous as a defender of the rights of the colonists against royal intrusions. In 1687 he urged the people to resist the poll and property taxes imposed by Governor Edmund Andros. When they did resist and when several other towns joined them, the government imprisoned and fined Wise and stripped him of his ministry. But when Andros was overthrown in 1689, Wise was exonerated and awarded a position as chaplain in the military expedition to Quebec, during which he distinguished himself for his sound advice and inspired preaching.

Returning to Boston just before the Salem witchcraft trials, Wise displayed courage and independence in defending his former parishioners John and Elizabeth Proctor, but to no avail (see Chapter 2). In fact, Wise may have been the only minister in the country who disavowed the proceedings from the beginning. Throughout his career, he consistently fought for democratic practices in government and the church. During the movement for clerical associations, Wise was in the opposition and wrote two books refuting the notion of a union of clergy as being narrow and undemocratic.

The first of these works, *The Churches Quarrel Espoused*, reportedly appeared in 1710, but the extant copies were published in New York in 1713 and reprinted in Boston in 1715. His second book, *A Vindication of the Government of New England Churches*, appeared in 1717 in Boston. In these tracts, Wise directs his arguments to ordinary church members, employing common images and pointed humor to sting his colleagues. Warning that the clergy's proposals "be but a Calf now, yet in time it may grow (being of a Thirsty Nature) to become a sturdy Ox that will know no Whoa," he charges that with their plan to consolidate power in associations the clergy have "Our Pope't the Pope Himself." Pretending to be making small repairs in the Cambridge Platform, the ministers, in Wise's view, were really dismantling it: they came with trowel in hand "to plaster over a chink or two, . . . but in Reality they have in their other hand a formidable *Maul* . . . to break Down the Building." Regarding one complicated proposal to emerge from the association meetings, he mocks, "a Riddle I found it, and a Riddle *I leave it*." In response to the clergy's argument that an association was needed to help ministers resolve disagreements that might arise in particular parishes, Wise said that any decent minister should not need "a Covering of Fig-Leaves" or a "Harbor to Cowards and Fools": "if men are plac'd at Helm, to steer in all weather which Blows, they must not be afraid of the Waves, or a wet Coat." No one ever published a reply to Wise's books, and they remained the last public word against the association movement.

Like Barnard, Wise also endorsed a form of sacred economics, and in his last publication he illustrates the economic side of his equation of religion and finance. In *A Word of Comfort to a Melancholy Country; Or, the Bank of Credit Erected in Massachusetts Fairly Defended* (1721), he defends the establishment of a private land bank that would issue paper currency as a way of stimulating the economy and unifying the colony's residents in active commerce and good faith. In Wise's schema, faith in an invisible God and trust in the bank's promised reserves operate in tandem for salvation and prosperity.

Whereas men like Barnard and Wise were known for their homey, direct language and humble personal style, Benjamin Colman was urbane, witty, and sophisticated and known for his poetic constructions, variety of diction, and eloquence. Born in Boston in 1673, to Elizabeth and William Colman, Colman studied under Ezekiel Cheever at Boston Latin School and graduated from Harvard in 1692. After receiving his MA in 1695, he departed for England but was captured by pirates and imprisoned for several months in France. He finally arrived in England sick and destitute but was soon taken in by fellow Protestant Dissenters who arranged for him to preach at Bath, where he spent two years. During his four years in England, Colman became acquainted with poets and artists and was befriended and tutored in the manners of London society by the poet Elizabeth Singer. Later, he encouraged the poetic pursuits of his own daughters (see Chapter 4). Upon his return to Boston and the establishment of his ministry, Colman married Jane Clark, with whom he had a son, who died in infancy, Jane, the poet, and Abigail. When his first wife died, Colman married the widow Sarah Clark (no relation to Jane) in 1732, and after she died, he married another widow, Mary Frost, in 1745. In a career that spanned nearly fifty years, Colman fashioned a delicate theological and political compromise by retaining the Calvinist doctrines of the founders while allowing the external forms of the church to be adapted to the psychological needs and social desires of his eighteenth century congregation. After the initial disturbance caused by his arrival, he formed friendships with most of the established ministers of Boston, and he even preached the funeral sermons for the Mathers and for many of their opponents, including Stoddard, Thomas Brattle, Dudley, and Leverett. He corresponded with Jonathan Edwards and welcomed Whitefield and Tennent to Boston. In the pulpit, Colman performed in a style that contemporaries called "grand and polite," and he encouraged his parishioners to think confidently of themselves as saints who had been lifted by grace above anxiety. While Increase Mather was still ranting about sin and backsliding, Colman recommended balance, calm, and assurance in Christ.

In his most famous series of sermons, *A Practical Discourse on the Parable of the Ten Virgins* (1707), Colman urged his listeners to try to "resemble virgins in purity" because then they will benefit from the joys of being with Christ in life and death. In selecting this biblical text, on which Thomas Shepard had preached a famous sermon series between 1636 and 1640, Colman shrewdly allied himself with the Puritan heritage and with Shepard's renowned balance of fervor and reason. Rather than focusing upon the evils of sin and damnation, he attempted to entice souls, with a degree of eroticism, to the beauty of Christ:

> Like espoused virgins we should be expecting, desiring, waiting, and preparing for the coming of our Lord... How much more should we with raptures think of and wish for heaven, the place and time of full communion and vision? In this we groan earnestly in the hope and expectance of an expecting love, the preparations against the day of the consummations of our desires, and how joyfully it is welcomed when arrived; nor is there any indecency herein. Can the bride forget to provide her ornaments and attire against the time? No more the believer his, the graces of the spirit of God, and the rightness which is through the faith in Christ.... Why should we not run to meet the smiling vision, as those that are found alive at Christ's second coming will fly up to meet him in the air?

Even as he apologizes for the possible "indecency" of the sexual implications of the image of the groaning, impatient bride, Colman proceeds in his balanced and melodious prose to images of comfort and safety. Ordinary emotions presented in fluid and clear language inscribed Colman's writing with an urbane grace that set it apart from the choppy and relatively crude directness of ministers such as Barnard, Wise, and Increase Mather.

Just as stylistic changes had begun to appear in the early eighteenth-century sermons, other writers were developing new techniques in other genres. For modern readers, one of the liveliest and most delightful pieces of prose narrative of the period is *The Journal of Madam Knight*, written by Sarah Kemble Knight (1666–1727) in 1704 and 1710 and later edited and published in 1825 by Theodore Dwight, Jr. Sarah Kemble was born in Boston in 1666 to Thomas Kemble, a merchant, and Elizabeth Treice. Although it is not known to which Boston church the Kembles belonged, it is very likely that as the daughter of a successful merchant, Sarah grew up hearing Puritan sermons in one of the congregational churches. From her journal, it is evident that she had associations with several ministers, for she makes a point of visiting clergy on her journey. Sometime before 1689, she married the much older Richard Knight, who was a shipmaster and London agent for an American firm; they had one child, Elizabeth, in 1689. It is also likely that the financially comfortable Knights would have been members of one of the major Boston churches in the 1690s.

Some years before her husband died in 1706, Knight was forced to assume many of his business responsibilities. Within the context of the growing social and religious acceptance of public roles for women, she kept a shop and house on Moon Street in Boston, took in boarders, and taught children handwriting. Because she learned much about business and the law from her work, Knight decided to travel to New Haven in 1704 to help settle the estate of her cousin for his widow. Recognizing that it was rare for a woman to undertake such a journey alone, she decided to keep a narrative of her travels. Her journey covers two periods: from October 2 through October 7 and several selected days between December 6 and January 6, 1704–05.

Adopting techniques of the mock-epic and elements of the picaresque, Knight wrote a humorous, direct, and concrete account having only traces of the moral didacticism that forms the center of most Puritan autobiographies. Highly self-conscious as a narrator, even self-mocking and ironic at times, Knight demonstrates a self-reflective awareness that her narrative violates conventions. On her second night on the road, for example, she and her guide enter a dark forest. In language that anticipates the techniques of the gothic style later in the century, she recalls this frightening experience before making the religious point her contemporaries might expect:

> Now returned my distressed apprehensions of the place where I was:
> the dolesome woods, my Company next to none, Going I knew not
> wither, and encompassed with Terrifying darkness; the least of which
> was enough to startle a more Masculine course. Added to which [were]
> the Reflections, as in the afternoon of the day, that my Call was very
> Questionable which till then I had not so Prudently as I ought considered.

Although she makes it clear here, though as an afterthought, that her fear has aroused a spiritual concern about her calling, when they reach a clearing at the top of a hill, she does not first praise God for deliverance; instead, she is enraptured with "the Sight of that fair Planet," the moon, to which she then writes a poem. When she does credit God for her safe return home at the end of the journal, she correspondingly sounds more like a Franklinian Deist than a proper Puritan: "But [I] desire sincerely to adore my Great Benefactor for thus graciously carrying forth and returning in safety his unworthy handmaid."

In earthy language and with robust energy, Knight records her experiences with her guides, saucy servants in country inns, ignorant, gruff innkeepers, and boisterous tenants who kept her awake at night. She recounts her delight in the beauty of nature but also interpolates troubling images of rural poverty:

> This little Hut was one of the wretchedest I ever saw [as] a habitation for
> human creatures. It was supported with shores enclosed with Clapboards,
> laid on Lengthways, and so much asunder, that the Light come throu'
> every where.... The floor the bare earth; no windows.... The family were
> the old man, his wife and two Children; all and every part being the
> picture of poverty.... I Blest myself that I was not one of this miserable
> crew.

Although she tends to foreground consciousness of economics and class, she frequently displays the prejudices of her own class in her view of the world; her descriptions of country "bumpkins" are forerunners of later depictions of the backwoodsmen in works of American humor. Sharing the racial prejudices of her white society, she accepted slavery, and she wrote with scorn of Native Americans: "There are every where in the Towns as I passed, a Number of Indians the Natives of the Country, and are the most savage of all the savages of that kind that I had ever Seen: little or no care taken (as I heard upon enquiry) to make them otherwise." The details she selected to report about Native Americans correspond to her received stereotypes of their sexual promiscuity, general immorality, and need for white supervision.

Knight often expresses her sense of moral superiority, but she also makes religion the butt of her humor. On her third day, she and her guide endure a thirty-mile stretch of highway with no accommodations. When she complains, her guide tells her that they would reach "Mr. Devills" in a few miles. She answers in the terminology of Puritan sermons: "But I questioned whether we ought to go to the Devil to be helpt out of affliction. However, like the rest of Deluded souls that post to ye Infernal den, We make all possible speed to this Devil's Habitation, where alighting in full assurance of good accommodations we were going in." Her description of this stop at the Devil's house mingles elements of the journey motifs of Greek mythology and the typology of spiritual passage in Christian conversion narratives that had been used in such works as *Everyman*, the *Divine Comedy*, and *Pilgrim's Progress*. In a later episode, in another comic jibe at religion, she describes the prosperity of the town of Fairfield and mocks the constant controversies over clerical salaries: "They [the townspeople] have abundance of sheep, whose very Dung brings them, great gain, with part of which they pay their Parson's salary, And they Grudge that, preferring their Dung before their minister."

It is not known if Knight produced other writings, for if she did, they have been lost. When her daughter married into the powerful Livingston family of Connecticut, Knight moved to New London in 1714, where she owned several farms and an inn. Her success as a businesswoman in these ventures, which surely must have been partly the result of her sharp wit and keen observations of society, enabled her to leave a considerable estate when she died in 1727.

Mary White Rowlandson's captivity narrative and Sarah Kemble Knight's journal both illustrate and critique dominant culture and ideology. Another substantial autobiographical text by a woman before 1750 similarly enriches early American literature. Although Elizabeth Sampson Ashbridge (1713–55) was a Quaker in the middle colonies and not a New England Puritan, her work, *Some Account of the Fore Part of the Life of Elizabeth Ashbridge* (1774), deserves mention within the context of Puritan literature because in her search for the best religion, Ashbridge explicitly considered Calvinism and rejected it, and her reasons for doing so suggest some of the problems the congregational ministers encountered during the period.

Elizabeth Sampson was born in Middlewich, Cheshire, England, in 1713 to the physician Thomas Sampson and his wife, Mary. She was the only child of this union, but her mother, a widow, had a son and daughter by her first husband. Perhaps Elizabeth inherited a propensity for travel from her father, who, she reports, "sometime after my birth, . . . took to the sea and followed his Profession on board ship, in many long voyages, till I arrived to the age of twelve years." Similar to the tales of adventure and hardship of the romances of the period such as those of Defoe's *Moll Flanders*, Richardson's *Clarissa Harlowe*, and Susanna Rowson's *Charlotte Temple*, Ashbridge's narrative recounts complicated events that leave her a woman on her own in the world. When she was fourteen, she eloped with a poor stocking-weaver, whom she called the "darling of my heart." When he died five months later, Ashbridge's family exiled her to Ireland to live with Quakers, whom she initially found repulsive, a point that has ironic reverberations later in her narrative. She wanted to return home, but when her father refused to forgive and accept her, she arranged to go to America as an indentured servant.

During her years of indentureship, Ashbridge served different male masters, including a clergyman who, she reports, tried to seduce her. She observed that many ministers displayed an external righteousness whereas they were secretly corrupt and immoral. Still, on her quest for her spiritual calling, she investigated various current religions. While she was living in New Jersey, she learned of a trial of a Presbyterian minister accused of drunkenness, and she attended in the hope of learning something about that Protestant sect. Observing "great Divisions among the People about who Should be their Shepherd," she quickly grew disillusioned with the Presbyterian clergy: "I greatly Pitied their [the congregation's] Condition, for I now saw beyond the Men made Ministers, & what they Preached for." Ashbridge observes that the main interest of the clergy was to gain the highest salary but that the congregation could not see this motive because "the prejudice of Education, which is very prevalent, blinded their eyes."

In the controversy, some argued for keeping the old minister, others were for hiring "a young man had upon trial for some weeks," and "a third Party was for sending for one from New England." One member objected to the high cost of the last option: "Sir, when we have been at the Expense (which is no Small Matter) of fetching this Gentleman from New England, may be he'll not stay with us." When another answered that the way to make him stay is to "give him a good Salary," Ashbridge laments "these Mercenary creatures: they are all Actuated by one & the same thing, even the Love of Money, & not the regard of Souls." She goes on to explain the bidding war for ministers that involved hiring a famous minister away from another parish, where the people had "almost Impoverished themselves to keep him." Rejecting Presbyterianism, she says, "their Ministry all proceeded from one Cause" – "the Shepard that regards the fleece more than the flock, in whose mouths are Lies."

In a brisk and lively style, *The Life of Elizabeth Ashbridge* depicts her unusual experiences, including her brief career on the New York stage and her marriage to a schoolmaster named Sullivan who abused her. After her second husband died, Ashbridge worked as a seamstress to pay off his many debts. She then married Aaron Ashbridge in 1746, converted to Quakerism, and was ordained; with Aaron, she then returned as a Quaker missionary to Ireland, where she died in 1755. Although she moved away from

Puritan New England geographically, her observations and opinions on the clergy exemplify the reasons for the increasing anticlericalism and suggest the magnitude of the problem that the New England clergy and their middle-colony colleagues faced at the time. Ashbridge's text reveals how a bold and perspicacious woman in early America could see "beyond the Men made Ministers," demystify masculine authority, and feel compassion for those whose educations had "blinded their eyes."

In the face of such critiques, one clergyman who struggled to preserve a positive image for the New England clergy both by his personal example as a temperate, sober leader devoted to the needs of his flock and through his writings was the Reverend Charles Chauncy (1705–87). Author of dozens of books and pastor of the First Church of Boston from 1727 until 1787, Chauncy played an important role in almost all of the formative events of his time: the French and Indian Wars, the resistance to an Anglican episcopacy in America, the Stamp Act controversy, the rise of science, the American Revolution, and the beginnings of Deism and Unitarianism. Whereas Edwards has been identified as a literary genius and his works have been established in the American literary canon, Chauncy's contributions as a thinker and author have remained in Edwards's shadow. In the views of some historians, however, Chauncy – along with Franklin – was much more the representative eighteenth-century American, and his career and writings bear examination in their own right.

Like Cotton Mather, Chauncy was born into a Boston family with impressive leadership and clerical credentials. He was the great-grandson of the second president of Harvard, the grandson of a controversial London minister, and the son of a leading Boston merchant. His mother, Sarah Walley, was the daughter of a Massachusetts Supreme Court judge. Chauncy graduated from Harvard in 1721, a year before Jonathan Edwards graduated from Yale, and after six more years of study and teaching, he joined Thomas Foxcroft at Boston's First Church, which people had come to call the "Old Brick." Widowed twice, he was married three times, first in 1727 to Elizabeth Hirst, with whom he had three children, then to Elizabeth Townsend in 1738, and last to Mary Stoddard in 1760.

The congregation of the Old Brick was made up of wealthy, educated, and by then long-established Boston families. Chauncy, who was by temperament and intellectual leaning a strong advocate of the New England congregational way and of Calvinism, faced the problem that had troubled New England clergy ever since the 1650s. He sought to maintain his own integrity as a strict Calvinist while preaching to a congregation that prized worldly comforts and modern ideas. Ranting sermons with images of hellfire were not to the taste of the kind of people who attended the Old Brick, yet for clergy simply to assure such people of their salvation because they were financially comfortable and performed works of charity was to approach Arminianism. Although Chauncy believed that he avoided an Arminian doctrine of works, religious historians still debate whether Edwards was not correct in detecting that heresy in Chauncy's reassurances to his wealthy parishioners.

Advocating a "commonsense" approach to theology that would gain currency among congregationalists influenced by the Scottish Common Sense Realist philosophy in the latter decades of the century, Chauncy encouraged his congregation to "trust in Christ the Redeemer" and not to fret over the "metaphysical niceties" of theology. Within his church, he sought harmony and temperance in all things, and he tried to avoid religious disputes. In his own personal life, he also practiced a strict moderation, for which he was greatly admired. Conservative in doctrine but liberal in church polity and membership, Chauncy represented the balanced establishment ideal. As a friend admiringly described him, Chauncy was "little of stature. God gave him a slender, feeble body, a very powerful, vigorous mind, and strong passions; and he managed them all exceedingly well. His manners were plain and downright, – dignified, bold, and imposing. In conversation with his friends he was pleasant, social, and very instructive." Certainly, it was in admiration of his will and endurance and not for his physical size, that Chauncy himself came to be called Old Brick.

The New England clergy had been hoping for a renewal of religion for many decades, and perhaps for that reason Chauncy at first joined nearly all of his fellow ministers in welcoming the revivals in 1740 and 1741. By 1742, however, he had become apprehensive that those being converted "placed their Religion so much in the Heart and Fervour of their Passions, that they too much neglect their Reason and Judgement." Whereas some antirevivalist clergy opposed the movement because they feared loss of their authority to lay enthusiasts, Chauncy's motives appear to have been less self-interested. He sincerely believed that the "religious Phrenzy" and "ecstatic violence" would destroy the "reasonable peace of soul and mind" of individuals and disrupt the harmony of communities, which he cherished as the two great personal and social benefits of Christianity. He also found those converted by the revivals to be overly confident, proud, "impatient of contradiction, censorious, and uncharitable." When Edwards published *Some Thoughts Concerning the Present Revival of Religion in New England* in 1742 defending the Great Awakening, Chauncy, who had had some previous exchanges with Edwards over these issues, took up the challenge to be the spokesman of the Old Light liberals.

To gather evidence for his writing against Edwards and the Great Awakening, Chauncy traveled throughout New England in 1743 recording accounts of the "convulsions and distortions" and "quaking and trembling" that resulted from "deluded imagination[s]." Composed as a rebuttal or "antidote" to Edwards's work, Chauncy's Seasonable Thoughts on the State of Religion in New England attempts to reinscribe the traditional Puritan position: "there is the Religion of the Understanding and Judgment, and Will as well as of the Affections, and if little account is made of the former while great Stress is laid upon the latter, it can't be but People should run into Disorders." Chauncy's position on the perennial head versus heart debate within Puritanism seemed perfectly reasonable to many of Chauncy's congregation – but not to Thomas Foxcroft, his colleague in his own church, who continued to support the revivals. It is a mark of the even temperaments of both men that they remained cooperative over the years in spite of their opposition on this and on other divisive issues. In subsequent works against enthusiasm, Chauncy tried to expose the dangers posed by the untrained, itinerant clergy, the weaknesses of lay preachers, and the damage that religious disagreements might do to the churches in general.

In his preaching, Chauncy always advocated the plain style, and he prided himself in avoiding rhetoric and "all pomp of words, all show of learned subtlety by artful use of the scholastic, systematical, and metaphysical terms." Oratorical eloquence, he felt, had no place in the pulpit, and he said of his own sermons: "If I have wrote in a mystical, perplexed, unintelligible way, I own it is a fault not to be overlooked." Thus, one of his main objections to the New Light preachers was that they were mere performers, resorting to inflamed theatrical rhetoric and pulpit histrionics to stir the passions instead of informing the mind.

Although Chauncy believed that it was unnecessary to burden his congregation with the details of religious and philosophical thought, he held that sermons, though plain and lucid, should be founded upon deep and extensive learning. In his own constant study, he labored to reconcile the fundamental doctrines of congregationalism with new developments in philosophy and with the spiritual needs of the people. Relying heavily upon John Locke and the Scottish Common Sense philosophers such as Francis Hutcheson, Thomas Reid, and Henry Home, Lord Kames, he composed a series of theological works that reveal rather remarkable shifts in his theological positions over time. Viewing God as a benevolent "Divine Administrator," he developed quite radical ideas, such as the rejection of the arbitrary God of Calvinism and the elimination of the doctrines of election and Original Sin, which he perceived as casting infants into hell for "a sin which they certainly had no hand in." Rejecting predestination, Chauncy said: "A more shocking idea can scarce be given to the Deity than that which represents him as arbitrarily dooming the greater part of the race of men to eternal misery." Although he did not eliminate other fundamental ideas – such as the existence of hell, the need for faith and works for salvation, and the necessity that the sinner undergo painful repentance – he came to believe in universal salvation, or what came to be called Universalism, holding that Christ had died for everyone's sins and that God wants all to be saved. Thus, in doctrine and polity, Chauncy led the First Church of Boston from the seventeenth-century world of the Mathers toward the Deism of Jefferson and Franklin and the Unitarianism of Emerson. By the time of his death, Chauncy had come to be viewed as the most influential minister of his time and one of the most significant figures in eighteenth-century America. In the twentieth century, Chauncy's contributions have been much overshadowed by the luminous work of Jonathan Edwards, whose mysticism, poetic vision, and originality informed some of the most challenging and intriguing texts in American literature, which have had particular appeal to critics of the last fifty years.

Born to the Reverend Timothy and Esther Stoddard Edwards in East Windsor, Connecticut, on October 5, 1703, Jonathan was the middle child and only boy in a family of eleven children. He was the grandson of Solomon Stoddard, whose liberal church admission practices had kept him in long-standing controversies with Edward Taylor and Increase Mather. Known as the "Pope [and sometimes the 'bastard'] of the Connecticut River Valley," Stoddard was a formidable, rebellious figure for Edwards to emulate. Upon graduating from theologically conservative Yale in 1722, Edwards spent four more years there teaching and completing his MA before answering Stoddard's call in 1727 to be his assistant at Northampton. In the same year, Edwards married Sarah Pierrepont, with whom he had eleven children.

A devoted student of Calvin and the early Puritan theologians, Edwards was a firm believer in the religion of his ancestors in an age of its diminishing power. To increase church membership Stoddard had opened communion to all who wished for conversion as early as the 1670s, but the more theologically conservative young Edwards recognized that this tactic had only temporary positive effects and potential long-term risks. Similarly, in Edwards's view, ministers like Chauncy who preached moral propriety as a likely path to heaven were deluding their congregations in order to retain them. In contrast, Edwards always directed his philosophical gaze toward God, heaven, and eternity. Within his eschatological schema, Edwards believed the present weakened condition of Christianity in his New England to be a mere moment of lapse in sacred history. As he sought to understand God's transcendent design for humanity, Edwards investigated the writings of Locke, Newton, and other contemporary philosophers. In so doing, he formulated a synthesis of Calvinism and Enlightenment ideas that in complexity and inventiveness far eclipsed the comparatively unsophisticated thought of Chauncy and that continues to challenge theologians and intellectual historians today.

After his personal spiritual struggles with the notion of God's divine sovereignty and his subsequent conversion, Edwards became committed to the idea of salvation by faith and grace alone and to the prime importance of a personally felt and understood conversion experienced through the senses as well as the reason. Espousing a position reminiscent of the original Pauline spirit of the first-generation fathers, Edwards believed that grace empowers every saint with a daily vision of the beauty of nature, the joy of salvation, and the peace of God's heavenly glory. Thus, the sanctified Christian should not give primacy to moral duties, good works, and tests of conversion. Such conscious human efforts are useful and good, but they are secondary to the ways that the lives of the saved are conspicuously transformed by grace. In their gracious ecstasy, the converted will necessarily bring order to their families and virtue to those around them. For Edwards, a congregation of such souls radiates sacred energy and assurance.

To revitalize this message for the early 1730s, Edwards invented a new language of sensory experience that stirred the passions of his country congregation. Although he actually distrusted enthusiasm and presented his sermons in a calm, deliberate manner, his use of innovative imagery to expound familiar themes struck his parishioners with a force they had never experienced. His best-known sermon, *Sinners in the Hands of an Angry God* (1741), is a jeremiad full of fire and brimstone, but that text is not typical of Edwards's style, and he reportedly delivered it in a monotone. More often he tried to make salvation and grace desirable through an invocation of positive, enticing imagery.

What Edwards's congregation also heard from him was news of the beauty and peace of the new life of grace, as in *God Glorified in the Work of Redemption, By the Greatness of Man's Dependence* (1731), which stresses human powerlessness in the process of salvation. After reading a series of scriptures depicting the saved as a "new creature," "created again," "the new man," "raising from the dead," Edwards explains:

> Yea, it is a more glorious work of power than mere creation, or raising a dead body to life, in that the effect attained is greater and more excellent. That holy and happy being, and spiritual life which is produced in the work of conversion, is a far greater and more glorious effect, than mere being and life. And the state from whence the change is made – a death in sin, a total corruption of nature, and depth of misery – is far more remote from the state attained, than mere death or non-entity.

After a few years of hearing this message of humanity's dependency and God's saving grace, the people in Edwards's parish began to experience the "surprising conversions" that marked the beginning of the Great Awakening. In 1735, in response to Benjamin Colman's request for an accounting of the phenomenon, Edwards wrote a letter to Colman explaining that over the course of the last few years he had noticed that the town had "gradually been reforming," that the "contentious disposition" had quieted, that "young people . . . left off their frolicking," and that "heads of families . . . agreed every one to restrain their families." He had found a "remarkable religious concern" and new questions "about Arminianism [and] the way to salvation." He also indicates that he preached on grace and salvation, which was "found fault with by many elsewhere" but "was most evidently attended with a very remarkable blessing from heaven to the souls of the people in this town." Soon, many, including "those that were most disposed to contemn vital and experimental religion," such as the "highest families," were "affected remarkably" by "the Spirit of God." Edwards reports that this enthusiasm spread quickly to surrounding towns, where people were "confessing their faults to one another" and "neglecting their worldly business" in order to "mind nothing but religion." So powerful were the emotions that many were weakened physically, as were "three young persons in this town walking together of the dying love of Christ till they all fainted away." Edwards also notes an element that must have been good news to many clergy during a time of growing anticlericalism: that since the awakenings began, the people "have greater respect to ministers" so that "there is scarcely a minister preaches here but gets their esteem and affection." Edwards concludes that his report is a true "account of this affair which Satan has so much misrepresented."

A few weeks later, Edwards wrote to Colman again but this time less confidently, for he had to report a tragic event that had soon cooled his congregation's enthusiasm for the revival. Edward's own uncle, Joseph Hawley, had committed suicide as a result of his "deep melancholy" and "despairing thoughts," apparently stirred by his concern about "the condition of his soul." But rather than becoming wary of the revival, Edwards remained committed to it: "the devil took the advantage and drove him into despairing thoughts . . . Satan seems to be in a great rage at this breaking forth of the work of God. . . . We have appointed a day of fasting. . . . by reason of . . . other appearances of Satan's rage amongst us against poor souls." Hawley's death and the other acts of "Satan's rage" seem to have stunned many, for the excitement subsided by 1736, and it would be five years before Edward's church would experience another awakening.

In the meantime, reports of revivalism began to arrive in Massachusetts from England and from the American southern and middle colonies, where preachers such as George Whitefield, Gilbert Tennent, and James Davenport employed powerful oratory to engage and convert hundreds at a time. Reports of excesses of emotionalism led Edwards to repeat his earlier warnings against deliberate ministerial attempts to appeal only to the affections, yet he did invite Whitefield to preach in his parish and did himself employ terrifying rhetoric and imagery in some of his sermons of this period, including *Sinners in the Hands of an Angry God* (1741) and *The Future Punishment of the Wicked* (1741). Because of his belief in divine sovereignty and his expectation that the Apocalypse was imminent, Edwards could not conceive that the evidence of the Holy Spirit was other than the work of Providence. When critics of the revival, such as Chauncy, began to berate the emotional excesses, Edwards became the leading spokesman of the Awakening forces. Even after the revival cooled and the beginning of King George's War became the focus of public attention in 1744, Edwards continued to defend the Great Awakening in his *Treatise Concerning Religious Affections* (1746).

In a series of sermons he composed while preparing that work, Edwards presented in greater detail the ideas on church membership and salvation he had been developing. The members of his congregation were shocked to discover that he had rejected his grandfather's liberal policies of open church membership and communion. People were especially disturbed by Edwards's proposal that the church must revert to public professions of faith for full church membership. The parishioners were attached to Stoddardism, which had distinguished the Northampton parish for fifty years, and they were furious with Edwards for his arbitrary changes in the church rules. The controversy smoldered between 1744 and 1748 because no one presented themselves for membership, but the issue exploded in 1748, revealing that Edwards's congregation had turned bitterly against him. Historians and Edwards's biographers observe that other factors contributed to the break, such as local factional jealousies, various resentments, and a scandal involving a "dirty book." Edwards discovered that some young people had been circulating *Midwifery Rightly Represented*, and even though the group included some from the families of prominent church members, Edwards read their names from the pulpit and chastised them for immorality. In the months that followed, the outraged parents banded with those parishioners who had begun to doubt Edwards's spiritual leadership and formed a faction that outnumbered Edwards's supporters. While Edwards was in his study developing his most impressive ideas about psychology, nature, and God, which would bring him lasting fame, his congregation was plotting his expulsion. By 1750, Edwards's church voted for his dismissal, and after delivering his famous *Farewell Sermon*, in which he said that God would decide who was right, he stepped down.

The demise of Edwards's ministry served as resounding evidence to Chauncy and other Old Lights that Edwards and the Great Awakening were certified failures. After turning down several offers to move to other parishes, including the option of starting a second church for his supporters in

Northampton, Edwards made the surprising choice of electing to take Sarah and his eleven children to the isolated frontier town of Stockbridge, where he became a missionary to the Housatonic tribe. During his seven years there, Edwards continued to experience many difficulties in the area of public relations. The Solomon Williams clan, a white family who wielded great power in Indian affairs and who antagonized the Indians, made Edwards's missionary work difficult, and the outbreak of the French and Indian Wars in 1754 made conditions dangerous. Still, in spite of his trials, Edwards spent these years of exile in his study composing the great works of his life. Although most of these books would not be published until after his death, he did manage to have his *Freedom of the Will* printed in Boston in 1754. This impressive work added so substantially to his reputation among New Light clergymen that in 1757 he was invited to be president of the College of New Jersey (later Princeton). At first Edwards resisted, saying that he lacked talent for the job, suffered poor health, and wished to remain absorbed in his studies. At that time, a college president taught a full schedule of courses in addition to his administrative duties. Offering to reduce his teaching load, the trustees persuaded him to accept, and he was inaugurated in February 1758. An outbreak of smallpox that winter led Edwards and the trustees to decide that he should be inoculated; however, soon after the inoculation, he contracted an infection and died on March 22, 1758.

Edwards's remarkable and, in many ways, regrettable public career provides an important context for understanding his towering intellectual achievement. His less public, inner narrative really began in his childhood home in East Windsor, Connecticut, where both his father, who conducted the parish grammar school, and his mother instructed their precocious son, preparing him to enter Yale at the age of twelve. From early on, Edwards seemed inclined toward scientific investigation and philosophical argumentation. Edwards's protege and early biographer Samuel Hopkins reported that "in his second year at college, and thirteen of his age, he read Locke on the human understanding with great delight and profit." It was an important innovation that Locke and Newton were introduced in 1717 at Yale, where Edwards then studied them intensively. Edwards disagreed with Locke on many issues, but he borrowed from both thinkers and found Locke's *An Essay Concerning Human Understanding* especially valuable. Edwards's earliest known intellectual investigations were in some short scientific papers: "On Insects," "Of the Rainbow," "Of Being," "Of Atoms," a paper on light rays, a series of essays entitled "Natural Philosophy," and his "Notes on the Mind." These early writings display a fascination with nature that characterizes much of his writing. He was particularly interested in spiders, which he described with obvious delight:

> Of all insects no one is more wonderful than the Spider.... they may be
> seen well enough by an observing eye at noon Day by their Glistening
> against the sun and what is more wonderful I know I have several times
> seen in a very Calm and serene Day ... multitudes of little shining webs
> and Glistening Strings of a Great Length and at such a height that one
> would think they were tack'd to the Sky.

Although Edwards ultimately saw no conflict between such enthusiasm for
physical nature and the Calvinist rejection of the world, he did think more
deeply about such pleasure and would return to analyze the ambiguity of
human delight in nature in his so-called *Personal Narrative*, published in *The
Life and Character of The Late Reverend Mr. Jonathan Edwards* (1765).

In the *Personal Narrative*, Edwards describes his conversion experience
in language through which he attempts to capture the transcendent, even
mystical, quality of the effects of grace. Although the *Personal Narrative* is
structured, rather like earlier Puritan conversion accounts, by his struggle
to discover the truth of his calling, the work departs significantly from the
traditional form in conveying passion for God in terms of human affection
and love. He explains that the greatest obstacles to his conversion were his
"objections to the doctrine of God's sovereignty," but he gradually came to
see that "the doctrine has very often appeared exceeding pleasant, bright,
and sweet." This change enabled him to read the scriptures with a "new
sense," which thereby prepared his heart for grace. After talking to his father
one day, he was walking in the pasture and "looking up on the sky and
clouds, [when] there came into my mind so sweet a sense of the glorious
majesty and *grace* of God that I know not how to express." Whereas before
his experience he used to shrink from thunderstorms, he now "felt God,
so to speak, at the first appearance of a thunder storm; ... and [could] hear
the majestic and awful voice of God's thunder. [And] while thus engaged,
it always seemed natural to me to sing, or chant for my meditations; so,
to speak my thoughts in soliloquies with a singing voice." Having had this
awakening, he became enchanted by its beauty: "It appeared to me that
there was nothing in it but was ravishingly lovely; the highest beauty and
amiableness ... a divine beauty." For him now, the natural world is infused
with elements of the supernatural:

> The soul of a true Christian ... appeared like such a little white flower as
> we see in the spring of the year; low and humble on the ground, opening
> its bosom to receive the pleasant beams of the sun's glory; rejoicing as it
> were in a calm rapture; diffusing around a sweet fragrancy; standing
> peacefully and lovingly in the midst of other flowers ... to drink in the
> light of the sun.

As an artist of language, Edwards appears to take pleasure in the words themselves as he invokes natural imagery to conflate the realms of the worldly and the divine. He found the image of light, in particular, to be an apt metaphor for evoking the sublime and mystical. His technique for capturing reverie in language is most evident in the famous passage he composed about his beloved future spouse, Sarah, at about the time of his conversion. He praises her for her love of God and also for her "sweetness, calmness, and universal benevolence of mind," which led her to "go about from place to place singing sweetly" and to walk in the fields and to seem "to have someone invisible always conversing with her." After having had years of the aging Reverend Solomon Stoddard in the pulpit, the congregation of Northampton must have been quite startled to have young Edwards and his wife preaching, singing, and expressing the ecstasy of the "new life" of salvation.

Edwards's first two great sermons of doctrinal analysis were *God Glorified in the Work of Redemption, By the Greatness of Man's Dependence* (1731) and *A Divine and Supernatural Light, Immediately Imparted to the Soul by the Spirit of God* (1734). The first is a systematic explication of the doctrine of divine sovereignty in which Edwards uses biblical imagery to set forth his arguments against Arminianism: "But now when fallen man is made holy, it is from mere and arbitrary grace: God may forever deny holiness to the fallen creature if he pleases." But in the second sermon Edwards comes close to expressing his responses to the mystical experience of the moments of his encounter with grace that he had recorded in his *Personal Narrative*.

Here, his language reveals a struggle for words adequate to describe the ineffable nature of his religious experiences. His focus moves to the physical and sensual changes after spiritual rebirth, and he distinguishes between "natural men," who have not experienced grace, and those illuminated by it. Using highly figurative and lyrical language, he struggles to find words capable of conveying the complexity of his emotions. There is a vast difference, he says, between the perception of one whose imagination has been "affected" by "the story of Christ," which like a "romance" or a "stage play" may create strong feelings that are "wholly graceless," and the true vision of a saint. To describe this new life, Edwards moves to employ a poetic language that many readers have seen as anticipating the style of the Transcendentalists:

> There is a difference between having a rational judgment that honey is
> sweet, and having a sense of its sweetness. . . . there is a difference between
> believing that a person is beautiful, and having a sense of his beauty. . . .
> There is a wide difference between mere speculative rational judging
> any thing excellent, and having a sense of its sweetness and beauty.
> The former rests only in the head, speculation only is concerned in it;
> but the heart is concerned in the latter.

The person who has grace has a "sensibleness of the excellency of divine objects, dwells upon them with delight"; in this new state all things are "sweet and pleasant to his soul," and the person "feels pleasure in the apprehension [of] the beauty and sweetness of the objects."

Regarding the supernatural light itself, he is at pains to make the point that the light does not depend upon reading the scriptures or upon anything in the natural world but comes entirely from the supernatural. The difference between seeing with the power of the divine light and seeing without it is like beholding "the objects on the face of the earth when the light of the sun is cast upon them" and viewing "them in a dim starlight or twilight." Edwards's use of natural imagery to emphasize the world's beauty as reflective of God's glory and his expression of what has been called his "aesthetic ecstasy" introduce original elements into Puritan theology. Edwards did understand nature to be "power" rather than substance, but he never confused God with nature, for the world consisted always, in his Christian-Platonic mode of thinking, of images and shadows of the divine real things of God. Celebrating ecstatic piety as life's true goal, Edwards's language made the more tepid moral religion being fostered in many Boston churches seem dull and legalistic by comparison.

What is the proper response of a congregation of saints struck with the supernatural light of conversion? Just as in his *Personal Narrative*, where he responded to grace by singing and chanting, so too he encouraged his congregation to sing out their joyous pleasure in their rebirth. He later reported on this time of awakening: "Our public assemblies were then very beautiful . . . there has [been] scarce any part of divine worship wherein good men amongst us have had grace so drawn forth . . . as in singing. . . . they were . . . wont to sing with unusual elevation of heart and voice." The idea that people can somehow return something to God by glorifying him in song underlies Edwards's important concept of reemanation, perhaps the most profound idea that he was to develop in subsequent works.

In making conversion so emotionally and aesthetically appealing, Edwards certainly motivated his listeners to desire grace, but he also faced the predicament that had confronted the Puritan clergy from the beginning. What can the sinner do to be saved? As a strict Calvinist who adhered to the doctrines of absolute divine sovereignty and humanity's complete helplessness, Edwards could not advise people to take actions to enable them to earn salvation, but he retained the preparationist idea that "if we would be saved, we must seek salvation" by listening to God's word preached, praying for grace, and contemplating God. For the saved, this process will be in harmony with God's predestined salvation. For the unregenerate, the attempt will necessarily fail, but their efforts will make them better members of the community.

When in 1734 and 1735, Edwards witnessed the surprising beginnings of the revival and was asked by Colman to account for those events, he began to formulate the synthesis that would explain and preserve Calvinism to modern times. This intellectual feat has earned Edwards his high place in the history of religion and philosophy. In a series of works beginning with *A Faithful Narrative of the Surprising Work of God in the Conversion of Many Hundred Souls* (1737) and continuing in *Some Thoughts Concerning the Present Revival of Religion in New England* (1742) and especially in *A Treatise Concerning Religious Affections* (1746), Edwards developed his synthesis of Calvinism and modern philosophy. While preserving some of the elements of seventeenth-century faculty psychology that was the basis for the theories of Thomas Shepard and the early divines, he used Locke's theory of human understanding to complicate the system. He retained the idea that the intellect and the will are the primary elements of the soul, but he viewed them as acting synchronically, in Locke's terms, as powers of a unified soul and understanding. Whereas the old system had depicted the affections as separate faculties sometimes in conflict with understanding, Edwards, following Locke, saw the affections not only as part of the will but as a "vigorous exercise" of the will.

In *Religious Affections*, Edwards makes one of his more important theological leaps, one that for many scholars is his most significant contribution and one that will reappear in Emerson in the idea of the genuine poet as a genius with a special higher vision. Edwards's key concept is that of reemanation. Using Locke's idea that the intellect not only receives information but has a "power" to act upon it, Edwards argued that as grace emanates from God to the saved individual, so too the saint may reemanate the grace back toward the world and to God and thereby participate actively in expressing salvation. The soul, he writes,

> receives light from the Sun of Righteousness in such a manner that its nature is changed, and it becomes properly a luminous thing: not only does the sun shine in the saints, but they also become little suns.... The manner of their derivation of light is like that of the lamps in the tabernacle rather than a reflecting glass.

As Edwards developed this idea of active reemanation in later works, it takes on ethical and aesthetic dimensions.

After the end of the second set of revivals and his dismissal from Northampton, Edwards continued writing his major works, most of which were published after his death: *The Great Doctrine of Original Sin* (1758), *Two Dissertations: I. Concerning the End for which God Created the World. II. The Nature of True Virtue* (1765), *A History of the Work of Redemption* (1774), and *Images and Shadows of Divine Things* (1948). Resisting the human-centered elements of the Enlightenment philosophies, Edwards remained self-consciously theocentric. His aim was to keep finding intellectually convincing ways to retain God at the center of his system while developing a more complete – and more complicated – explanation of humanity's relation to God. His study of the mind led Edwards to insights in epistemology. He came to believe in the autonomy of the mind from external reality and the indeterminacy of language and of experience, concepts that would later be developed by Kant and Emerson. Yet Edwards believed in the literal truth of the Bible, in the predestined design of sacred and human history, in acts of divine Providence, in Original Sin, in the coming Millennium and Apocalypse, in angels, and in Satan's active role in the world. His work explores the nature of God, Christ, and the Trinity, and it investigates the problem of evil and the proper nature of the Christian community.

Scholars debate how attached Edwards's thought remained to his Calvinist doctrines and to what degree his writings express the potential of human power that would be fully expounded in the Romantic age. Those who see his ideas as in some ways anticipating Emerson and the Romantics argue that although Edwards insists that God has predetermined all things, he does allow that human beings have free will to make choices. The pre-Romantic Edwards may be characterized in the following terms: God has always known how a person will choose, but for Edwards, the person still has the freedom to do the choosing. Arguing that the will always motivates the understanding to choose what it perceives to be good, Edwards says that both "natural" people and saints perceive objects as good and are motivated to choose them. Others may judge the morality and ethics of those choices and praise or punish accordingly. The saint, however, sees the world with a heightened perception and will necessarily choose the good in ways that are "virtuous" and "gracious." Thus, the incandescent virtuous saint reemanates God's glory through acts of virtue that are themselves "beautiful." Beauty itself is an important concept for Edwards, one that he develops throughout his writings. When illuminated with grace, every human act of love and virtue becomes a gracious work of art, spreading God's beauty in the world. In this way, Edwards celebrates the human capability for artistic creativity and spiritual transcendence – the human power to give something back to God. There is little indication in current scholarship that the question of whether Edwards is the last great Puritan or the first American Romantic, or both at once, will soon be resolved.

The following passage on the beauty of the world does illustrate, however, why Edwards's aesthetics have earned him recognition as a literary theorist:

> There are beauties that are more palpable and explicable, and there are hidden and secret beauties. . . . We find ourselves pleased in beholding the color of the violets, but we cannot know what secret regularity or harmony it is that creates that pleasure in our minds. These hidden beauties are commonly by far the greatest because the more complex the

> beauty is, the more hidden it is.... That mixture we call white is a
> proportionate mixture that is harmonious, as Sir Isaac Newton has
> shown, to each particular simple color ... and each sort of rays play a
> distinct tune to the soul, besides those lovely mixtures that are found in
> nature. Those beauties, how lovely is the green of the face of the earth in
> all manner of colors, in flowers the color of the skies, and lovely tinctures
> of the morning and evening.

Chauncy lived thirty years beyond Edwards and helped usher in the liberal Protestantism that would dominate the American eastern seaboard for the next two centuries. But it was Edwards who had the greater impact on American culture and thought. He led the first of what would become repeated religious awakenings in America. From Princeton, where his life ended so tragically, young preachers traveled to the South and the Southwest to generate the Second Great Awakening, while New Lights from Edwards's alma mater Yale spread religious fervor across the "burned over" areas of upper New York State. Edwards's followers and admirers edited and published his books and manuscripts; his *Miscellanies*, which contains the material for his unwritten magnum opus, is only now being edited for publication; literary scholars have recognized him to be a major figure in American literature.

In our secular society, so much the product of the purely rationalist elements of the Enlightenment that Edwards resisted, it may be difficult to grasp how Edwards, who was a narrow Calvinist, in many ways looking back to the Puritan founders, could also have possessed a deep love of language, metaphor, ideas, and, thus, of the world. That, however, is one of the most arresting features of the man: the mixture of Ramistic logic with poetic visions that are at once medieval and modernist, as in the closing paragraph of "The Beauty of the World":

> Corollary. Hence the reason why almost all men, and those that seem to
> be very miserable, love life, because they cannot bear to lose sight of such
> a beautiful and lovely world. The idea, that every moment whilst we live
> have a beauty that we take distinct notice of, brings a pleasure that, when
> we come to the trial, we had rather live in much pain and misery than lose.

In spite of all the theological and political disputes that racked the Puritan experiment from its earliest moments and in spite of all the pain and anxiety the Puritans inflicted upon their enemies and each other, perhaps it is their extraordinary ability to believe themselves a special people that draws readers still to their writings and to the records of their ordeals. The image of Jonathan Edwards at his desk in the frontier village of Stockbridge thinking of the awesome power of the Creator and the "lovely world" in which he would "rather live in much pain and misery than lose" in some way captures the peculiar ambiguity of Puritan literary history.

Chapter Eight

Toward the formation of a United States

England's Glorious Revolution of 1688–89 marked a significant turning point in the development of American culture. Before that event, the thought and writing of those living in the New World, and in New England in particular, had begun to develop in ways that were increasingly autonomous and, from a contemporary Englishman's viewpoint, rather peculiar. Throughout the seventeenth century, the political turmoil in England and some shrewd New England diplomacy had enabled the northern colonists to develop their own religious ideas, political structures, and of pre-nationalist pride, which was expressed in works such as Cotton Mather's *Magnalia Christi Americana* (1702). Even in the southern colonies, where the ties to the Church of England and the Crown remained stronger, conditions of life in the New World – the land, the Native peoples, the distance from Europe – led to variations in taste and forms of expression that give Ebenezer Cook's *The Sot-Weed Factor* (1708) and William Byrd's *The Secret History of the Line* (circa 1730) their particular literary character. By 1689 in New England, the Puritan jeremiads, spiritual autobiographies, captivity narratives, and spiritualized histories and biographies possessed recognizable features of a distinctive literary tradition. In the southern and middle colonies, the literary forms were more secular, but the style and content of the writings were also different enough for the English to be identified as Colonial American.

The establishment of a stable parliamentary government in England in the 1690s, however, had a profound and lasting impact upon intellectual and cultural life in England and America. A heightened awareness in Europe of the value of the American colonies and the increased political control that followed served to transform the colonies from a set of relatively separate entities to a subculture of Europe. Meanwhile, the Spanish continued to colonize the areas of the Southwest and the West, and the French developed their system of forts and outposts from Canada to New Orleans and from western New York to the Mississippi. The area from Maine to Florida and between the Atlantic shore and the Allegany mountains became what historians have come to call "English America."

During the first half of the eighteenth-century, the British, French, and Spanish governments took a much greater interest in their investments in the Americas than they had previously. Conflicts between the French and the Spanish in the areas between what are now the states of Florida and Texas had continued since the early sixteenth century, and by 1770, Spain controlled most of the territory west of Louisiana. Although many of the Native peoples suffered losses from war, disease, and enslavement, many tribes remained strong throughout the territories occupied by the Spanish and French in the southern and western sections of what is now the United States. As increasing numbers of Africans were transported to the Americas in the eighteenth century, the cultures of the French, Spanish, African, and Native American peoples became engaged in the long process of biological blending and cultural syncretism that resulted in what scholars have called the culture of the Black Atlantic. By the early nineteenth century, an outsider entering the city of New Orleans or other parts of what are now Texas and Louisiana would have found it quite difficult to identify the culture or the people to be of French, Spanish, African, or Native American origin, for already it had become a hybrid or Creole culture. In areas of the southwest, including what is now Mexico, New Mexico, Arizona, and California, over a hundred years of blending of Spanish and Native American had already produced an "American" who was not Indian or Spaniard and who was also not the same "new American" of the northeastern colonies that Michel-Guillaume Jean de Crevecoeur (1735–1813) described in his *Letters From an American Farmer* (1782).

These developments would continue in the south and southwest into the mid-nineteenth century and would ultimately have a major impact on the future of what would become the complex and diversified culture of the United States today. Yet, in the 1700s, immigrants from northern and central Europe, from England, Germany, Ireland, Holland, Scotland, France, and Poland, who were arriving by the thousands in Boston, New York, Philadelphia, Baltimore, and Charleston would have a more immediate impact on the formation of the thirteen colonies that would become the United States. The dominant non-indigenous languages and cultures on the eastern seaboard in the eighteenth century were, English, French, German, Scottish, and Dutch rather than Spanish, Portuguese, and Italian. Just as government officials, military leaders, and bankers of these various European countries watched the growing productivity and markets of the economically vital eastern colonies, so too the religious and cultural leaders recognized the growing population of the colonies to represent both an opportunity and a responsibility. The colonists joined and contributed to the various religious denominations; they bought European books and art works, and they wanted their sons to be educated in accord with the latest European theories and their daughters trained in the domestic arts and refinements of polite society. Thus, between 1700 and 1725, the Europeans became the arbiters of literary and artistic taste, and they attempted to establish the standards and the forms for the literature and arts that would be produced in America and purchased by the colonists.

But the success of European culture importation was somewhat limited. For eight decades between 1620 and 1700, New England had enjoyed a high degree of cultural autonomy as a result of the relative geographical isolation and the desire for political and religious independence of the colonial Congregationalists. As a result, New England had experienced a nascent form of American cultural independence about which many took personal pride. Cotton Mather was not alone in expressing the resistance that many New Englanders felt toward European influences on their lives when he signaled in his *Magnalia Christi Americana* that the colonists would do well not to imitate the Europeans for "the *Wonders* of the CHRISTIAN RELIGION, [were] flying from the Depravations of *Europe*, to the American Strand."

At the same time, the problem of American cultural dependence on Europe was present from the start of the colonies and would continue long after the Revolution and political independence. Seventeenth-century New England poets such as Anne Bradstreet and Edward Taylor had been strongly influenced by European writers such as Robert Burton, John Donne, Michael Drayton, Guillaume du Bartas, John Milton, Benjamin Quarles, Shakespeare, Sir Philip Sidney, and Edmund Spenser; even though the Puritan writers of the seventeenth century felt neither the desire nor the obligation to imitate English models directly. Their religious dictates told them that the Bible was the only literary text to be revered and that the best writings of men and women were mere drivel compared to the beauty of the words of God. By the early eighteenth century, on the other hand, the preacher-poet Mather Byles (1707–28) of Massachusetts, composed verse in careful imitation of the works of Alexander Pope and American prose writers kept their copies of the essays of Addison and Steele on their writing desks. As English and Scottish philosophers, critics, and writers elaborated the criteria for politeness and elegance in polite society and for orderliness, decorum, wit, and taste in literature and the arts, the American provincials strove to adhere to these standards and to emulate their European betters. Still, the cultural situation remained ambiguous, and a form of British-American *belles lettres* sprung forth in the New World.

As a result of these complex historical developments, American literature really had multiple originating sources: before 1700, there are the various forms of artistic expressions of the Native peoples; the writings of the Spanish explorers; the accounts of the French trappers and priests; and the diaries and journals of the Dutch, Portuguese, and Italian adventurers. On the eastern seaboard in the seventeenth and eighteenth centuries, there are two very different literary beginnings: one deriving from the austere rhetoric and sacred imagery of the Puritan sermon and the personal narrative of New England; another fostered by Enlightenment thought, neoclassical literary principles, and language play and humor of Augustan England. While the blending of these heritages would ultimately provide rich verbal and imaginative resources for later American writers, the situation presents the student of eighteenth-century American literature with complex questions of literary history. For example, because of the powerful impact of preachers such as Jonathan Edwards and George Whitefield during the religious revivals of the Great Awakening in the 1740s, the imagery, myths, and verbal structures of the Puritan sermon remained vital elements of American writing. The sermon continued to be a very important literary form throughout the eighteenth century as thousands in the middle and southern colonies as well as in New England learned the rhetoric of sin and salvation and of personal calling and communal mission from itinerant New Light clergy who traveled the circuits as far west as Ohio and Kentucky preaching the Gospel. By the 1770s and 1780s, the vision of the sacred destiny of the "Chosen People" of America as depicted in the Puritan idiom became central to the political tracts and speeches of the American Revolution, persistent even in the works of a deist and rationalist such as Thomas Paine, and present still today in the political rhetoric of the United States.

At the same time, by the mid-1700s the classics and the works of contemporary Scottish and English writers such as Aphra Behn, Robert Burns, William Congreve, Daniel Defoe, and Jonathan Swift were widely available in the colonies. An increasing number of American bards experimented with heroic couplets, sonnets, and odes. Images and tales of London coffee houses and Edinburgh literary clubs inspired groups of young American writers to form their own literary societies. In Philadelphia a circle of poets and artists studied under an unusually fine writer, President William Smith (1727–1803) at the College of Pennsylvania, and founded a literary club named "The Swains." Among its members were such promising artists and writers as Joseph Duche, Nathaniel Evans, Thomas Godfrey, Francis Hopkinson, Joseph Reed, and Benjamin West. West became world famous for his painting while the others were much respected in their time for achievements in literature, music, and the arts. Throughout the American province, literary clubs sprang up in all of the major cities, and both men and women formed such societies with some clubs admitting members of both sexes. Beginning in the 1760s, the colleges in America instituted major curriculum reforms, introducing the classics along with the critical and philosophical works of contemporary European thinkers, especially those of the Scottish Commonsense School of thought, who would come to have a major impact upon American literature in the eighteenth and nineteenth centuries.

Throughout the eighteenth century, there occurred a gradual and subtle blending of religious and classical elements, so that by the 1770s and 1780s, young writers such as Philip Freneau and Joel Barlow created nationalistic epics and satires that are neoclassical in form but echo Puritan writing in content and imagery. What precedes this aesthetic revolution, however, are four decades of literary history that continue to challenge the scholar who seeks to understand the complex intellectual and literary conditions in the mid-eighteenth century and the relationship of this period to the development of American literature and culture as a whole.

At the head of this new tradition in American literature stands Benjamin Franklin. With his graceful style and wit, Franklin typified the cosmopolitan ideal in both his life and his writing, and he personally challenged the assumption that persisted in England and Scotland during the century that no one would ever find merit or beauty in an American book. But before turning to Franklin and the writers who tried to establish a national literature after the American Revolution, it is necessary to describe the intellectual context into which they came of age.

The designation "Age of the Enlightenment" describes over a century of one of the most profound philosophical changes in Western culture. The remarkable movement from the holy wars and witch burnings in seventeenth-century Europe to the establishment of secular republican governments and the spread of religious skepticism by the last third of the eighteenth century stemmed from complex causes. Of prime importance was the pervasive impact of the philosophical and scientific works of Francis Bacon, Isaac Newton, René Descartes, Thomas Hobbes, and John Locke. These philosophers created new ways of seeing the world and provided texts that offered new philosophical grounds for social and political change. The enlightenment of the minds to the errors of religious superstition, the power of human reason, the order of the universe, and the progress of the sciences and the arts: these were the objectives that the writers, artists, and scholars pursued with astonishing energy and optimism.

The impact of these developments upon intellectual life in British America in the eighteenth century has been a subject of considerable research and scholarship. The picture these and earlier studies presents is a complicated one. On the one hand, religious authority remained very strong in the colonies until the decade of the Revolution. Wherever the Calvinist spirit prevailed, there was resistance to philosophical change unless new theories could be reconciled with established doctrines. On the other hand, the main figure of the Great Awakening revivals in America, Rev. Jonathan Edwards, was clearly influenced by experiments and theories of Locke and Newton. From Edwards's perspective, Locke provided a more sophisticated way of understanding God's plan for the universe and His use of nature, which was itself only one of the tools through which the creator expressed his divine sovereignty. Yet some of Edwards's critics, ministers and theologians, who were disturbed by the emotionalism of the Great Awakening, found in the rationalist ideas of Locke an argument against the perceived pietistic excesses of Edwards and the New Light clergy. Others found Locke's thought tending too much toward the philosophical extreme of materialism, and they found attractive the philosophical idealism of Bishop George Berkeley. There had always been a strain of Platonism in American Puritan thought, articulated most clearly in the vision of the City on a Hill and a New World Zion as an ideal communal destiny to which to aspire. Berkeley's well-known poem, "Verses by the author on the prospect of Planting Arts and Learning in America," had for its theme the ancient notion of *transliltio studii* or the westward movement of culture from the Near East westward. Berkeley depicted this movement as going beyond the western shores of Europe to the eastern coast of America. This vision appealed to the Platonist strain of Puritanism, as well as to American pride, and thereby served to heighten Berkeley's appeal in the colonies.

Edwards' influence diminished after the Great Awakening, however, as a result of his untimely death in 1758 soon after he assumed the presidency of the College of New Jersey (later to become Princeton University). In the nineteenth century, Ralph Waldo Emerson, would take Edwards' mantle as original American thinker. In an age marked by strong currents of philosophical change as the eighteenth century, however, young scholars, especially those training for the clergy and the professions, demanded knowledge of current theories and contemporary answers to their nagging questions and doubts.

For the American colleges in the mid-eighteenth century, the solutions to bewildering, philosophical concerns seemed to be best provided by the group of Scottish Realists of what came to be called the Commonsense School. The leaders of this group steered a middle course between the idealism of Berkeley and the tendency toward skepticism most fully expressed in the works of David Hume. The Commonsense doctrines, which emphasized "experience and fact interpreted by plain common sense," also reconciled the apparent conflict between natural philosophy and religion by arguing that reason could find practical value in both of these existing systems of thought. The clergy who presided over the American colleges in the 1760s and 1770s found the writings of John Reid, Lord Henry Home Kames, and other Scottish thinkers most appealing because they provided a new philosophical legitimization for maintaining religious orthodoxy.

One of the key figures in the transmission of the Commonsense precepts to America was Rev. John Witherspoon, who arrived from Scotland to become president of the College of New Jersey in 1768. Witherspoon established a new curriculum, which stressed the classics, poetry, eloquence, and the arts as disciplines that would improve the moral sense. With these changes Witherspoon started an educational reform that quickly spread to Yale, Harvard, and the College of Philadelphia (later the University of Pennsylvania). This new curriculum was eventually codified in a text by Hugh Blair, *Lectures on Rhetoric and Belles Lettres* (1783). This work increased the dissemination of Commonsense Realism throughout the American colleges, a process that continued until the middle of the nineteenth century. In 1803 when Samuel Miller composed his small cultural history, *America, A Brief Retrospect of the Eighteenth Century*, he asserted that Witherspoon's arrival in the colonies was a turning-point in "the advancement of literature and science in our country." Leading political figures of the Revolution and the New Republic, such as Thomas Jefferson, Benjamin Franklin, James Madison, and George Washington, were deeply influenced by the writings of John Locke and of the Commonsense philosophers, and every American writer of the period of the Revolution embraced a notion of the moral value of *belles lettres* that they had learned from teachers such as Witherspoon at Princeton, William Smith at Pennsylvania, and Ezra Stiles at Yale.

The decades between 1760 and 1800 may have produced only a few significant figures of American writing, but it is a formative period for American culture and one that set the stage for the emergence of an identifiably American literature in the nineteenth century. Writers such as Poe, Hawthorne, Melville, Fuller, Stowe, Douglass, Thoreau, Emerson, Whitman, and Dickinson knew the works of the writers who preceded them and the particular forms of resistance they faced as artists in America. Historians approach these decades as being the "critical period" of American history where the fundamental structures of politics and society took shape, and certainly the same is true for literature.

As the political leaders fashioned the founding documents of the emerging Republic, the poets, novelists, and playwrights were attempting to render a distinctive American voice, expressive of the characteristics, dreams, and particular difficulties of an American people. This literary origin was as crucial to the development of a distinctive American culture and national identity as the *Bill of Rights* and the *Constitution* were to the creation of the political system. To understand these writings and assess the achievement of the Republic's first men and women of letters, however, it is useful to organize the abundant and varied forms and texts into three categories. There are certainly many works that belong under more than one heading, such as Michel Guillaume Jean de Crevecoeur's *Letters From an American Farmer* (1782) and William Bartram's *Travels* (1791), which qualify as imaginative narratives as well as works of historical and scientific discourse, but for introductory purposes classification is useful.

The first of these categories includes the writings that have received the most public attention: the political and philosophical essays and documents, such as Thomas Paine's *Common Sense* (1776), Thomas Jefferson's *Notes on Virginia* (1785), the *Declaration of Independence* and the *Constitution*, and *The Federalist Papers*, co-authored by Alexander Hamilton, John Jay, and James Madison. Many students of the period see the prose essay as its highest form of literary achievement and thus celebrate these works and other political prose as the best and most influential writing of the period. Yet the magnificence of these political works should not lead to an undervaluing of other genres. The religious and oratorical writing of the decades and the studies of language by Noah Webster and Jedidiah Morse should also be included in this class of nonfiction prose. During the last twenty-five years, historians and literary scholars such as Bernard Bailyn, Sacvan Bercovitch, Edmund Morgan, and Gordon Wood have examined the verbal and ideological continuities that link the political writings of the early Republic to the pamphlets, sermon literature, and religious tracts of the early and mid-eighteenth century.

Attention to this literary foreground deepens our appreciation of the American democratic literary heritage. Unlike in England where some wrote for the royal court and aristocrats while other more popular writers of plays, novels, broadsides, and pamphlets addressed the common people, in America writers were expected to address the entire population – those formally educated, and those who were self-taught; those of the landed gentry as well as their servants; merchants and farmers and day laborers. In order to achieve their political effect and move people to action, the prose works of John Adams, Jefferson, and Paine had to appeal to and be understood by a wide spectrum of readers, and these writers managed to achieve a powerful combination of reason and logic with stirring imagery and diction. They thereby established a benchmark for rhetorical and literary skill for a democratic society that would challenge every writer of non-fiction and fiction come after them.

Until very recently, the only rival to political discourse as the epitome of literary achievement in the 1780s and 1790s was the poetry of the so-called "Connecticut Wits" and a handful of "pre-Romantic" poems by Philip Freneau, such as his well-known lyric, "The Wild Honey Suckle." For the poets themselves, the period after the Revolution was a time of both excitement and disappointment. In a host of celebratory poems that carried such titles as "The Rising Glory of America," poets proclaimed the dawning of a new age in America that would witness the glorious establishment of the most productive and successful political and economic system in the world. These poems and many other expressions of the period also called for the creation of a cultural climate in America in which the arts and letters would reach their highest form. In this spirit, Joel Barlow composed his epic, *The Columbiad,* and Timothy Dwight his *Conquest of Canaan,* and others composed their own epic poems celebrating the ascendance of the arts in the new nation. By the mid-1790s, however, these writers had come to recognize that whatever benefits the new nation might bestow, increased support for the arts and letters was not to be one of them. The contrast between the hopefulness of Barlow's early poem, *The Prospect of Peace* (1778), and the discouragement he expressed in his "Advice to a Raven in Russia" (1812) illustrates the arc of disillusionment that occurred for many artists during those two decades. A chronological survey of the *oeuvre* of Philip Freneau reflects the same slide from enthusiasm to frustration and disappointment. As a result of this loss of confidence, the poetry and the imaginative prose essays of the period took on new dimensions of irony and ambiguity and some acquired a questioning, somewhat bemused, comic tone – a recognizable feature of the works of many later American writers and artists.

Within the last two decades, scholars and critics have developed new respect for American writing in the decades between 1770 and 1820. In addition to studies of the poets Barlow, Dwight, and Freneau, the works of the satirist John Trumbull, especially his *The Progress of Dulness* (1772–73) and his *M'Fingal* have received attention. The remarkable career and writing of Phillis Wheatley have moved to the center of discussions of poetry in the era, and her works are now well established in anthologies and college courses.

New attention has been given to the playwrights, William Dunlap, Thomas Godfrey, Royall Tyler, and Mercy Otis Warren. Thomas Godfrey's *The Prince of Parthia,* published in 1765 and produced in 1767, was a popular tragedy that draws much upon Shakespeare and is considered to be the first professionally produced play by an American. A patriotic propagandist for American independence, Warren wrote plays that satirized Boston politics and attacked the English loyalists. Her *The Adulateur* (1773) mocks the Massachusetts governor Thomas Hutchinson for being a puppet of the King while her 1775 play, *The Group,* ridiculed politicians who continued to be loyal to King George III in spite of his broken agreements. Her plays, *The Blockheads* in 1776 and *The Motley Assembly* in 1779, continued her sharp commentary on political folly. Royall Tyler's play, *The Contrast,* is a sophisticated comedy of manners produced in New York in 1787. Tyler created what would become stock American characters, such as Jonathan, the type of the Yankee figure, and Colonel Manly who teaches his daughter to keep her eye on making a good marriage as the "main chance" for a young woman in middle-class America. These figures reappear in slightly different forms in plays throughout the nineteenth century.

Within the emerging prose narrative form of the novel, the reputations of Hugh Henry Brackenridge and especially Charles Brockden Brown have been furthered by numerous studies demonstrating the verbal, structural, and thematic complexities of their works and revealing them to be much more artistically self-conscious than previously assumed. As this effort to reassess the early novel has proceeded, the canon of American literature has expanded to include other works and writers previously overlooked. Writers such as Susanna Rowson, Sarah Wentworth Morton, Hannah Webster Foster, and Olaudah Equiano have been rediscovered, and genres previously excluded from anthologies, college courses, and serious literary study for being aesthetically unsophisticated, such as slave narratives, Gothic novels, domestic novels, and so-called "sentimental romances" of the period, are now being widely read and studied for their literary merits as well as their historically valuable content.

Also, given far more attention in the last twenty years have been the American Indian orators and oral historians of the time. Now appearing in college anthologies are Senecan and Cherokee oral histories that have been preserved and sermons by Samson Occom who was converted to Christianity by missionaries and was the first Native American to publish in English. Also restored to its rightful place in American literature is the *Speech at the End of Lord Dunmore's War* by Logan, the name the colonists used for Chief Tachnechdorus of the Mingo people, whose moving plea to end the injustice and violence against his people became part of the popular schoolbook, the *McGuffey Reader*. Unfortunately, his appeal did not prevent the devastating Indian Wars that raged across America throughout the nineteenth century.

Probably the most enduring figure of eighteenth-century writing in America has been Benjamin Franklin whose works were admired as much in the nineteenth and twentieth centuries as they are in the twenty first. In remarkable ways, Franklin's life and thought sharply reflect the American amalgam of the Puritan work ethic and self-discipline and the Enlightenment rationalist zeal for science, technology, and order that emerged in the latter half of the eighteenth century. For many in Europe during his lifetime and to many Americans in the twentieth century, Franklin has typified the new American. Both in his life and in his extraordinarily popular and influential *Autobiography*, Franklin had performed an array of characteristics that were seen by his contemporary European and American admirers and millions of students since as being representative of an American national identity.

Franklin was born in Puritan Boston in 1706 at the dawn of the Enlightenment, and he died in his adopted Philadelphia, a city that he helped to make the most culturally rich city in the United States during his lifetime. As a young man, he heard the preaching of the Reverend Cotton Mather, and from him Franklin learned of the power of charity and public service. Although Franklin was a Deist and a skeptic who believed in no single religion, he was moved emotionally upon hearing the revivalist preacher Reverend George Whitefield, to the point of making a contribution to the collection. Thus, he is a figure of the Age of Reason who understood well the power of religious emotion. In the later third of his long life, he was feted in European capitals as that rarest of Americans: one who was a sophisticated, multi-lingual, learned, witty, and open-minded American scientist-artist-statesman. Most important of all, he was walking proof that the American Dream existed, the idea that one could begin in America without wealth, family name, property, or aristocratic friends, and rise on the basis of one's own talent and labor to become rich and famous.

As one of fifteen children of a shop owner who had come to America in 1682 and a working mother who was a schoolteacher, young Ben attended the Boston Grammar School for a few years because his parents strongly believed education to be the key to success in America. When he had to leave school to begin work at the age of twelve, he was first employed in his father's shop and then became a printer's apprentice under his older brother James. When Ben was sixteen, James was arrested in 1722 for offending Massachusetts' authorities, leaving Ben to publish his brother's newspaper. Following a common practice of the time of writing under a pseudonym, he adopted the name of "Silence Dogood" and began to write essays in the paper. This name was inspired by his Puritan New England roots and by Cotton Mather's well-known book, *Bonifacius: An Essay Upon the Good.* By the time he was seventeen, Franklin had gained enough confidence to strike out on his own, and so he deserted his apprenticeship, a violation of Massachusetts law, and escaped by ship to Philadelphia to begin anew.

In the early pages of his *Autobiography*, Franklin depicts himself as a nervous young man arriving in Philadelphia on a Sunday in October, 1723, with only the clothes on his back and a few coins in his pocket. As a striking image of plight and survival that would inspire millions of future immigrants, he was "fatigued with travel" and "very hungry" and purchased a meal of "three great Puffy Rolls" with his last pennies. In these first moments in his new life, he sees a young woman, Deborah Reed, and falls in love at first sight; she soon became his common law wife and life's partner until her death in 1774. As a Deist and radical thinker in the Age of Reason, Franklin, like many intellectuals and working people of the time, did not see religion or marriage as being necessary for a lasting relationship.

From such humble beginnings, Franklin rose quickly in Philadelphia to become a printer and then publisher of the successful *Pennsylvania Gazette*. As an author in his newspaper and various other publications, he gained a reputation for his biting wit, satiric tone, and incisive social criticism. The voices of the many pseudonyms that he created through which to instruct the public and attack folly were always multi-leveled: a mix of sharp scolding tempered by fondness for humanity; wicked debunking balanced by fatherly concern; the superior, sometimes egotistical, manner of a brilliant, confident leader undercut by self-effacement, expressions of guilt and failure, and self-criticism. In sum, he shrewdly blended the Enlightenment confidence in the perfectibility of himself and humanity with the Puritan fear of failure and self-deception and an awareness of the innate corruption of human beings.

The many qualities of Franklin's writing are present in a wide range of genres and texts that are included in American literature anthologies today. These include his masterful and popular *Poor Richard's Almanac* which appeared regularly from 1733 to 1758, and his many satiric essays such as "The Speech of Polly Baker" and "Rules by Which a Great Empire May Be Reduced to a Small One." A scientist and inventor, Franklin was also a social reformer who critiqued the injustices of the white society toward the native peoples and who was an outspoken opponent of slavery. In 1789, the year before his death at age eighty-four, Franklin wrote "An Address to the Public from the Pennsylvania Society for Promoting the Abolition of Slavery, and the Relief of Free Negroes Unlawfully Held in Bondage," in which he urged the creation of a "national policy" to insure against the indentured bondage of former slaves and to help them find proper employment and the means "to procure their children an education."

As a wise observer of human nature, Franklin contributed many memorable remarks to American literature, such as his famous quip: "If you would not be forgotten, as soon as you are dead and rotten, either write things worth reading, or do things worth the writing." As a guarantee against the chance that he might be forgotten, Franklin did both, and in his most famous work, *The Autobiography*, he immortalized himself by writing a rich and complex narrative that combines the historical and biographical facts of a diary with the personal revelations of a conversion narrative and the drama and excitement of a novel.

Breaking new ground for American life narratives, he invented himself as a character who is the narrator of the tale and the hero. The voice that we hear has much in common with Benjamin Franklin the man but is also a speaker who is not entirely forthcoming about everything in his life and who is in the process of forging a myth of himself even as he claims to be totally honest and forthright.

Using such a *persona* was already common in fictional narratives such as Henry Fielding's *Tom Jones* and *Joseph Andrews*, Defoe's *Robinson Crusoe*, and Jonathan Swift's *Gulliver's Travels*, but it was not yet a device used in autobiography where readers expected to find a completely guileless speaker.

Evidently, Franklin recognized that Americans needed role-models and that his rags-to-riches life and career would inspire emulation especially if he erased some of the mistakes he made – what he called *errata* – and created a self that epitomized the virtues of diligence, temperance, and self-reliance. Thus, his *Autobiography* is both a report on a life and a brilliant act of pedagogy designed not just to instruct his son, as he claims, but to teach all readers to succeed in this new society of immigrants.

This playful and constructive masquerade is revealed most clearly in his tongue-in-cheek discussion of his efforts to attain moral perfection by keeping a chart of his virtues and vices and to erase his errors or sins with systematic discipline and self-examination. He says "I was surpriz'd to find myself so much fuller of Faults than I had imagined, but I had the Satisfaction of seeing them diminish." Describing his system for approaching moral perfection, he jokes that he recognized that it was not smart to be too perfect, so he was careful to retain a few flaws to protect himself from envy: "a perfect character might be attended with the Inconvenience of being envied and hated; and that a benevolent Man should allow a few Faults in himself, to keep his friends in Countenance." This joke on his effort to cultivate some imperfections draws attention to the kind of verbal trickery that his *character* of Ben Franklin engages in throughout the work. At one point, he reports that a friend pointed out that as he approaches perfection he might fall into the sin of pride, so he agreed to "add *Humility* to my List... [and while] I cannot boast of much Success in acquiring the *Reality* of this Virtue; but I had a good deal with regard to the *Appearance* of it." By this little comic lifting of the mask of his *persona*, Franklin conveys a knowing wink to readers who might know of his less than virtuous life, such as his many sexual affairs in Europe. This original masterpiece deserves to be studied for what it tells about the strategies of self-invention, about the interplay of appearances and realities in life, and about the possibilities for "new Americans" to be shrewd confidence men and women and clever deceivers as well as devoted, honest models of the Protestant work ethic.

Between 1765 and 1810, poetic expression in America took various forms. The most widely circulated poems were in the form of public verse celebrating "the rising glory of America," including epics like Joel Barlow's *The Vision of Columbus*, mock epics and other comic poems like his "The Hasty Pudding," and pre-Romantic lyrics such as those of Philip Freneau. For the most part, poetry by American writers of the period received little attention abroad and circulated among a limited number of educated readers in the colonies. The one exception to this pattern was the remarkable international reputation of Phillis Wheatley (1753–84). Although Wheatley lived only thirty-one years and lived the majority of her short life in bondage, the story of her achievements as a writer who received national and international recognition is also one that would inspire generations of aspiring authors who have come after her. Transported from Gambia, West Africa, to Boston in 1761, this seven-year-old girl was purchased by John and Susannah Wheatley and given the name of Phillis. When Phillis quickly learned to read and write English and began to study Latin, the Wheatleys recognized her remarkable intelligence, limited her domestic chores, and encouraged her interest in the Bible, English literature, and the classics.

When she began to compose poetry, the Wheatleys encouraged her to read her work to their friends and soon she gained a reputation as a literary prodigy. At the age of thirteen, Wheatley first published a poem: celebrating a remarkable tale of survival at sea, her "On Messrs. Hussey and Coffin" appeared in the Newport, Rhode Island, *Newport Mercury* on December 21, 1767. It was her next publication, "On the Death of Mr. George Whitefield" that brought Wheatley international acclaim. Celebrated for his evangelical preaching during the Great Awakening, Whitefield was famous in England and America, and Wheatley's poem circulated on both sides of the Atlantic. She was invited to London in 1773 where she met many English dignitaries and Benjamin Franklin. Unable to publish a book of her poetry in America, she was encouraged by a London printer and published a collection of her work, *Poems on Various Subjects, Religion and Moral* at the age of twenty. An American edition did not appear until 1786, when it was printed two years after her death.

When Wheatley returned to America, the colonies were on the verge of revolution, and her mistress was near death. At the urging of her admirers in England, John Wheatley freed Phillis in 1773, and for the next five years she was able to continue her writing and live in the Wheatley home. In 1775, she wrote one of her most famous poems in honor of George Washington who invited her to his headquarters where he and his fellow officers received her. But this relatively stable period of her life ended in 1778 when John Wheatley and his daughter died, leaving Phillis to provide for herself. She married a freedman named John Peters, but the couple struggled financially. Phillis had two children who died in infancy, and she tried to earn a living by opening a small school. When her husband was jailed for not paying his debts and her school failed, she opened a boarding house for African Americans. Always physically frail from childhood, she died at the age of thirty-one while trying to care for a third child who was mortally sick.

The first African American to publish a book, Wheatley achieved remarkable success in her own time, recognized by such figures as Voltaire and Franklin. But then, her work and career slipped into obscurity for nearly two centuries until the 1970s. When she was rediscovered, some readers at first thought that her use of traditional couplet rhymes and classical forms such as the elegy indicated that her work was merely imitative in form and that her themes and content only reinforced the dominant Anglo-European culture of her time.

As critics began to examine her work more closely, however, they discovered that her poetry was far more original and challenging to the dominant society and culture than is evident at first. With subtle and sophisticated aesthetic consciousness and diplomatic skill, she negotiated the racial politics of her day by criticizing slavery, challenging white supremacy, and subverting the assumptions about African people upon which the emergent racist culture was being established. In her poem "On Being Brought from Africa to America" (written in 1768 and published in 1773), the speaker says that she is grateful that she had been introduced to Christianity and thus redeemed from paganism, but then she stands upon her new identity as a Christian to criticize those whites who "view our sable race with scornful eye" and who say "'Their colour is a diabolic die,'" thereby making the false identification of dark skin color to evil. She closes by exhorting her white readers to "Remember, *Christians*, *Negros*, black as *Cain*, / May be refin'd, and join th' angelic train."

In many of her poems about the American Revolution, such as her "On the Death of General Wooster," Wheatley asks why God would help Americans to win freedom from English oppression while they themselves "hold in bondage Afric's blameless race." In some ways, even more unsettling to the "tyrannic sway" of the dominant white society are Wheatley's more subtle, philosophical and religious poems that display the undeniable brilliance of her intellectual powers. In such poems as "On Imagination" and "Thoughts on the Works of Providence," Wheatley syncretizes religious and philosophical elements of Christian, classical, and African thought and art to express universal themes of the grandeur of God, nature, human imagination, and art that transcend time and space, revealing a divine purpose that knows no social inequalities, but is "To nourish all, to serve on gen'ral end, / The good of man." After more than two hundred years, the work of one of America's earliest accomplished poets has now begun to receive the attention it deserves.

During the eighteenth century in England, narrative fiction and the novel emerged as the major genre of modern literature, and the works of Aphra Behn, Samuel Butler, Daniel Defoe, Henry Fielding, Samuel Richardson, Tobias Smollett, and Jonathan Swift circulated in cheap editions in the colonies since there were not yet copyright laws and American printers did not pay English writers royalties. The book widely accepted to have been the first American novel appeared in 1789, *The Power of Sympathy*, by William Hill Brown. Its sensationalized plot of adultery and incest established a type that was imitated in many novels that followed. The two best-selling American novels of the period were Susanna Haswell Rowson's

Charlotte Temple (1791) and Hannah Webster's *The Coquette* (1797), both of which followed the pattern of having a heartless seducer ruin the virtue, reputation and life an unwitting young woman. These novels of seduction or sentimental fiction served the social and educational function of alerting young women and their parents for the need to be alert to the new gender politics of marriage that accompanied the rise of the commercial and professional middle classes in Europe and America. A variation on the model was Judith Sargent Murray's *The Story of Margaretta* (1798) in which the main character, Margaretta Melworth, is educated and rational and is able to avoid the seducer and choose the virtuous man for her husband. Aimed primarily at women readers, such novels were often condemned by clergy and other moralists for leading to "female depravity" because they stimulated the imagination and romantic yearning of young women, but even the clergy eventually came to recognize that they could also serve a moral function. Certainly, the creation of a successful market for fictional works began to attract more male authors and also led to the development of new types of novels, of which gothic fiction of Mary Shelley's *Frankenstein* is a seminal example.

Two American novelists of the period, Hugh Henry Brackenridge and Charles Brockden Brown, aimed for a broader audience including male readers and sought to engage a broader range of social subjects with their works. In his multi-volume, serialized novel, *Modern Chivalry* (1792–1815), Brackenridge, a lawyer and judge in Pennsylvania, tried to educate his readers on a host of subjects about which he felt potential voters in a democracy needed information. Adding volumes to this rambling, satiric picaresque narrative over twenty-three years, Brackenridge claimed that his work was intended to illustrate his stylistic techniques and thus improve the writing style of American English.

The most ambitious and artistically successful novelist of these decades was clearly Charles Brockden Brown (1771–1810) who was born into a Quaker family in Philadelphia in 1771. Brown's training from his parents at Quaker school put him at odds with the dominant Calvinist puritan religious culture and taught him to focus on rationalism and individual morality. After preparing to enter the law, he changed his mind and moved to New York to begin a literary career. Brown was encouraged by several members of the Friendly Society, a group of freethinkers who were readers and admirers of Mary Wollstonecraft, author of the feminist text, *Vindication of the Rights of Women*, and Charles Godwin, an idealist who believed in the perfectibility of society and humanity. Brown believed that the novel form could become a powerful mode of persuasion for the political leaders of society and help open their minds to new ideas for solving human problems. Thus, he sought to address his works directly to the intellectual elite of the young republic with the hope that they might learn from his works more about the complexities of human nature.

After writing a fictional feminist work, *Alcuin: A Dialogue*, that consists of a long dialogue between a young man and an older woman in which she instructs him on the injustices that society, and especially marriage, imposes on women, Brown began in 1798 an extraordinary period of literary production. Within two years, he produced four novels while also editing the *Monthly Magazine and Literary Review*, in which he anticipated Emerson in urging fellow intellectuals to create with him an American literature independent of European ideas, and like Melville thirty years later, he called on American readers to support American writing.

The four novels that he produced during this period did not sell well during his lifetime, but his work did receive praise from some leading contemporary writers in England, such as John Keats, Percy Bysshe Shelley and William Godwin, and his works were admired decades later by such American writers as Edgar Allen Poe, Nathaniel Hawthorne, and Margaret Fuller. After a long period in which he received little attention, critics of the last three decades have rediscovered Brown's work, and he has gained a respectable place in literary history for his complex characterizations through which he explored important philosophical and psychological issues having to do with religion, gender, class, sexuality, race, and ethnicity. Of particular interest to him was the nature of American democracy and the moral and ethical responsibility of the individual to society as a whole.

Of his six published novels, the two that are considered his most interesting are *Wieland* and *Arthur Mervyn*, but his *Ormond* and *Edgar Huntly* are also much admired and often taught today. Though they are flawed by some inconsistencies of plot and employ devices of the gothic novel and novel of sensation, readers are surprised to discover him engaging subjects that are still of current and even compelling interest today. His novels clearly forecast many of the subjects and aesthetic concerns of later American writers such as Poe, Hawthorne, Melville, and even of modern and postmodern writers such as DeLillo, Morrison, Oates, O'Connor, Percy, and Pynchon.

Afterword

When Charles Brockden Brown died of tuberculosis in 1810 at the age of thirty-nine, American literature had not attained the lofty stature and respect that many writers of the 1770s had predicted it would achieve. To a considerable degree, however, neither the writers themselves nor unappreciative American audiences were entirely to blame. The lack of copyright regulations posed a major problem for American writers. Rather than pay royalties to American novelists for their works, American publishers simply purchased large numbers of successful English novels at bargain prices and sold them in America. For example, Susanna Rowson's *Charlotte Temple*, which was a best seller in America, earned the author no royalties because it was first published in England.

As cheap English books flooded the American market, English novelists such as Henry Fielding, Samuel Richardson, and Lawrence Stern became highly popular. There was no incentive for American publishers to print the works of American writers or for the public to seek them out. Not until 1830 when the first international copyright laws were established did the practice of pirating foreign books become illegal and did American writers have the possibility of earning a living from their writing. These financial realities provide a useful context for the famous insult of the Scottish critic, Sydney Smith, in 1820 in the *Edinburgh Review* where he wrote: "Who reads an American book? Or goes to an American play? Or looks at an American picture or statue?" Smith's answer, of course, was that nobody did, and even today, most who have read Smith's remarks assume that the reason was simply that American writing was inferior. In fact, matters of money and markets had much to do with cultural lag.

At the same time, Smith's quip also signals a cultural rivalry that began to emerge in the 1820s between the aspiring Americans and the established artistic and literary communities of Europe. In her often satiric memoir of her travels in the United States in the late 1820s, *Domestic Manners of the Americans*, Mrs. Frances Trollope judged the literature and art of the United States no better than "trash" or a "mass of slip-slop." Mrs. Trollope's son, Anthony (1815–82), would become one of England's major novelists and would compete for readers with Americans like Nathaniel Hawthorne and Henry James. Even the usually admiring and judicious observer of America, Alex de Tocqueville, could not resist writing about American culture from a position of European superiority: "It must be acknowledged that in few of the civilized nations of our time have the higher sciences made less progress than in the United States; and in few have great artists, distinguished poets, or celebrated writers been more rare." Given such harsh judgments, it is not difficult to understand why Americans in general developed a cultural inferior complex in relation to Europe that lasted well into the twentieth century.

In the spirit of the new American republic, many of the writers and artists were resolved to prove the European critics wrong. Among the few Americans who, between 1800 and 1830, did win recognition for American literature were Washington Irving (1783–1859) and James Fenimore Cooper (1789–1815). Both asserted anew the possibilities and promise of American literature with works of fiction and non-fiction that attracted readers at home and abroad. In content, narrative technique, and style, the fictions of Irving and Cooper were comparable to the novels of the famous Scottish author Sir Walter Scott and gained the admiration of Scott himself and many other European writers. In fact, Scott helped Irving protect his work from pirating by facilitating the arrangement for Irving to publish an English edition of his highly successful book, *The Sketch Book of Geoffrey Crayon, Gent.* The best known of Irving's prodigious list of titles, *The Sketch Book*, contains the famous stories "Rip Van Winkle" and "The Legend of Sleepy Hollow." Like Benjamin Franklin, Joel Barlow, Thomas Paine, and many American writers during his own time and since, Irving spent a lengthy period of his life in Europe. Returning with an honorary degree from Oxford after seventeen years in Europe, he appears to have been so bolstered by the admiration of his English audience that he felt confident he could flaunt his American identity. Thus, he turned his attention to writing several books about the American West and to paying homage to his heroic namesake by culminating his career with a magisterial five-volume *Life of George Washington* (1855–59).

The daughter of the other major figure of this period, Susan Cooper, recorded in her diary that her father, James Fenimore, began his writing career when he remarked to his wife that he could write a better book than the latest imported novel from England. Assuming this comment to be a joke, she laughed at such presumption. That first work, *Precaution* (1820), a novel of manners set in England, was so well received that he wrote three more novels in the next three years. Eventually, he would produce thirty-two novels and several volumes of commentary, histories, and social criticism. His most famous books are those in the series known as the "Leather-Stocking Tales," named after the hero, Natty Bumppo, who is nick-named

"Leather-Stocking." Romantic, melodramatic, and composed of elements from gothic and sentimental fictions of the time, these novels explore the American West during the early decades, depicting the struggles between the European pioneers and Native Americans over possession of the continent. Such works as *Last of the Mohicans* (1826) and the *Prairie* (1827) are among the best known American books in the world today.

Like Irving, Cooper also lived abroad for many years, the first stay between 1826 and 1833. When Cooper returned, however, he found an America that had changed greatly in seven years. Unlike the "era of good feeling" that had existed until the fateful 4th July in 1826 when both John Adams and Thomas Jefferson died within a few hours of each other, the years of Andrew Jackson's presidency had initiated an era of what Cooper considered to be democratic excesses, with lower standards of civility and ethics. In his books *A Letter to His Countrymen* (1834) and *The American Democrat* (1838), Cooper expressed his scorn for the new society of common men and women, and in so doing, he lost many of his former admiring readers. His response to his feeling of being out of place in this new America led him to retreat into his imagination and into an earlier world that existed in eighteenth-century America. The settings of these later novels was a simpler time when Leather-Stocking was young and America was still innocent and embraced more fully the American Dream.

Such frustration and despondence with a backsliding America was not new in American writing. Philip Freneau had expressed a similar sense of dismay fifty years earlier in his poem, "To An Author" (1788) where the speaker complains that in America the people had become too materialistic, complaisant, and occupied with business: they lack imagination and "can no poetic raptures feel." Around the same time that Cooper was lamenting that his shallow fellow Americans were losing their souls, a new voice in American literature was beginning to be heard, that of Ralph Waldo Emerson who called for a new confidence in American Genius. In lectures such as "The American Scholar" and "Self-Reliance," Emerson sought to inspire his countrymen and women to cast off their feelings of cultural inferiority and to recognize that they represented a new beginning in world history.

This familiar pattern in American public rhetoric – to critique the current state of society and to remind people of the high aims and accomplishments of their forefathers and mothers – was established on the Mayflower. This highly effective, formulaic verbal construction has been described as a ritual, a myth, and a jeremiad. A social and psychic algorithm deeply inscribed into American culture, this American jeremiad had its origins in those early Puritan writings by John Winthrop, William Bradford, Ann Hutchinson, Increase Mather, and Jonathan Edwards. The message that the errand had taken a wrong turn; that the lofty goals of the mission had been forgotten; that the purity of the community had been tainted; and that the zeal for success and victory had nearly extinguished occurs repeatedly in American literature.

Since the 1620s, the political and religious rhetoric of the New England Puritans has pervaded American expression, and even appears in the works of those like Franklin who would reject many other features of a Puritan worldview or ideology. The verbal formulas are there in the works of John Adams, Thomas Jefferson, and James Madison, as well as in the poetry of Phillis Wheatley and the fictions of Charles Brockden Brown. In the nineteenth century, the writings of Emerson, Hawthorne, Poe, Melville, Stowe, Thoreau, Whitman, and Dickinson are certainly surprising in their originality and innovations, so remarkably original that for many decades traditional critics thought they were untrained, careless, and exotic. But at the same time, their works are also part of a tradition of American writing that draws upon the writers of the seventeenth and eighteenth centuries. The stylistic and thematic components of that tradition, and the rhetorical structure of the jeremiad may still be heard and seen in the works of such contemporary writers as Toni Morrison, Thomas Pynchon, Philip Roth, Joyce Carol Oates, and Don DeLillo. Readers who engage the works of such writers without a sense of the American literary tradition that preceded them will, in Toni Morison's words, be just "playing in the dark."

Bibliography

Adair, Douglass. *Fame and the Founding Fathers*. ed. Trevor Colbourn. New York: Norton, 1974.

Adair, John. *Puritans: Religion and Politics in Seventeenth-Century England and America*. Gloucestershire: Sutton Publishing, 1998.

Anderson, Virginia D. *New England's Generation: The Great Migration and the Formation of Society and Culture in the Seventeenth Century*. Cambridge University Press, 1991.

Andrews, William L., ed. *Journeys in New Worlds: Early American Women's Narratives*. Madison: University of Wisconsin Press, 1990.

Arch, Stephen C. *Authorizing the Past: The Rhetoric of History in Seventeenth-Century New England*. DeKalb, Illinois: Northern Illinois University Press, 1994.

Axtell, James. *The Invasion Within: The Contest of Cultures in Colonial North America*. New York: Oxford University Press, 1985.

Bailyn, Bernard. *Education in the Forming of American Society*. Chapel Hill: University of North Carolina Press, 1960.

Bailyn, Bernard. *The Ideological Origins of the American Revolution*. 1967. Enl. ed. Cambridge: Harvard University Press, 1992.

Bailyn, Bernard. *The New England Merchants in the Seventeenth Century*. Cambridge: Harvard University Press, 1955.

Bell, Michael. *The Development of the American Romance*. Chicago University Press, 1980.

Bercovitch, Sacvan. *The American Jeremiad*. Madison: University of Wisconsin Press, 1978.

Bercovitch, Sacvan. *The Puritan Origins of the American Self*. New Haven, CT: Yale University Press, 1975.

Bercovitch, Sacvan, ed. *The American Puritan Imagination: Essays in Revaluation*. New York: Cambridge University Press, 1974.

Bercovitch, Sacvan, ed. *Typology and Early American Literature*. Amherst: University of Massachusetts Press, 1972.

Berens, John F. *Providence and Patriotism in Early America, 1640–1815*. Charlottesville: University Press of Virginia, 1978.

Berkin, Carol. *First Generations: Women in Colonial America*. New York: Hill and Wang, 1996.

Bonomi, Patricia U. *Under the Cope of Heaven: Religion, Society, and Politics in Colonial America*. New York: Oxford University Press, 1986.

Boorstin, Daniel J. *The Americans: The Colonial Experience*. New York: Random House, 1958.

Boyer, Paul and Stephen Nissenbaum. *Salem Possessed: The Social Origins of Witchcraft*. Cambridge: Harvard University Press, 1974.

Bozeman, Theodore D. *To Live Ancient Lives: The Primitivist Dimensions in Puritanism*. Chapel Hill: University of North Carolina Press, 1988.

Breen, T. H. *The Character of the Good Ruler: A Study of Puritan Ideas in New England, 1630–1730*. New Haven, CT: Yale University Press, 1970.

Breen, T. H. *Puritans and Adventurers: Change and Persistence in Early America*. New York: Oxford University Press, 1980.

Breitweiser, Mitchell R. *American Puritanism and the Defense of Mournings: Religion, Grief, and Ethnology in Mary White Rowlandson's Captivity Narrative*. Madison: University of Wisconsin Press, 1990.

Breitweiser, Mitchell Robert. *Cotton Mather and Benjamin Franklin: The Price of Representative Personality*. New York: Cambridge University Press, 1984.

Bremer, Francis J., ed. *Puritanism: Transatlantic Perspectives on a Seventeenth-Century Anglo-American Faith*. Boston: Massachusetts Historical Society, 1993.

Bremer, Francis J. *Congregational Communion: Clerical Friendship in the Anglo-American Puritan Community, 1610–1692*. Boston: Northeastern University Press, 1994.

Bremer, Francis J. *Shaping New Englands: Puritan Clergymen in Seventeenth-Century England and New England*. New York. Twayne, 1994.

Breslaw, Elaine G. *Tituba, Reluctant Witch of Salem: Devilish Indians and Puritan Fantasies*. New York University Press, 1996.

Brown, Kathleen M. *Good Wives, Nasty Wenches, and Anxious Patriarchs: Gender, Race, and Power in Colonial Virginia*. Chapel Hill: University of North Carolina Press, 1996.

Brown, Richard D. *Modernization: The Transformation of American Life, 1600–1865*. New York: Hill and Wang, 1976.

Brumm, Ursula. *American Thought and Religious Typology*. Trans. John Hooglund. New Brunswick, NJ: Rutgers University Press, 1970.

Buel, Richard. *Securing the Revolution: Ideology in American Politics, 1789–1815*. Ithaca: Cornell University Press, 1972.

Caldwell, Patricia. *The Puritan Conversion Narrative: The Beginnings of American Expression*. New York: Cambridge University Press, 1983.

Calloway, Colin G. *New Worlds for All: Indians, Europeans, and the Remaking of Early America*. Baltimore: Johns Hopkins University Press, 1997.

Calloway, Colin G., ed. *The World Turned Upside Down: Indian Voices from Early America*. Boston: Bedford, 1994.

Campbell, Mary B. *The Witness and the Other World: Exotic European Travel Writing, 400–1600*. Ithaca: Cornell University Press, 1988.

Cassirer, Ernst. *The Philosophy of Enlightenment*. trans. Fritz C.A. Koelln and James P. Pettegrove. Princeton University Press, 1951.

Castiglia, Christopher. *Bound and Determined: Captivity, Culture-Crossing, and White Womanhood from Mary Rowlandson to Patty Hearst*. University of Chicago Press, 1996.

Chai, Leon. *Jonathan Edwards and the Limits of Enlightenment Philosophy*. New York: Oxford University Press, 1998.

Cheyfitz, Eric. *The Poetics of Imperialism: Translation and Colonization from The Tempest to Tarzan*. New York: Oxford University Press, 1991.

Clark, J. C. D. *The Language of Liberty, 1660–1832: Political Discourse and Social Dynamics in the Anglo American World*. Cambridge University Press, 1994.

Clendinnin, Inga. *Ambivalent Conquests: Maya and Spaniard in Yucatan, 1517–1570*. New York: Cambridge University Press, 1987.

Cogley, Richard W. *John Eliot's Mission to the Indians Before King Philip's War*. Cambridge: Harvard University Press, 1999.

Cohen, Charles L. *God's Caress: The Psychology of Puritan Religious Experience*. New York: Oxford University Press, 1986.

Cooper, James F. *Tenacious of Their Liberty: The Congregationalists in Colonial Massachusetts*. New York: Oxford University Press, 1999.

Cowell, Pattie. *Women Poets in Pre-Revolutionary America: An Anthology*. Troy, NY: Whitson, 1981.

Cowing, Cedric. *The Saving Remnant: Religion and the Settling of New England*. Urbana: University of Illinois Press, 1995.

Cressy, David. *Coming Over: Migration and Communication Between England and New England in the Seventeenth Century*. New York: Cambridge University Press, 1987.

Cronon, William. *Changes in the Land: Indians, Colonists, and the Ecology of New England*. New York: Hill and Wang, 1983.

Daly, Robert. *God's Altar: The World and the Flesh in Puritan Poetry*. Berkeley: University of California Press, 1978.

Daniels, Bruce C. *Puritans at Play: Leisure and Recreation in Colonial New England*. New York: St Martin's, 1995.

Davidson, Cathy N. *Revolution and the Word: The Rise of the Novel in America*. New York: Oxford University Press, 1986.

Davidson, James W. *The Logic of Millennial Thought*. New Haven, CT: Yale University Press, 1977.

Davies, Horton. *Worship and Theology in England*. Princeton University Press, 1961–75.

Davies, Horton. *The Worship of the American Puritans, 1629–1730*. New York: Lang, 1990.

Davis, David Brion. *The Problem of Slavery in the Age of Revolution, 1770–1823*. Ithaca: Cornell University Press, 1975.

Davis, J. C. *Fear, Myth and History: The Ranters and the Historians*. New York: Cambridge University Press, 1986.

Dayton, Cornelius H. *Women Before the Bar: Gender, Law, and Society in Connecticut, 1639–1789*. Chapel Hill: University of North Carolina Press, 1995.

Delbanco, Andrew. *The Puritan Ordeal*. Cambridge: Harvard University Press, 1989.

Demos, John P. *A Little Commonwealth: Family Life in Plymouth Colony*. New York: Oxford University Press, 1970.

Demos, John P. *Entertaining Satan: Witchcraft and the Culture of Early New England*. New York: Oxford University Press, 1982.

Demos, John P. *The Unredeemed Captive: A Family Story from Early America*. New York: Knopf, 1994.

Dunn, Richard S. *Puritans and Yankees: The Winthrop Dynasty of New England, 1630–1717*. Princeton University Press, 1962.

Egan, Jim. *Authorizing Experience: Refigurations of the Body Politic in Seventeenth-Century New England Writing*. Princeton University Press, 1999.

Elliott, Emory. *Power and Pulpit in Puritan New England*. Princeton University Press, 1975.

Elliott, Emory. *Revolutionary Writers: Literature and Authority in the New Republic*. New York: Oxford University Press, 1982.

Elliott, Emory. *The Literature of Puritan New England*, in *The Cambridge History of American Literature*, Vol. I., ed. Sacvan Bercovitch. Cambridge University Press, 1994.

Elliott, Emory, ed. *American Colonial Writers, 1607–1734*. Detroit: Gale, 1984.

Elliott, Emory. *American Colonial Writers, 1735–1781*. Detroit: Gale, 1984.

Elliott, Emory. *American Writers of the Early Republic*. Detroit: Gale, 1985.

Elliott, Emory. *Puritan Influences in American Literature*. Urbana: University of Illinois Press, 1979.

Ellis, Joseph J. *After the Revolution: Profiles of Early American Culture*. New York: W. W. Norton & Company, Inc., 1979.

Emerson, Everett H. *Puritanism in America*. Boston: Twayne, 1977.

Emerson, Everett H., ed. *Major Writers of Early American Literature*. Madison: University of Wisconsin Press, 1972.

Erikson, Kai T. *Wayward Puritans: A Study in the Sociology of Deviance*. New York: Wiley, 1966.

Faust, Langdon L. *American Women Writers: A Critical Reference Guide from Colonial Times to the Present*. 4 vols. New York: Ungar, 1979–82.

Favret-Saada, Jeanne. *Deadly Words: Witchcraft in the Bocage*. Trans. Catherine Cullen. New York: Cambridge University Press, 1980.

Ferguson, Robert A. *The American Enlightenment*. Cambridge: Harvard University Press, 1994.

Ferguson, Robert A. *Law and Letters in American Culture*. Cambridge: Harvard University Press, 1984.

Fiedler, Leslie A. *Love and Death in the American Novel*. New York: Dell, 1966.

Fliegelman, Jay. *Declaring Independence: Jefferson, Natural Language, and the Culture of Performance*. Stanford University Press, 1993.

Fliegelman, Jay. *Prodigals and Pilgrims: The Revolution Against Patriarchal Authority, 1750–1800*. Cambridge University Press, 1982.

Foster, Stephen. *The Long Argument: English Puritanism and the Shaping of New England Culture, 1570–1700*. Chapel Hill: University of North Carolina Press, 1991.

Foster, Stephen. *Their Solitary Way: The Puritan Social Ethic in the First Century of Settlement in New England*. New Haven, CT: Yale University Press, 1971.

Franklin, Wayne. *Discoverers, Explorers, Settlers: The Diligent Writers of Early America*. University of Chicago Press, 1979.

Frey, Sylvia R. *Water From the Rock: Black 20 Resistance in a Revolutionary Age*. Princeton University Press, 1991.

Games, Alison. *Migration and the Origins of the English Atlantic World*. Cambridge: Harvard University Press, 1999.

Gay, Peter. *The Enlightenment: An Interpretation*. 2 vols. New York: Knopf, 1966–69.

Gildrie, Richard P. *Salem, Massachusetts, 1626–1683: A Covenant Community*. Charlottesville: University Press of Virginia, 1975.

Gilmore, Michael T., ed. *Early American Literature: A Collection of Critical Essays*. Englewood Cliffs, NJ: Prentice-Hall, 1980.

Godbeer, Richard. *The Devil's Dominion: Magic and Religion in Early New England*. New York: Cambridge University Press, 1992.

Gray, Edward G. *New World Babel: Languages and Nations in Early America*. Princeton University Press, 1999.

Greenblatt, Stephen. *Learning to Curse: Essays in Early Modern Culture*. New York: Routledge, 1990.

Greenblatt, Stephen. *Marvelous Possessions: The Wonder of the New World*. University of Chicago Press, 1991.

Greven, Phillip J. *Four Generations: Population, Land and Family in Colonial Andover, Massachusetts*. Ithaca: Cornell University Press, 1970.

Greven, Phillip J. *The Protestant Temperament: Patterns of Child-Rearing, Religious Experience, and the Self in Early America*. New York: Knopf, 1977.

Gummere, Richard M. *The American Colonial Mind and the Classical Tradition: Essays in Comparative Culture*. Cambridge: Harvard University Press, 1963.

Gura, Philip F. *A Glimpse of Sion's Glory: Puritan Radicalism in New England, 1620–1660*. Middletown, CT: Wesleyan University Press, 1984.

Gura, Philip F. *The Crossroads of American History and Literature*. University Park: Pennsylvania State University Press, 1996.

Hall, David D. *The Faithful Shepherd: A History of New England Ministry in the Seventeenth Century*. Chapel Hill: University of North Carolina Press, 1972.

Hall, David D. *Worlds of Wonder, Days of Judgment: Popular Religious Belief in Early New England*. New York: Knopf, 1989.

Hall, David D., ed. *The Antinomian Controversy, 1636–1638: A Documentary History*. 2nd ed. Durham: Duke University Press, 1990.

Hall, Timothy D. *Contested Boundaries: Itinerancy and the Reshaping of the Colonial American Religious World*. Durham: Duke University Press, 1994.

Hambrick-Stowe, Charles. *The Practice of Piety: Puritan Devotional Disciplines in Seventeenth-Century New England*. Chapel Hill: University of North Carolina Press, 1982.

Hansen, Chadwick. *Witchcraft at Salem*. New York: Braziller, 1969.

Hartman, James D. *Providence Tales and the Birth of American Literature*. Baltimore: Johns Hopkins University Press, 1999.

Heimert, Alan. *Religion and the American Mind: From the Great Awakening to the Revolution*. Cambridge: Harvard University Press, 1966.

Heimert, Alan, and Perry Miller, eds. *The Great Awakening: Documents Illustrating the Crisis and Its Consequences*. Indianapolis: Bobbs-Merrill, 1967.

Henderson, Katherine U., and Barbara F. McManus, eds. *Half Humankind: Contexts and Texts of the Controversy about Women in England, 1540–1640*. Urbana: University of Illinois Press, 1985.

Henretta, James A., and Gregory H. Nobles. *Evolution and Revolution: American Society, 1600–1820*. Lexington, MA: Heath, 1987.

Hoffer, Peter C. *The Devil's Disciples: Makers of the Salem Witchcraft Trials*. Baltimore: Johns Hopkins University Press, 1996.

Holifield, E. Brooks. *The Covenant Sealed: The Development of Puritan Sacramental Theology in Old and New England, 1570–1720*. New Haven, CT: Yale University Press, 1974.

Holstun, James. *A Rational Millennium: Puritan Utopias of Seventeenth-Century England and America*. New York: Oxford University Press, 1987.

Horton, James O. and Lois E. Horton. *In Hope of Liberty: Culture, Community and Protest Among Northern Free Blacks, 1700–1860*. New York: Oxford University Press, 1997.

Howard, Leon. *Essays on Puritans and Puritanism*. Ed. James Barbour and Thomas Quirk. Albuquerque: University of New Mexico Press, 1986.

Hulme, Peter. *Colonial Encounters: Europe and the Native Caribbean, 1492–1797*. London: Methuen, 1986.

Innes, Stephen. *Creating the Commonwealth: The Economic Culture of Puritan New England*. New York: Norton, 1995.

Jacobs, Wilbur R. *Dispossessing the American Indian: Indians and Whites on the Colonial Frontier*. 1972. Reprinted. Norman: University of Oklahoma Press, 1985.

Jaffee, David. *People of the Wachusett: Greater New England in History and Memory, 1630–1860*. Ithaca: Cornell University Press, 1999.

Jantz, Harold S. *The First Century of New England Verse*. Worcester, MA: American Antiquarian Society, 1944.

Jehlen, Myra. *American Incarnation: The Individual, the Nation, and the Continent*. Cambridge: Harvard University Press, 1986.

Jehlen, Myra and Michael Warner, eds. *The English Literatures of America, 1500–1800*. New York: Routledge, 1997.

Jennings, Francis. *The Invasion of America: Indians, Colonialism, and the Cant of Conquest*. Chapel Hill: University of North Carolina Press, 1975.

Johnson, Ellwood. *The Pursuit of Power: Studies in the Vocabulary of Puritanism*. New York: Peter Lang, 1995.

Jordan, Winthrop. *White over Black: American Attitudes toward the Negro, 1550–1812*. Chapel Hill: University of North Carolina Press, 1968.

Joyce, Lester D. *Church and Clergy in the American Revolution: A Study in Group Behavior.* New York: Exposition Press, 1966.

Joyce, William L., David D. Hall, Richard D. Brown, and John B. Hench, eds. *Printing and Society in Early America.* Worcester, MA: American Antiquarian Society, 1983.

Juster, Susan. *Disorderly Women: Sexual Politics and Evangelicalism in Revolutionary New England.* Ithaca: Cornell University Press, 1994.

Kamensky, Jane. *Governing the Tongue: The Politics of Speech in Early New England.* New York: Oxford University Press, 1997.

Kammen, Michael. *Mystic Chords of Memory: The Transformation of Tradition in American Culture.* New York: Knopf, 1972.

Karlsen, Carol F. *The Devil in the Shape of a Woman: Witchcraft in Seventeenth-Century New England.* New York: Norton, 1987.

Karsten, Peter. *Patriot-Heroes in England and America: Political Symbolism and Changing Values over Three Centuries.* Madison: University of Wisconsin Press, 1978.

Kaufmann, Michael W. *Institutional Individualism: Conversion, Exile, and Nostalgia in Puritan New England.* Middletown, CT: Wesleyan University Press, 1998.

Kerber, Linda. *Women of the Republic: Intellect and Ideology in Revolutionary America.* Chapel Hill: University of North Carolina Press, 1980.

Kibby, Ann. *The Interpretation of Material Shapes in Puritanism: A Study of Rhetoric, Prejudice, and Violence.* New York: Cambridge University Press, 1986.

Knight, Janice. *Orthodoxies in Massachusetts: Rereading American Puritanism.* Cambridge: Harvard University Press, 1994.

Koch, Adrienne. *Power, Morals and the Founding Fathers: Essays in the Interpretation of the American Enlightenment.* Ithaca: Great Seal Books, 1961.

Koehler, Lyle. *A Search for Power: The "Weaker Sex" in Seventeenth-Century New England.* Urbana: University of Illinois Press, 1980.

Kolodny, Annette. *The Lay of the Land: Metaphor as Experience and History in American Life and Letters.* Chapel Hill: University of North Carolina Press, 1975.

Kramer, Michael P. *Imagining Language in America: from the Revolution to the Civil War.* Princeton University Press, 1992.

Kupperman, Karen Ordahl. *Settling with the Indians: The Meeting of English and Indian Cultures.* Totowa, NJ: Rowman & Littlefield, 1980.

Lambert, Frank. *Inventing the "Great Awakening".* Princeton University Press, 1999.

Lang, Amy S. *Prophetic Woman: Anne Hutchinson and the Problem of Dissent in the Literature of New England.* Berkeley: University of California Press, 1987.

Leach, Douglas E. *Flintlock and Tomahawk: New England in Kind Philip's War.* New York: Macmillan, 1958.

Lemay, J. A. Leo. *A Calendar of American Poetry in the Colonial Newspapers and Magazines and in the Major English Magazines through 1765.* Worcester, MA: American Antiquarian Society, 1972.

Lemay, J. A. Leo, ed. *Deism, Masonry, and the Enlightenment: Essays Honoring Alfred Owen Aldridge.* Newark: Delaware University Press, 1987.

Lemay, J. A. Leo. *Men of Letters in Colonial Maryland.* Knoxville: University of Tennessee Press, 1972.

Leon-Portilla, Miguel. *The Aztec Image of Self and Society: An Introduction to Nahuatl Culture.* Edited and with an introduction by J. Jorge Klor de Alva. Salt Lake City: University of Utah Press, 1992.

Lepore, Jill. *The Name of War: King Philip's War and the Origins of American Identity.* New York: Knopf, 1998.

Lestringant, Frank. *Le Huguenot et le sauvage: L'Amerique et la controverse coloniale, en Grance, au temps des Guerres de Religion.* Paris: Aux Amateurs de livres, 1990.

Leverenz, David. *The Language of Puritan Feeling: An Exploration in Literature, Psychology, and Social History.* New Brunswick, NJ: Rutgers University Press, 1980.

Levernier, James, and Douglas Wilmes, eds. *American Writers before 1800: A Biographical and Critical Dictionary.* 3 vols. Westport, CT: Greenwood, 1983.

Lewalski, Barbara Kiefer. *Protestant poetics and Seventeenth-Century Religious Lyric.* Princeton University Press, 1979.

Limon, John. *The Place of Fiction in the Time of Science: A Disciplinary History of American Writing.* New York: Cambridge University Press, 1990.

Lockridge, Kenneth A. *A New England Town: The First Hundred Years, Dedham, Massachusetts, 1636–1736.* Exp. ed. New York: Norton, 1985.

Looby, Christopher. *Voicing America: Language, Literary Form, and the Origins of the United States.* University of Chicago Press, 1995.

Lowance, Mason I. *The Language of Caanan: Metaphor and Symbol in New England from the Puritans to the Transcendentalists.* Cambridge: Harvard University Press, 1980.

Martin, Calvin, ed. *The American Indian and the Problem of History.* New York: Oxford University Press, 1987.

Martin, Wendy. *An American Triptych: Anne Bradstreet, Emily Dickinson, Adrienne Rich.* Chapel Hill: University of North Carolina Press, 1984.

McDermott, Gerald R. *Jonathan Edwards Confronts the Gods: Christian Theology, Enlightenment Religion, and Non-Christian Faiths.* New York: Oxford University Press, 2000.

Meinig, D. W. *The Shaping of America: A Geographical Perspective on 500 Years of History. Vol. I, Atlantic America, 1492–1800.* New Haven, CT: Yale University Press, 1986.

Merrell, James H. *Into the American Woods: Negotiators on the Pennsylvania Frontier.* New York: Norton, 1999.

Merrell, James H. *The Indians' New World: Catawbas and Their Neighbors from European Contact through the Era of Removal.* Chapel Hill: University of North Carolina Press, 1989.

Meserole, Harrison T., ed. *Seventeenth-Century American Poetry.* New York University Press, 1968.

Middlekauff, Robert. *The Mathers: Three Generations of Puritan Intellectuals,*
    1596–1728. New York: Oxford University Press, 1971.
Miller, Perry. *Errand into the Wilderness.* Cambridge: Harvard University Press,
    1956.
Miller, Perry. *The New England Mind: From Colony to Province.* Cambridge:
    Harvard University Press, 1953.
Miller, Perry. *The New England Mind: The Seventeenth-Century.* New York:
    Macmillan, 1939.
Miller, Perry. *Orthodoxy in Massachusetts, 1630–1650.* Cambridge: Harvard
    University Press, 1933. Reprinted, with a new preface, Boston: Beacon,
    1959.
Morgan, Edmund S. *The Puritan Dilemma: The Story of John Winthrop.* Boston:
    Little, Brown, 1958.
Morgan, Edmund S. *The Puritan Family: Religion and Domestic Relations in*
    Seventeenth-Century New England. Rev. ed. New York: Harper & Row, 1966.
Morgan, Edmund S. *Visible Saints: The History of a Puritan Idea.* Ithaca, NY:
    Cornell University Press, 1963.
Morison, Samuel Eliot. *Harvard College in the Seventeenth Century.* 2 vols.
    Cambridge: Harvard University Press, 1936.
Morison, Samuel Eliot. *The Intellectual Life of Colonial New England.* 2nd ed. New
    York University Press, 1956.
Murdock, Kenneth B. *Literature and Theology in Colonial New England.* Westport,
    CT: Greenwood Press, 1949.
Murray, David. *Forked Tongues: Speech, Writing, and Representation in North*
    American Indian Texts. Bloomington: Indiana University Press, 1991.
Nash, Gary B. *Race and Revolution.* Madison: Madison House, 1990.
Nash, Gary B. *The Urban Crucible: Social Change, Political Consciousness and the*
    Origins of the American Revolution. Cambridge: Harvard University Press, 1979.
Nelson, Dana D. *The Word in Black and White: Reading "Race" in American*
    Literature, 1638–1867. New York: Oxford University Press, 1992.
New, John F. H. *Anglican and Puritan: The Basis of Their Opposition.* Stanford
    University Press, 1964.
Norton, Mary Beth. *Liberty's Daughters: the Revolutionary Experience of American*
    Women, 1750–1800. Boston: Little, Brown, 1980.
Nye, Russel B. *American Literary History: 1607–1830.* New York: Knopf, 1970.
Nye, Russel B. *The Cultural Life of the New Nation, 1776–1830.* New York:
    Harper, 1960.
Oberg, Michael L. *Dominion and Civility: English Imperialism and Native America,*
    1585–1685. Ithaca: Cornell University Press, 1999.
O'Gorman, Edmundo. *The Invention of America: An Inquiry into the Historical*
    Nature of the New World and the Meaning of Its History. Bloomington: Indiana
    University Press, 1961.
Palmer, Stanley H., and Dennis Reinhartz, eds. *Essay on the History of North*
    American Discovery and Exploration. College Station: Texas A&M University
    Press, 1988.

Parry, J. H. *Europe and a Wider World, 1415–1715*. Edited by Sir Maurice
Powicke, 1949. Reprinted as *The Establishment of the European Hegemony,
1415–1715: Trade and Exploration in the Age of the Renaissance*. New York:
Harper & Row, 1961.

Patterson, Mark R. *Authority, Autonomy, and Representation in American Literature,
1776–1865*. Princeton University Press, 1988.

Pearce, Roy H. *Savagism and Civilization: A Study of the Indian and the American
Mind*. Berkeley: University of California Press, 1988. (First published as *The
Savages of America*, 1953.)

Peterson, Mark A. *The Price of Redemption: The Spiritual Economy of Puritan New
England*. Stanford University Press, 1997.

Pettit, Norman. *The Heart Prepared: Grace and Conversion in Puritan Spiritual Life*.
New Haven, CT: Yale University Press, 1966. 2nd ed. Middletown, NT:
Wesleyan University Press, 1989.

Peyer, Bernd C. *The Tutor'd Mind: Indian Missionary-Writers in Antebellum America*.
Amherst: University of Massachusetts Press, 1997.

Pope, Robert G. *The Half-Way Covenant: Church Membership in Puritan New
England*. Princeton University Press, 1969.

Porterfield, Amanda. *Female Piety in Puritan New England: The Emergence of
Religious Humanism*. New York: Oxford University Press, 1992.

Powell, Sumner C. *Puritan Village: The Formation of a New England Town*.
Middletown, CT: Wesleyan University Press, 1963.

Quinn, David B. *North America from Earliest Discovery to First Settlements: The Norse
Voyages to 1612*. New York: Harper & Row, 1977.

Quinn, David B. *Set Fair for Roanoke: Voyages and Colonies, 1584–1606*. Chapel
Hill: University of North Carolina Press, 1985.

Quinn, David B., ed. *New American World: A Documentary History of North America
to 1612*. 5 vols. New York: Arno, 1979.

Regis, Pamela. *Describing Early America: Bartram, Jefferson, Crèvecoeur, and the
Rhetoric of Natural History*. DeKalb: Northern Illinois University Press, 1992.

Reid-Maroney, Nina. *Philadelphia's Enlightenment, 1740–1800: Kingdom of Christ,
Empire of Reason*. Westport: Greenwood Press, 2001.

Reis, Elizabeth. *Damned Women: Sinners and Witches in Puritan New England*.
Ithaca: Cornell University Press, 1997.

Rice, Grantland S. *The Transformation of Authorship in America*. University of
Chicago Press, 1997.

Richter, Daniel K. *The Ordeal of the Longhouse: The Peoples of the Iroquois League in
the Era of European Colonization*. Chapel Hill: University of North Carolina
Press, 1992.

Rinaldi, Ann. *Hang a Thousand Trees with Ribbons: The Story of Phillis Wheatley*.
San Diego: Harcourt Brace & Co., 1996.

Ringe, Donald A. *American Gothic*. Lexington: Kentucky University Press, 1982.

Round, Phillip H. *By Nature and by Custom Cursed: Transatlantic Civil Discourse and
New England Cultural Production, 1630–1660*. Hanover, NH: University Press
of New England, 1999.

Rowe, Karen E. *Saint and Singer: Edward Taylor's Typology and the Poetics of Meditation.* New York: Cambridge University Press, 1986.

Ruether, Rosemary Radford, and Rosemary Skinner Killer, eds. *Women and Religion in America: The Colonial and Revolutionary Periods.* San Francisco: Harper & Row, 1981–6.

Rutman, Darrett B. *American Puritanism: Faith and Practice.* Philadelphia: Lippincott, 1970.

Ruttenberg, Nancy. *Democratic Personality: Popular Voice and the Trial of American Authorship.* Stanford University Press, 1998.

Salisbury, Neal. *Manitou and Providence: Indians, Europeans, and the Making of New England, 1500–1643.* New York: Oxford University Press, 1982.

Sayre, Gordon M. *Les Sauvages Americains: Representations of Native Americans in French and English Colonial Literature.* Chapel Hill: University of North Carolina Press, 1997.

Scanlan, Thomas. *Colonial Writing and the New World, 1583–1671.* New York: Cambridge University Press, 1999.

Scheick, William J. *Authority and Female Authorship in Colonial America.* Lexington: University of Kentucky Press, 1998.

Scheick, William J. *Design in Puritan American Literature.* Lexington: University Press of Kentucky, 1992.

Schweitzer, Ivy. *The Work of Self-Representation: Lyric Poetry in Colonial New England.* Chapel Hill: University of North Carolina Press, 1991.

Seelye, John. *Prophetic Waters: The River in Early American Life and Literature.* New York: Oxford University Press, 1977.

Selement, George. *Keepers of the Vineyard: The Puritan Ministry and Collective Culture in Colonial New England.* Lanham, MD: University Press of America, 1984.

Shea, Daniel B., Jr. *Spiritual Autobiography in Early America.* Princeton University Press, 1968.

Shields, David S. *Civil Tongues and Polite Letters in British America.* Chapel Hill: University of North Carolina Press, 1997.

Shields, David S. *Oracles of Empire: Poetry, Politics, and Commerce in British America, 1690–1750.* University of Chicago Press, 1990.

Shields, John C. *The American Aeneas: Classical Origins of the American Self.* Knoxville: University of Tennessee Press, 2001.

Shuffleton, Frank. *A Mixed Race: Ethnicity in Early America.* New York, NY: Oxford University Press, 1993.

Silverman, Kenneth. *A Cultural History of the American Revolution.* New York: T. Y. Crowell, 1976.

Slotkin, Richard. *Regeneration through Violence: The Mythology of the American Frontier, 1600–1860.* Middletown, CT: Wesleyan University Press, 1974.

Smith, James W. and A. Leland Jamison, eds. *Religion in American Life.* 4 vols. Princeton University Press, 1961–.

Sobel, Mechal. *The World They Made Together: Black and White Values in Eighteenth-Century Virginia.* Princeton University Press, 1987.

Sobel, Mechal. *Trabelin' on: The Slave Journey to an Afro-Baptist Faith.* Westport: Greenwood P, 1979.

Spengemann, William C. *A New World of Words: Redefining Early American Literature.* New Haven: Yale University Press, 1994.

Spengemann, William C. *A Mirror for Americanists: Reflections on the Idea of American Literature.* Hanover, NH: University Press of New England, 1989.

Staloff, Darren. *The Making of an American Thinking Class: Intellectuals and Intelligentsia in Puritan Massachusetts.* New York: Oxford University Press, 1998.

Steele, Ian K. *Warpaths: Invasions of North America.* New York: Oxford University Press, 1994.

Stevens, Henry. *Historical and Geographical Notes on the Earliest Discoveries in America, 1453–1530.* 1869. New York: Burt Franklin, 1970.

Stone, Lawrence. *The Family, Sex and Marriage in England, 1500–1800.* New York: Harper & Row, 1977.

Stout, Harry S. *The New England Soul: Preaching and Religious Culture in Colonial New England.* New York: Oxford University Press, 1986.

Swann, Brian, and Arnold Krupat, eds. *Recovering the Word: Essays on Native American Literature.* Berkeley: University of California Press, 1987.

Szasz, Margaret C. *Indian Education in the American Colonies, 1607–1783.* Albuquerque: University of New Mexico Press, 1988.

Tebbel, John. *A History of Book Publishing in the United States. Vol. I. The Creation of an Industry, 1630–1865.* New York: Bowker, 1972.

Thickstun, Margaret O. *Fictions of the Feminine: Puritan Doctrine and the Representation of Women.* Ithaca: Cornell University Press, 1988.

Thomas, Isaiah. *The History of Printing in America with a Biography of Printers & an Account of Newspapers.* Edited by Marcus A. McCorison. New York: Weathervane, 1970.

Thompson, Roger. *Mobility and Migration: East Anglian Founders of New England, 1629–1640.* Amherst: University of Massachusetts Press, 1994.

Thornton, Russell. *American Indian Holocaust and Survival: A Population History Since 1492.* Norman: University of Oklahoma Press, 1987.

Tichi, Cecilia. *New World, New Earth: Environmental Reform in American Literature from the Puritans through Whitman.* New Haven, CT: Yale University Press, 1979.

Todorov, Tzvetan. *The Conquest of America: The Question of the Other.* Translated by Richard Howard. New York: Harper & Row, 1984. (Translation of *La Conquete de l'Amerique.* Paris: Editions du Seuil, 1982.)

Tompkins, Jane. *Sensational Designs: The Cultural Work of American Fiction, 1790–1860.* New York: Oxford University Press, 1985.

Toulouse, Teresa. *The Art of Prophesying: New England Sermons and the Shaping of Belief.* Athens: University of Georgia Press, 1987.

Ulrich, Laurel Thatcher. *Good Wives: Image and Reality in the Lives of Women in Northern New England: 1650–1750.* New York: Knopf, 1982.

Van Sertima, Ivan. *Early America Revisited*. New Brunswick (USA): Transaction Publishers, 1998.

Vaughan, Alden T. *New England Frontier: Puritans and Indians, 1620–1675*. Rev. ed. New York: Norton, 1979.

Vaughan, Alden T., ed. *The Puritan Tradition in America, 1620–1730*. Hanover, NH: University Press of New England, 1972.

Vaughan, Alden T., and Francis J. Bremer, eds. *Puritan New England: Essays on Religion, Society, and Culture*. New York: St Martin's, 1979.

Vaughan, Alden T., and Edward W. Clark, eds. *Puritans among the Indians: Accounts of Captivity and Redemption, 1624–1674*. Cambridge: Harvard University Press, 1981.

Vizenor, Gerald. *The Heirs of Columbus*. Hanover, NH: Wesleyan University Press, 1991.

Wald, Priscilla. *Constituting Americans: Cultural Anxiety and Narrative Form*. Durham: Duke University Press, 1995.

Wall, Helena M. *Fierce Communion: Family and Community in Early America*. Cambridge: Harvard University Press, 1990.

Walters, Kerry S. *The American Deists: Voices of Reason and Dissent in the Early Republic*. Lawrence: Kansas University Press, 1992.

Warner, Michael. *The Letters of the Republic: Publication and the Public Sphere in Eighteenth-Century America*. Cambridge: Harvard University Press, 1990.

Washburn, Wilcomb E. *The Indian in America*. New York: Harper & Row, 1975.

Watts, Emily S. *The Poetry of American Women from 1632–1945*. Austin: University of Texas Press, 1977.

White, Peter, ed. *Puritan Poets and Poetics: Seventeenth-Century American Poetry in Theory and Practice*. University Park: Pennsylvania State University Press, 1985.

Wilson, Lisa. *Ye Heart of Man: The Domestic Life of Men in Colonial New England*. New Haven: Yale University Press, 1999.

Winship, Michael P. *Seers of God: Puritan Providentialism in the Restoration and Early Enlightenment*. Baltimore: Johns Hopkins University Press, 1996.

Wright, Louis B. *The Cultural Life of the American Colonies, 1607–1763*. New York: Harper & Row, 1957.

Wright, Thomas G. *Literary Culture in Early New England, 1620–1730*. New Haven, CT: Yale University Press, 1920.

Youngs, J. William T. *God's Messengers: Religious Leadership in Colonial New England, 1700–1750*. Baltimore: Johns Hopkins University Press, 1976.

Zakai, Avihu. *Exile and Kingdom: History and Apocalypse in the Puritan Migration to America*. New York: Cambridge University Press, 1992.

Ziff, Larzer. *Literary Democracy: The Declaration of Cultural Independence in America*. New York: Viking Press, 1981.

Ziff, Larzer. *Puritanism in America: New Culture in a New World*. New York: Viking, 1973.

Zuckerman, Michael. *Peaceable Kingdoms: New England Towns in the Eighteenth Century*. New York: Knopf, 1970.

Index

Abenakis 10
Act of Uniformity 90
Adams, John 131, 160, 161, 162, 163,
    165, 166, 170, 171, 172, 173
Adams, William 106; *The Necessity of*
    Pouring Out of the Spirit from on
    High upon a Sinning Apostatizing
    People 106
Addison 155
Africa 3, 30, 118
Africans *see* Africa
Age of Reason 163
Alaska 3
Alger, Horatio 122
Algonkian 10, 111, 157
Allin, James 101
America 1, 2, 4, 5, 6, 10, 13, 17, 40,
    58, 77, 81, 82, 88, 108, 109, 112,
    115, 119, 132, 138, 144, 153,
    155, 156, 161, 162, 163, 165,
    166, 170, 171, 172, 173
American Dream 163
Ames, William 32
Andros, Edmund 102, 107, 113, 120,
    132
Anglican 1, 32, 48, 71, 89, 102, 106,
    121, 126, 128, 129
Anglicans *see* Anglican
Anne 64
anti-slavery *see* slavery
anticlericalism 139, 144
antinomian *see* antinomianism
antinomianism 33, 42, 66, 82
Appleton, Aaron 138
Appleton, Nathaniel 127

Arabella 36, 39, 40, 62, 65, 81
Arizona 5, 154
Arminianism 33, 41, 44, 131, 140,
    144, 148
Ashbridge, Elizabeth 137–38; *The*
    Life of Elizabeth Ashbridge
    137–38; *Some Account of the*
    Fore Part of the Life of Elizabeth
    Ashbridge 137
Asia 5
Augustan movement 97
Augustine 61; *City of God* 61
Avery, Sybil 55
Aztec 3

Bacon, Francis 34, 157
Bahamas 2
Bailey, John 107; *Man's Chief End to*
    God's Glory 107
Bailyn, Bernard 160
Barker, William 27
Barlow, Joel 157, 161, 165, 171;
    "Advice to a Raven in Russia"
    161; *The Columbiad* 161; *The*
    Prospect of Peace 161; *The Vision of*
    Columbus 165
Barnard, John 130, 131–35; *The Throne*
    Established by Righteousness 131;
    A Zeal for Good Works, Excited and
    Directed 132
Barth, John 15; *The Sot-Weed Factor* 15
Bartram, William 159; *Travels* 159
Baxter, Richard 73–74, 77, 91; *The*
    Saint's Everlasting Rest 73
Bay Psalm Book 72–73

CPSIA information can be obtained at www.ICGtesting.com
Printed in the USA
LVOW10s2002101115

461900LV00002B/188/P